The Pedagogy of Pop

The Pedagogy of Pop

Theoretical and Practical Strategies for Success

Edited by Edward A. Janak and Denise Blum

LEXINGTON BOOKS
Lanham • Boulder • New York • Toronto • Plymouth, UK

KH

Published by Lexington Books
A wholly owned subsidiary of The Rowman & Littlefield Publishing Group, Inc.
4501 Forbes Boulevard, Suite 200, Lanham, Maryland 20706
www.rowman.com

10 Thornbury Road, Plymouth PL6 7PP, United Kingdom

British Library Cataloguing in Publication Information Available

Library of Congress Cataloging-in-Publication Data

Library of Congress Cataloging-in-Publication Data Available

ISBN 978-0-7391-7600-9 (cloth : alk. paper)—ISBN 978-0-7391-7601-6 (electronic)

♾™ The paper used in this publication meets the minimum requirements of American
National Standard for Information Sciences—Permanence of Paper for Printed Library
Materials, ANSI/NISO Z39.48-1992.

Printed in the United States of America

11/12/13

Dedication

This book is dedicated to all the educators in the United States who were ever moved by a song, film, or episode of a television series . . .

and then immediately wondered "Now how can I use that with my students?"

Contents

Preface

Somehow, it has become trendy to attack education today; there is almost no discussion of the state of our public schools that doesn't involve establishment of alternatives, such as charter school and voucher conversations, or sweeping statements of accountability-based reform. Contemporary discussions surrounding school reform rather shortsightedly revolved around two issues: how to make students test better and how to use schools to make the economy stronger. Strangely, these two rather unimportant views govern most of the little attention given by scholars and the general public regarding schooling. Rather than focus on minutiae such as test scores, instead teachers should be thinking about ways to produce lifelong learners, to really hook student attention and find the most effective means to tap into their interests to base curriculum.

This trend toward teaching for test scores is disturbing; as Henry Giroux (2010) chides, it is the youth of this nation in which the future lies. However, they are being bombarded by pro-neoliberal media messages and representations of themselves as flawed, failing, and broke, leading to a sense of powerlessness that requires drastic alteration. As Giroux argues, "[i]n order to strengthen the public sphere, we must use its most widespread institutions, undo their metamorphoses into means of surveillance, commodification, and control, and reclaim them as democratic spaces" (23). There must be a way to re-empower the youth of the United States to improve the nation—and our schools are the best means to do so at this time for, as Giroux further argues, due to the "contradictions and their democratic potential, their reality and their promise" (23), schools offer the best way to re-empower American youth and thus the nation.

Sadly, schools are not helping their case very much in much of their current approach. As discussed by Diane Ravitch in 2007's *The Language Police*, students live in two worlds that provide a "strange contradiction" (p. 162), home versus school. While at home, students watch television, surf the Internet, and receive updates on unfiltered stories about "terrorism, hijackings, massacres, famines, and political upheavals." They attend, rent, or stream movies in which they enter "a world of fantasy, romance, passion, excitement, and action" (p. 162). Their music, whether hip-hop, emo, pop, or any of the other myriad subgenres popular at any given time sends messages about how the world works and in what they should be paying attention. And, of course, whereas in the past at night millions of American school children would hide under the blankets with a flashlight and a comic or other taboo reading material, today's children hide under the blankets with their smart phones or tablets, sharing gossip and status updates via social networking sites and viewing videos instantly. School, however, provides a completely different media experience for them. As painfully, but accurately, explained by Ravitch, the typical American school child goes to school Monday through Friday:

> There she will open her literature textbook to a story that has been carefully chosen for its inoffensive language. The teacher points out that the story was written by a woman; the student doesn't care. It's boring. She will read entries written by students her age. She will quickly skip over all the pedagogical junk about critical thinking, looking for something interesting. She won't find it. Then she moves to history class, where the class is studying the role of women in the Revolutionary War; the text says that twenty thousand women fought in the war. Really? Hmmm. Yawn. (p. 162)

For students such as this—and all too many millions more across the country—school has become, in Ravitch's words, "the Empire of Boredom." In the drive to standardize and protect students, the corporations that produce textbooks and the schools that adopt them have completely insulated students "from any contact in their textbooks with anything that might disturb them, like violence, death, divorce, or bad language." However, educators must remember that "[t]hey are safe, but they are bored." Students then return home to complete the contradiction; while school materials are boring and safely homogenized, in reality students live "within the context of adolescent culture in which anything goes" (p. 162).

Schools cannot compete, nor is it the intent of this work to argue that they should. However, schools can provide students with more interesting, more real curricular materials from which they can draw, showing students the world as it is, not some utopian vision. This book is an attempt to turn this model on its ear, discussing a variety of strategies and approaches to use the very mass media that have come to attach education as tools through which to improve it. Using popular culture in classrooms is nothing new; as we are most recently reminded by Ray Browne, the concept of popular culture can be traced back to the ancient Roman concept of *vox populi*, literally the voice of the people. In the modern United States, one way that this has evolved is from "people on the street" interviews to reality television in all its forms—which, in turn, are less *vox populi* and more *tumultuositas vulgi semper insaniae proxima sit* as Alcuin of York reminded us in the year 798: the riotousness of the crowd is always close to madness. The popularity of shows such as *Jersey Shore* demonstrates the truth to Alcuin's assertion.

Rather than combat it, teachers on all levels have been trying for decades to tap into this riotousness, attempting to capture the zeitgeist of their students' lives, and have been sharing their methods and theories, successes and failures, in a variety of forums. A keyword search of one state university library's electronic catalog for "popular culture + teaching" returned an unwieldy 73,388 results; narrowing the scope to a search of the Education Index returned a more manageable 439 entries, and an ERIC search returned 659. Even a brief scan of the titles clearly demonstrates that teachers on all levels in all fields are engaged in this work, from agriculture (Bruce & Ewing, 2009) to physiology (Paul, 2011), from early childhood education (Flores-Koulish et al., 2011) to postsecondary (Smith, 2002), and much written on all levels of teacher education (Trier, 2007). In addition, it is teachers in popular culture who also tend to push boundaries the most, from teaching ethnic studies (Troutman, 2009) to teaching about transgender issues (Boucher, 2011) to teaching for social justice (Hattam et al., 2009).

In addition, the field has evolved from studies about how to tap into popular culture into analyses of the implications of teaching with popular culture. Using the teaching of literacy as an example, literature in the field has its roots in articles such as Robert Myers' 1974 ERIC report "The Popular Arts and the Teaching of Literature." Myers made the case for using popular music lyrics as a means of teaching poetry—a common technique in English classrooms across the United States today. However, recent scholarship includes such postmodern deconstructions of the field as Adam Lefstein and Julia Snell's "Promises and Problems of Teaching with Popular Culture: A Linguistic Ethnographic Analysis of Discourse Genre Mixing in a Literacy Lesson" in which the authors analyzed an elementary-level teacher's lesson that tapped into the popular British talent show *The X-Factor* to teach writing. The article problematizes the approach because, while it did lead to increased student involvement and more interactive learning, the learning it led to was not substantive, and the interactions between the students not contributive to legitimate academic learning.

With the vast body of literature in the field, what makes this collection stand out? It differs in two substantive ways, to borrow terms from the field of curriculum development: scope and sequence. In terms of scope, this work is unique in two facets: first, it presents both theory and practice in one volume, bridging the two worlds; and second, it includes lessons from secondary and postsecondary classrooms, allowing teachers on all levels to learn from each other. In terms of sequence, this work is different as it draws a lesson from the past. When sharing the results of his 1945 "Design for America" project, Theodore Brameld cautioned that educators on all levels "seem to have forgotten that time consists of three dimensions rather than two" (p. 2). At that time it was the future that was lost; however, in today's world we are so busy looking to the future we have lost sight of yesterday's habits and practices. This book remedies this oversight by presenting teaching with popular culture in "3-D": past, present, and future.

In addition to scope and sequence, this work is unique in its multiplicity of voices. Readers will note a variety of authorial voices throughout the book. Rather than edit the contributions to reflect the styles of the editors, contributor voice was privileged whenever possible as the variety of backgrounds and experiences of the authors and their various classrooms are a critical strength of the work. Indeed, it is the authors that have successfully integrated popular culture into their teaching, and therefore it is their voices explaining how.

Introduction: The Past as Prologue

The introductory section of this book presents a pair of papers that use somewhat different approaches to examine the historical roots of contemporary critique. These first two chapters provide a bit of context behind where we are today and reason for the direction in which we are heading. The first chapter in this section, Jennifer Edelman and Edward Janak's "Can We Win the Future By Living in the Past? A Preliminary Exploration of Nostalgia in Education" examines the role popular culture plays in forming nostalgia, particularly in regards to the public schools. Interestingly, nostalgia was originally thought to be a physical and psychological illness, over time defined as homesickness, melancholy, and depression (Wildschut, Sedikides, Arndt, & Routledge, 2006). Presently, nostalgia has gained conceptual status defined not in terms of illness, rather in terms of experience. This chapter defines nostalgia as a longing for an idealized past, whether real or imagined, that is used as a benchmark to measure the quality of current and future experiences against. It also critiques this model, examining the validity of memory as it pertains to formation of nostalgia in public perception of schooling.

The second chapter, Sheila Delony and Mikee Delony's "Professional Paradox: Teachers in Film and Television," explores how the history of teaching in the United States, the feminization of the profession, and public perceptions of education are evident in popular media, particularly television and film. From Helen Crump of the Andy Griffith Show (1963) to Michelle Pfeifer's portrayal of an inner-city teacher (1995), the media has depicted teachers in ways that reflect the public and political perceptions of the day. The Delonys argue that, of course, media is never a unidirectional influence. Thus, they explore how the interdependent relationships among history, media, and perception reflect and often perpetuate pedagogy and public opinion.

Part I: Theoretical Analyses of Pop Culture

The first section of this book presents a series of chapters designed to provide guidelines and theories through which educators on all levels can think about their practice. While some include suggestions and lesson plans, these pieces tend to focus more on the "why" of their approach than the "how." It begins with Julie Prieto turning a critical eye on the House of Mouse in "Making a Modern Man: Disney's Literacy and Health Education Campaigns in Latin and South America during WWII." As Prieto explains, in 1942 the Office of Inter-American Affairs (OIAA), a war-time agency run by Nelson Rockefeller charged with increasing Pan-American unity in the face the total breakdown in Europe, signed a contract with Disney Studios to produce and distribute educational curricula and films for Latin and South America. Rockefeller signed with Disney not only because it was one of the few studios with the capacity to create large amounts of media content relatively quickly, but because Disney films already enjoyed immense popularity and recognition throughout the hemisphere. Under contract, Disney created two feature films for distribution, *Saludos Amigos* and *The Three Caballeros*, in order to introduce U.S. and Latin American audiences to the history and culture of Mexico and Brazil. In addition, Disney films launched a campaign based on phonics and visual media to teach both adults and children simple reading skills in Spanish, and a large series of health and hygiene films. These films, including *The Unseen Enemy*, *Cleanliness Brings Health*, and *Planning for Good Eating*, covered a variety of topics such as the avoidance of infectious disease, nutrition, sanitation, and the proper planting and care of corn. "Making a Modern Man" argues that the OIAA used U.S. popular culture to promote their vision of a transnational, Pan American culture based on "modern" forms of social, cultural, and economic organization throughout the hemisphere. In distributing Disney educational materials, the U.S. government hoped to change not only individual practices and beliefs but to provide Latin and South American governments with alternative pedagogical models designed to temper educational practices that the State Department considered to be radical, while at the same time avoiding charges of cultural imperialism.

From the House of Mouse, Sylvia Mac and Denise Blum turn to an examination of preservice teacher education. Instead of looking at film as a tool of colonization, Mac and Blum extend their analysis to a critical exploration of gender roles. "Uncovering Images of Teaching: Towards a Teacher-Activist Ideal" provides guidelines for incorporating the use of pop culture as a method to prepare preservice teachers. Studies show that both preservice and veteran teachers have been deeply socialized to treat boys and girls differently (Sadker, Sadker & Klein, 1991) thereby conditioning them for stereotypical gender roles and likely limiting students' potentials. Based on a survey administered in March 2011, few preservice teachers gain knowledge or experience in teacher preparation learning how to use pop culture to teach the curriculum. It guides students to use critical media literacy skills (Kellner & Share, 2005) and ends by interrogating the role of the teacher in guaranteeing gender equity in the classroom.

Joanna Davis-McElligatt and Forest Roth approach bridging critical race theory with pop culture in " 'The Words We Write for Ourselves': Confronting the Myths of Race, Education, and American Genius in *Finding Forrester.*" A popular "feel good" movie portraying the mentor-student friendship between an African-American teenage prodigy and an older, self-tortured famous author, Gus Van Sant's *Finding Forrester* (2000) addresses how race and education can successfully coalesce outside the traditional classroom setting through William Forrester, a J.D. Salinger-esque figure who retreats from the world in bitter reclamation of the discourse of his work. The protagonist's search for educational freedom in his writing, denied by his skeptical teacher and coming under strict rules applied by Forrester in his seclusion, closely mirrors the plantation slave's search for Hegelian transformative self-consciousness vis-à-vis Frederick Douglass's *Narrative*. This chapter, reflecting on both Salinger and Douglass's example, addresses the larger (and perhaps conflicting) messages of *Finding Forrester* as it follows Jamal's travails at an elite Manhattan prep school. It also shows how the movie employs an authenticating structure reminiscent of the classic American slave narrative to depict a white man—in this case, Forrester—escaping the confines of his self-imposed obscurity and, hence, his own physical confinement thanks to a young black man's act of academic defiance.

Turning from film to television, while much has been written about Bart Simpson and his willingness to misbehave, Brian Duchaney's "'If You Should Die Before You Wake…' Bart Simpson, Family Dynamics, and the Genesis of Rebellion" looks to identify how Bart's upbringing directly contributes to his own misbehavior and his further influence on his siblings Lisa and Maggie. Looking at how Bart was raised by Marge and Homer, and his subsequent response to the birth of Lisa, this chapter explores how Bart's earliest memories illustrate the problems of poor decision making by his parents. While *The Simpsons* is largely concerned with parental choice and acknowledges the difficulties of parenting, Bart's situation is unique in that the show over-dramatizes parental reaction, employing a wish-fulfillment fantasy in reacting to misdeeds. This is countered with a need for extensive displays of love. However, both extremes are resolved in a manner resembling the ideal reality of parents. By exploring the various manners by which the stories of the Simpson children are told, we can identify that creator Matt Groening uses his characters to explain childhood terrors and the methods that children use to counteract or come to embrace their adult selves.

Continuing with the theme of using popular culture in gender studies, Amy Rakowsky Neeman and David Newman tap into the medium of television in "From *Desperate Housewives*—Past and Present—to *The Real Housewives of New Jersey* to Simply *House*: Views on Family and Gender in Popular Culture" in which they argue popular television shows and literature can often be analyzed in terms of how the characters fill certain roles, be it gender roles or family roles. By looking at specific examples, this chapter examines gender roles and family roles, which can be exemplified even when the characters are unrelated, but behave as family members. This analysis is particularly useful in the college classroom for generating discussion, especially on issues surrounding gender and family roles in cross-cultural contexts. Connections to the sociology and English classroom, as well as specific assignments, are also discussed.

Part II: Improving Instruction, The Pop of Pedagogy

While Neeman and Newman's chapter, amongst others in the first part, includes specific suggestions in implementing popular culture, the second part of the book presents more of a "hands-on" approach by sharing a variety of specific strategies for incorporating pop culture in all its forms (technology, music, mass media, etc.) in classrooms of a variety of contexts and applications. The idea for Rich Ellefritz's chapter "Editorial Cartoons as Education: History, Politics and Popular Culture of Political Cartoons" came to him during a research project for a course titled "Popular Culture and Education." He had collected hundreds of editorial cartoons about the 2010 BP/Deepwater Horizon oil spill, and found that these and other editorial cartoons might have the potential to be used pedagogically. Upon digging further into the world of editorial/political cartoons, he discovered the rich history behind their production and use in the mass media, implementing them in two ways: first, to engage students in a study of political messages conveyed through these historical popular culture texts; and second, to discuss the relationship between politics, history, and popular culture in the form of print media. Lessons can include uncovering the context of certain cartoons; representations of race, class, gender, etc.; how cartoons changed over time; and how cartoons are related to their historical eras and tracing the origins of modern tabloids back to the "yellow journalism" of Joseph Pulitzer and William Randolph Hearst. One of the key elements in doing this well is balancing conservative vs. liberal and democratic vs. republican oriented messages so that students do not feel alienated based upon their political leanings and avoids blatant political bias with this teaching program.

The next chapter taps into awareness of the Millennial Generation's learning styles as impacted by their use of pop culture in technology and gaming. Bob Reese's "Using Technology to Engage Millennials in Learning" begins with the argument that Millennial's seem addicted to technology. They sit in class, laptops or iPads open, peering at screens rather than the professor. As the professor speaks, they are busy tapping the keyboard. Are they taking notes, or are they texting, tweeting, or e-mailing? One way to garner attention in the classroom is by using the technology of student response systems (iClicker) within PowerPoints. Two models of use are presented. First, a model for assessing real-time learning in which students are quizzed throughout the lecture on information they just received. Based on the immediate results, material can be reemphasized or clarified if needed. Second is a model for stimulating discussion and thought in the classroom. This model elicits anonymous responses to topics students may initially be hesitant to discuss and promotes discussion in class. Distance learning and hybrid courses also have challenges keeping students involved. Voice-Over PowerPoint (VO-PPT) is an important tool for engaging learners in all online settings. The professor's voice enhances the PowerPoint and complements visual learning already addressed with the text, printed lectures, video links. Pedagogically, VO-PPT is a flexible, learner-centered tool. It utilizes a mastery approach to learning as the student can access individual slides, replay a slide repeatedly, and view slides with or without the audio. Ongoing research continually shows that both iClicker use and VO-PPTs are efficacious in assisting learning, enhancing student participation, and students find them engaging and entertaining.

Fred Waweru and Mwenda Ntarangwi take a somewhat different approach in their "Amending Eurocentric Narratives of African History in the U.S. Classroom: A Popular Culture Approach." In this chapter, Waweru and Ntarangwi argue that the Western world is strongly influenced by mainstream media stereotypes that paint the image of Africa as occupied by a monolithic, primordial, and uncivilized society. Moreover, much emphasis continues to be placed on constructed and selective events that have struck Africa over time. Three features—slavery, war, and hunger—continue to dominate the history of Africa both in the American curriculum and in the educational media programs. The lack of positive representation of African history has many effects, particularly in the twenty-first century where the new world order is to create a "global village"—the interconnectedness of global economies through enhanced communication technologies. Precisely, the tired stereotypes of African history reinforce a Western superiority while socializing those of African origin to accept the lesser role. They argue for an appreciation for African history that taps into popular music from Bob Marley to present an exciting lesson on African history, specifically the history of Ethiopia. The history of Ethiopia is of significance to Africa for three main reasons. First, Ethiopia was one of the two countries in African that were never colonized. Second, Ethiopia is the only country in Africa that conquered colonization through military means. Third, the history of Ethiopia is connected to that of Haile Selassie, the first African emperor whose enduring legacy became inextricable in the African continent and the postindustrialist world. He was the first African leader to address the League of Nations (the predecessor of the United Nations) in 1936. The lesson plan involves using the famous speech given by Selassie when he addressed the United Nations General Assembly in 1963. The accompanying popular music to the lesson plan is Bob Marley's "War," the lyrics of which are based on that speech.

Part II also includes content-specific studies. Beginning this approach, Ludovic Sourdot's work, "Popular Culture and Teacher Education in the Twenty First Century: The Pedagogical Possibilities of *Aliens in America*" shows that using the sitcom *Aliens in America* with preservice educators may help them to apply culturally responsive teaching strategies and in turn empower students to embrace diversity in our multicultural society. He has used *Aliens in America* with preservice teachers for several years; the data collected shows an active engagement of students in the activity and discussions. Data collected also reveals that teacher candidates are more comfortable deciphering and dissecting the teaching strategies utilized on screen instead of assessing their peers. While the content and pedagogical possibilities of television shows had been investigated by educators and scholars in the past (Jhally and Lewis, 1992; Cortés, 2000; Freedman, 2000; Trier, 2005), this study adds to the research on the possibilities, challenges, potential uses and implications of popular culture for teacher education in the twenty-first century.

From teaching writing in university classrooms to secondary schools, Jennifer Culver's "'How Does This Sound?' Using Language to Characterize Race in Middle-Earth" invites students to apply their understanding of syntax and diction to better understand Tolkien's characters. Because each race in Middle-earth contains its own unique syntactical structure and word choice, the students begin to understand how understanding this uniqueness helps understand characterization in a deeper and more profound way. Complete with handouts, examples, and rubrics, this unit of study is ready to go. Suggestions for other novels studied successfully in this way accompany the unit as well.

Michelle Parke's "'World Goin' One Way, People Another': Using *The Wire* and Other Popular Culture Texts to Teach College Writing" assesses the success and challenges of using a range of popular culture texts in the first-year college writing classroom. In particular, Parke focuses on how well programs like *The Wire* and *Buffy the Vampire Slayer* have worked to teach critical thinking skills, rhetorical analysis, and analytical writing skills. The author discusses the tribulations encountered when using various episodes of Seinfeld in class— the obstacles that faced the students and the instructor. She also emphasizes how to use video games in this type of course with a spotlight on games such as *Call of Duty: Modern Warfare* and *Fable 3*. Finally, Parke hopes to share with colleagues what texts work and why, as well as certain writing assignments that allow students to have the freedom of choice while also accomplishing the course objectives.

Conclusion: The Future as Epilogue

Praxis, defined in the neo-Marxist sense, is what happens when theory is put into practice; the conclusion of the book shows the praxis of teaching with popular culture. It presents two discussions that demonstrate the enormous potential of what can happen when pop culture is applied educationally. The first such example is Jade Lynch-Greenberg and esteban garcia's "I Don't Get It, and That's Okay: Teaching Experiential Film Interpretation," which presents the idea that some films, defined in the chapter as "experiential films," should not be viewed in the critical or analytic manner as is typically taught in film studies courses and argues "if it is not necessary to autopsy a cow in order to enjoy a steak, it shouldn't be necessary to analyze a film to appreciate it." This piece then presents a pedagogical alternative to currently prescribed film studies practices, focusing on utilizing a film's rhetorical situation, which can be applied across the curriculum. Their thinking presents somewhat of an interesting counterpoint to much of the current thought regarding popular culture studies in the classroom.

The second is an example of an emerging subgenre known as "creative life writing." This approach to such fields as memoir and biography knowingly infuses elements of creativity when necessary for literary license purposes. Contrary to the controversy surrounding James Frey's *A Million Little Pieces*, this field is both provocative and informative. Emblematic of both is Yvette Benavides' discussion of her daughter in "My Conversations with Ben: What This Mother Learned from a Ghost Boy about Bullying." A work of critical importance to teachers at all levels, Benavides reminds us that the American Justice Department recently published a report indicating that during this month, one out of four kids from grades six through ten will be abused mentally, verbally, and physically. She is fairly certain that one of those kids will be her own wholly idiosyncratic twelve-year-old daughter. At a middle school dance which she chaperoned, classmates ignored her daughter, laughed at her dancing, and called her names. It was the latest in a long line of instances of quietly simmering abuse she's endured her entire life. Later that evening, Benavides told her daughter a white lie: that a boy at the dance had asked about her, wanted to know her name, was interested in her. Momentarily elated, she thought about the possibility of such an exchange for a minute and then surmised an equally plausible scenario—that the boy was really a ghost who visited upon the middle school gymnasium to assure the author that her daughter would be okay. Thus began Benavides' relationship with a ghost boy she named Ben who led to the inevitable truth that bullied children—and their parents—can indeed survive such treatment.

Taken in the aggregate, this work is intended to serve a variety of practical purposes for teachers at all levels. Indeed, while many chapters address incorporating popular culture in one specific content or at one particular level, it is the most sincere hope of the editors that teachers at all levels will find the ideas shared throughout this text immediately adaptable to their particular teaching situation. For example, teachers of elementary age students, while not showing a television show like *The Wire* as it is completely age inappropriate, can take some of Parke's approaches, find television shows that similarly reflect the lives and stimulate the imaginations of their students, and develop conversation even with young children. Junior high world geography and world history teachers can take a lesson from Waweru and Ntarangwi and, even if they choose not to teach Selassie or Marley, critically examine the curricular choices within their Africa units and explore ways to debunk stereotype. And teachers of all levels can read pieces such as Sourdot's or Benavides' and think about their practice in broad terms, asking how can they improve how they connect with students and how can they ensure a safe, interesting learning environment for all students at all levels.

References

Boucher, M.J. (Spring 2011). Teaching "Trans Issues": An intersectional and systems-based approach. *New Directions for Teaching and Learning*, 125, 65- 75.

Brameld, T. (1945). *Design for America: An educational exploration of the future of democracy*. New York: Hinds, Hayden and Eldredge, Inc.

Browne, R.B., edited by Ben Urish. On redefining cultural studies. *The Journal of American Culture*, 34(1), 13-16.

Bruce, J.A., and Ewing, J.C. (December 2009). Popular culture media as a teaching tool in agricultural and extension education. *NACTA Journal* 53 (4), 8.

Cortés, C.E. (2000). *The children are watching: How the media teach about diversity*. New York: Teachers College Press.

Flores-Koulish, S. A., et al. (Summer 2011). After the media literacy course: Three early childhood teachers look back. *Action in Teacher Education*, 33(2), 127-143.

Freedman, D. (2000). *(Re)presentations of education: Pre-service teachers' interpretations of* Dangerous Minds *through the lens of media cultural studies*. Unpublished doctoral dissertation, The University of Texas, Austin.

Giroux, H. (2010). *Youth in a suspect society: Democracy or disposability?* New York: Palgrave Macmillan.

Hattam, R., Brennan, M., Zipin, L., and Comber, B. (September 2009). Researching for social justice: Contextual, conceptual, and methodological challenges. *Discourse: Studies in the Cultural Politics of Education*, 30 (3), 303-316.

Jhally, S., and Lewis, J. (1992). *Enlightened racism:* The Cosby Show, *audiences, and the myth of the American dream*. Boulder, CO: Westview Press.

Kellner, D., and Share, J. (2005) Toward critical media literacy: Core concepts, debates, organizations, and policies. *Discourse: Studies in the Cultural Politics of Education*, 26(3), 369–386.

Lefstein, A., and Snell, J. (January-March 2011). Promises and problems of teaching with popular culture: A linguistic ethnographic analysis of discourse genre mixing in a literacy lesson. *Reading Research Quarterly*, 46(1), 40-69.

Myers, R.B. (April 1974). The popular arts and the teaching of literature. *ERIC Digest Report*: ED091699.

Paul, Z.E. (March 2011). From Claude Bernard to the Batcave and beyond: Using Batman as a hook for physiology education. *Advances in Physiology Education*, 35(1), 1-4.

Ravitch, D. (2003). *The language police: How pressure groups restrict what students learn.* New York: Alfred A. Knopf.

Sadker, M., Sadker, D. and Klein, S. (1991). The issue of gender in elementary and sec- ondary education. In Grant, G. (Ed.), *Review of Research in Education.* Washington, D.C.: American Educational Research Association.

Smith, D. (Summer 2002). Popular culture and pedagogy: An interview with Peter McLaren. *Journal of Curriculum Theorizing,* 18 (2), 59-63.

Trier, J. (2005). 'Sordid fantasies': Reading popular 'inner-city' school films as racialized texts with pre-service teachers. *Race Ethnicity and Education,* 8(2), 171-189.

Trier, J. (2007). Teaching theory through popular culture texts. *Teaching Education,* 18(2), 151.

Troutman, J.W. (May 2009). Indigenous popular culture. *World Literature Today,* 83(3), 41.

Wildschut, T., Sedikides, C., Arndt, J., and Routledge, C. (2006). Nostalgia: Content, triggers, functions. *Journal of Personality and Social Psychology,* 91(5), 975-993.

Acknowledgments

The editors wish to express tremendous thanks to the American Culture Association/Popular Culture Association, without whom this motley collection of contributors and editors would never have come together; to Lenore Lautigar, Johnnie Simpson, and all at Lexington Press for their inspiration for the project and great patience as deadline after deadline came and passed; to Fred Waweru, formatting genius, without whom the project would not likely have seen its completion; and to Sylvia Mac, for the wonderful artwork for the cover.

In addition, Denni wishes to thank Oklahoma State University for providing her the freedom to teach a course in Popular Culture and Education, and all the incredible students that have been enrolled in it thus far. Ed wishes to thank the University of Wyoming College of Education for supporting his work in the ACA/PCA and all the Education students, undergraduate and graduate, whom he taught using popular culture through the previous decade: thanks for your patience!

Introduction: The Past as Prologue

It is no longer trendy to study foundations when preparing to become a teacher. Due to a confluence of events including corporate meddling, federal control, preservice teacher education mandates, and the silencing of unions, the current generation of classroom teachers has become expert at the technical role of teaching and lacking in the social, philosophical, and historical foundations of education. For example, teachers may know how to implement Character Counts and other similar programs, but they can't identify why John Dewey's notions of democracy and education are so critical in today's climate, let alone discuss the relevance of George Counts's work on teaching for democracy. They can "successfully" implement a proscriptive curricula (i.e., read a script and follow a timer) and discuss backwards design, but may feel stymied by the idea of developing their own unit plans, let alone discuss how the term backwards design is apt as it inverts the Tyler Rationale.

This lack of foundational knowledge is problematic on many levels, not the least of which being professional recognition. Teaching arguably is a semi-profession, not a full profession, lacking in control over its preparation and certification standards. One substantive lack are these very foundations; while other professions that require the same kind of intense, clinical, and ongoing preparation incorporate and infuse historical and philosophical elements throughout their training in the lifetime of their membership, teachers have willingly lost all sense of who they are and how they came to be. Until teachers can stand up and explain why they do what they do in terms philosophic and historical, until all preservice teacher education programs re-emphasize this knowledge, teaching will never achieve fully the status of a profession.

The first two chapters in this work demonstrate attempts at using pop culture to remind educators of the necessity of knowing the past when engaging in contemporary discussions. The chapters talk about the historic development of role formation — the role that politics plays in dictating education policy, and the role the media has played in the development of teachers — and how these roles influence public perception of schooling. Whether examining the role nostalgia plays in current calls for educational reform or how the feminization of the teaching profession influences current debate, both chapters serve as a reminder that those who don't know the past are doomed to repeat it.

Chapter One

Can We Win the Future by Living in the Past? A Preliminary Exploration Of Nostalgia in Education

Jennifer Edelman and Edward Janak

In the 2011 State of the Union Address, President Obama told the country that "The future is ours to win" (White House.gov). Like many presidents before, his outlined plan for winning the future includes innovation in industry and education taken in conjunction. In the minds of many citizens of the United States, progress in education is indelibly linked to economic progress in methodology and results. However, unlike economic innovation that makes significant gains almost on a weekly basis, history has proven that innovative education policies and methods are difficult to sustain (Pinar, Reynolds, Slattery, & Taubman, 2006). We are faced with a rapidly changing global society and economy, yet the system of public education in the United States today looks very similar to the one in place one hundred years ago (Kliebard, 2004). Indeed, if the story of Rip Van Winkle were to occur in the modern age—with Rip awakening in 2012 after twenty years of slumber—it would be the public schools in which Rip finds solace as being wholly unchanged.

There is a need for our public schools to evolve beyond what they have, to become truly progressive once again. Despite this, a nostalgic trend has arisen with calls for a return to a golden age of education and back-to-basics schooling for all students (Shapiro, 1993). In one sense, education is simply falling in line with the greater movement across the United States, one that historian Gavriel Rosenfeld refers to as a "memory industry" (Rosenfeld, 2009). This movement is due to two separate factors: "first, the worldwide proliferation during the last two decades of public controversies over divisive historical legacies and, second, the emergence of scholarly interest in studying memory as a broader social and cultural phenomenon" (Rosenfeld, p. 124).

However, as Rosenfeld cautions, while this trend continues to surge in education (including academia), in the other social aspects it can be seen as a "boom" which has peaked and is in the process of abating. This abatement is due to many factors: differing interpretations of the past, differing philosophical outlooks of changing generations, the rise of identity politics, the exhaustion of nationalism, the politicalization of memory, the increasing acceptance of post-modern deconstructions, and the end of the Cold War. Interestingly, while considered individually, each of those factors has made some impact on education. However, when taken collectively, while they have led to a decrease in nostalgia in other fields, they have led to an increase in nostalgia in education. What makes education so different? Why do citizens of the United States remain so wedded to nostalgia when considering schooling, but willing to abandon it in other respects? And how valid are the memories that fuel it?

This chapter will explore four themes surrounding nostalgia in education. First, we will examine how nostalgia defines the public perception of what a "real" school is. The goal of a "real" school is to create students who have not only adequate knowledge for success, but also a love of learning and creative thinking skills necessary to succeed in a global economy. The idea of "real" schools is hard to overcome when parents and older stakeholders have pre-determined opinions based upon their nostalgic school experiences. Second, we will explore the idea that nostalgia acts as blinders to keep the public from realizing what is actually happening in schools. By elevating the nostalgic image of school to cultural myth, we preclude the possibility of looking critically at what schools actually are. Third, we will investigate the nostalgia for competition. In the United States, "school" is also a place where our culture competes with the world. As Petersson et al. (2007) said, "in most political contexts the 'social losses' of past values—solidarity, trust, fellow-feeling, authority, informal social control, and so on—are recalled and projected as social tools in narratives of the present and the future" (p. 60). President Obama also referred to a "Sputnik moment," which is meant to remind people of a time when the American people were united behind a singular purpose to win the space race (White House.gov). This is what Petersson et al. (2007) mean by "solidarity" as a tool of social control. Without recognition and analysis of these tools, education will not evolve past its nostalgic limitations. Fourth and finally, this chapter examines the validity of memory, the very stuff that fuels the nostalgic pushes in education.

Cultural and Educational Applications of Nostalgia

Originally thought to be a physical and psychological illness, nostalgia has been defined as homesickness, melancholy, and depression (Wildschut, Sedikides, Arndt, & Routledge, 2006). Presently, nostalgia has gained conceptual status, defined not in terms of illness, rather in terms of experience. This chapter defines nostalgia as a longing for an idealized past, whether real or imagined, that is used as a benchmark to measure the quality of current and future experiences against.

Nostalgia can serve several functions in a culture. Nostalgia can be used to define a culture's past and present (Petersson, Olsson, & Popkewitz, 2007). By remembering a common past, a group of people can delineate themselves as different from other groups based on their common experiences. Additionally, when faced with an uncertain and unfamiliar future, a cultural practice can emerge whereby the past is re-memorialized. "Nostalgia is a cultural practice that opens up the possibility of managing the present by reconstructing a past that is accessible and that can inspire mobilization for the future" (Petersson et al., 2007, p. 49).

Nostalgia can also be used to create a benchmark with which to measure current progress. As Dudden (1961) stated, "by contrast with the state of things as they are, there comes beseechingly to mind a preference for things as they once were, or, more importantly, a preference for things as they are believed to have been" (p. 517). Nostalgia is most often applied to education in this method. By "remembering" past school experiences, older generations choose to perpetuate the same system of public education that did not work in the past into the future.

In a country of over 300,000,000 people, institutional schooling is a nearly universal experience and a powerful cultural construct making it ripe for nationwide nostalgia. According to the U.S. Census Bureau, 59.9 million people, ages 3-34 were enrolled in school during the fall of 1969. In 2006, that number had increased to 79.1 million ("School Enrollment in the United States," 1970, p. 1). As nearly everyone has experience with the public school system, the concept of "school" has been defined by memories of experiences. Indeed, schooling is as close to a universal experience as can occur in the increasingly diverse United States. Cultural practices define what school is, what it looks like and how it operates. "Practices such as age-graded classrooms structure schools in a manner analogous to the way grammar organizes meaning in verbal communication. Neither the grammar of schooling nor the grammar of speech needs to be consciously understood to operate smoothly" (Tyack, 1995, p. 85).

Due to this universality, everyone has an idea of what a "real" school should be. Often, that image of a "real" school is a homogenous population of students, all of whom are on grade level, well fed, and ready to learn. Standing before them is a somewhat dowdy schoolmarm, a Rockwell-esque vision of uprightness and virtue. Dangerously, when depicting school environments that deviate from the white, middle class, suburban model that dominates thinking on the matter, the mass media portray students as being "at-risk," dangers to themselves, and in need of a young, attractive, white teacher to serve as educational messiah to the poor students of color—a concept explored more thoroughly in the next chapter of this volume.

Anyone working in schools today knows these are not realities. Poverty and racism still exist. Schools are expected to teach children not only the 3Rs, but to also teach children the social norms of modern society. One suggestion as to why parents are holding schools more accountable for the socialization of their children is the reduction in time that parents and children spend together as both parents need to work longer and harder to make ends meet. This information is not new; back in 1991, Henry Perkinson cautioned that the public schools were becoming viewed as panaceas, being forced to assume a messianic role in society. This role is both unrealistic and unprecedented: schools cannot be expected to fulfill all of the academic and social obligations being thrust upon them, and they are the only agency in U.S. society expected to do so, likely due to their universality.

Competition Nostalgia

Competition has been at the heart of most education reforms since the National Defense Education Act, signed into law in 1958. This is the rhetoric of "falling behind" and "competing in a global economy." In our search for a unifying narrative, competition has become central to education, economy, and security. This narrative means the American people long for the days when they knew (or, at least they *think* they knew) their country was the most powerful in the world. Prior to Sputnik, Americans were sure of their place in the world. Their military superiority was proven in countless global conflicts, then ultimately when the United States developed the nuclear bomb before any other country. Their economy was strong, providing work for every able-bodied man who wanted to work other than in relatively brief moments of recession and depression. Their families were strong, expanding in the post-war years via the "baby boom." Education was adequately preparing their students to take their place in what was perceived as the greatest nation on Earth. It is hard not to long for a return to a time when everyone was so very sure of everything.

This all changed with the launching of Sputnik, in 1957. Suddenly, the United States was not the innovator, no longer the first in everything. What stung even more was that it was the Soviet Union who beat us, a country whose culture and beliefs were almost complete opposites of our own. An obsession with "winning the future" began and has not yet ended. We are constantly measuring our public institutions, businesses, and people so a rank order of success can be created for the world. Indeed, Sputnik has become a sort of battle cry used by presidents, particularly the most recent administrations.

However, events that elicit strong emotional reactions such as Sputnik (or King's assassination, or the Challenger explosion, or 9/11) tend to create what Roger Brown and James Kulik (2000) refer to as "flashbulb memories," memories that emerge from "surprise, an indiscriminate illumination, and brevity" (p. 51). However, as writers in multiple fields have noted, these accounts are often inaccurate (see the inaccuracy of eyewitness accounts); the less personal the memory, the less accurate the memory. When it comes to something like "schooling," without a strong emotional trigger to flash the memory, accounts are subject to suggestion and bias.

Hinging contemporary views of what schooling should be on memories created in such circumstances is folly at best, yet it remains current practice. Examples of competition in education abound. For instance, from the Department of Education's High Priority Goals:

> The U.S. Department of Education seeks to promote student achievement and preparation for **global competitiveness** by fostering educational excellence and ensuring equal access. President Obama's vision is that by 2020, **America will again have the best-educated, most competitive workforce** in the world with the highest proportion of college graduates of any country. To do this, the United States must also close the achievement gap, so that all youth—regardless of their backgrounds—graduate from high school ready to succeed in college and careers. (2010, emphasis added).

Competition is built into the very mission statement of the government agency tasked with improving public education. But, as Michael Apple (1996) and others ask, since when is it ok to have winners and losers in education?

Beyond Apple's criticism, this master narrative of American superiority falls into the trap of the metanarrative as explained by Kerwin Lee Klein (1995). Americans desired this metanarrative of educational superiority to become "institutionalized, canonical, and legitimizing...in a position of intellectual mastery" (p. 282). However, to do so comes at the expense of the local narratives— in this case, the narratives of all of the groups that were being marginalized, colonized, deculturalized, and otherwise excluded from the public schools of the time. These "subaltern" texts remain sublimated by the blinding nostalgia of the time.

Blinded by Nostalgia

The public's attention is engaged with the past. For instance, the Dick and Jane readers were rereleased in 2002. By 2004, 2.5 million copies of these books had been sold (Toppo, 2004). Entire television networks dedicated to reruns of "classic" television programs have evolved. Studios released remakes of old movies and television shows to audiences. How are schools portrayed in these productions? Overwhelming, the schools in these nostalgic indulgences routinely show classrooms where racially homogenous, well-fed and dressed students sit in forward-facing desks. A teacher often stands at the front of the room, looking out over her charges, shiny faced and ready to learn. Order ruled in these classrooms. Everyone was on grade level, everyone followed the rules, and the worst problem for some students seemed to be deciding where to "look, Jane, look."

There is a danger in these images. By focusing attention on these romanticized images of the past, communities are denying that there are any problems lurking just out of sight. As Otto (2005) said, "The reinforcement of a fictitious past in the present, and presumably into the future, functions as an insidious form of propaganda" (p. 465). She continues, "(nostalgia) protects the public from knowing or thinking about what is really happening within schools as a result of this (NCLB) legislation (i.e. teaching only to the test, the testing of tiny children, evaluation costs bankrupting state budgets and so on)" (Otto, 2005, p. 465).

Nostalgia not only serves as a benchmark with which to judge the current state of school, it serves to distract stakeholders from what is actually occurring in public schools today. If a school can look like the schools in the Dick and Jane readers, then parents can know that it is a "real school" and is doing an adequate job. "Anyone who would improve schooling is a captive of history in two ways. All people and institutions are the produce of history (defined as past events). And whether they are aware of it or not, all people use history (defined as an interpretation of past events) when they make choices about the present and future. The issue is not whether people use a sense of the past in shaping their lives, but how accurate and appropriate are their historical maps?" (Tyack & Cuban, 1995, p. 6). In a media-driven culture that privileges the visual, many historical maps are drawn from what appears on TV and in books.

Beyond its immediate factor in shaping nostalgia, this media-driven culture has had a deeper, somewhat more insidious impact on human memory. If, as Brown and Kulik argue, memory comes in flashbulb moments, it has in the past been reliant on what the authors refer to as a "Now Print!" mechanism, by which the human brain actively retains memories felt to be necessary. However, as we live in an ever-emerging media culture that serves as the collective memory, we have had less and less need for this "Now Print!" mechanism. "It seems to be an irony of evolution" argues Brown and Kulik, "that it is just the central newsworthy events that no longer need to be retained because cultural devices have taken over the job" (p. 63). Worse, not only have we stopped trying to allow ourselves to be impacted by events in favor of just looking them up, we have lost sight of the value of living in the moment, appreciating things as they happen rather than how they are played back: "the automatic recording of the circumstances, concomitant to the main event, is what captures our interest and calls for attention" (p. 63). Unfortunately, while we live in a TiVo world, our brains still operate on a direct signal. How many people today live their lives through their screens rather than their eyes? And what impact is this lack of direct experience going to have on the memories and nostalgia of the next generation?

Validity of Memory, Validity of Nostalgia

A detailed examination of the impact of nostalgia would be incomplete without a critical examination of memory, the very stuff that feeds nostalgia. Indeed, the study of memory is taking on growing importance in the fields of history. Scholars such as Kerwin Klein refer to examination of memory as "the leading term in our new cultural history" (Klein, 2000, p. 128) and Charles Maier argues "memory has become the discourse that replaces history" itself (Maier, 1993, p. 143). While both of these phrases may be seen as hyperbolic, the fundamental belief that underpins them—that memory is worthy of study in itself—is valid.

The validity of examination of memory in educational nostalgia is particularly relevant. The history of schooling in the United States easily fits Rosenfeld's definition of being an

> unmastered history... a historical legacy that has acquired an exceptional, abnormal, or otherwise unsettled status in the collective memory of a given society. This distinct status arises from the fact that the particular past in question typically involves the commission of a historic injustice—an act of war, genocide, or political oppression—that has been remembered differently by, and has caused discord between, the original perpetrators, victims, and their respective descendants. (p. 127)

Indeed, the history of schooling in the United States, particularly when viewed through the lenses of historically marginalized groups, is one of a series of acts of historic injustice and political oppression which often get overlooked when applying the warm sepia tones of nostalgia. Rosenfeld's further argument—that such unmastered histories typically become silenced or repressed as neither perpetrators nor victims choose to further explore it—is a fitting description of the current state of discourse in the study of the history of education. Across the United States, colleges of education have become so focused on contemporary trends they have willingly abandoned historical foundations. This lack of foundational knowledge permits those who argue in nostalgic tones to voice their opinions uncontestedly.

Indeed, memory studies in general, nostalgic trips specifically, have become suspect by some scholars, ironically their lack of innovation. As explained by Banaji and Crowder (2000), those who study memory have provided no means of hypothesis validation—no means of proving the validity of the studies. By the turn of the millennium, in the fields related to memory studies, "No theories that have unprecedented explanatory power have been produced; no new principles of memory have been discovered; and no methods of data collection have been developed that add sophistication or precision" (p. 20). Short of using the qualitative researcher's tool of triangulating data, there is no means of confirming memory—and often nostalgia is the result. The average American citizen is not going to find multiple sources of information against which they can judge the validity of their memory on a day-to-day basis; they believe what they remember, and they remember what they believe.

"Unreflected nostalgia breeds monsters" (Boym, 2002, p. xvi)

Nostalgia is said to create positive feelings. "The nostalgic feeling is infused with sentiments of past beauty, pleasure, joy, satisfaction, goodness, happiness, love, etc.; in sum, any or several of the positive affects of being" (Davis, 1977, p. 418). Nostalgia, when applied to education, brings feelings of dissatisfaction, casting schools in a negative light. In Rosenfeld's terms, there still lacks reconciliation between conflicting groups with conflicting views of history causing discord in educational nostalgia. While educators see change occurring in schools, parents no longer share the belief that schools will be successful because they are so different than their own experiences. In actuality, schools have not changed much over the years. The Carnegie unit still applies, students continue to primarily use books to learn, and a teacher is still judged on his or her ability to maintain order. Perhaps the disillusion that many people feel about education comes not from dissatisfaction with how school is today, but with how it has always been.

Most troubling of this trend is the fundamental question: do the adult stakeholders in education—the parents, politicians, professors, and teachers—actually remember what they think they remember? Raymond Nickerson and Marilyn Adams (2000) argue that while people are convinced they know certain things—their example is a penny—whether they actually do or not is another matter entirely. To fully and accurately understand memories, one must determine if they actually remember the object—or the context, the "conceptual category" (p. 125) in which the person places the object. In addition, they must determine how much of an object they remember—or if they just remember enough to differentiate it in some way. Schooling is exactly such an object. Like a penny, it is common and familiar, yet complex and interesting. And just like a penny, everyone thinks they remember it accurately—but few actually do. Worse, without any foundational backing to provide context, people's memories of schooling—particularly, what schooling should be—become jumbled in with every other memory, every other flashbulb moment, until what constitutes effective teaching comes equally from their media exposure as their actual exposure.

Nostalgia for schools that never were is a dangerous thing. Schools are compared to impossible ideals. This sense of collective nostalgia as evidenced by references to Sputnik, back-to-basics curricula, and even Dick and Jane add ammunition to the arguments against public schools and the people who work in them. It is only in examining what this nostalgia means and what it serves to distract from that we will liberate our education system from unrealistic ideals and allow innovative ideas to take hold. After all, "See Jane fill in the bubble" never appeared in any of the Dick and Jane readers.

References

Apple, M.W. (1996). *Cultural politics and education*. New York: Teachers College Press.

Banaji, M.R., and Crowder, R.G. (2000). The bankruptcy of everyday memory. In Neisser, U. and Hyman, I.E., eds. *Memory observed: Remembering in natural contexts*. New York: Worth Publishers, 19-27.

Boym, S. (2002). *The future of nostalgia*. New York: Basic Books.

Brown, R. and Kulik, J. (2000). Flashbulb memories. In Neisser, U., and Hyman, I.E., eds. *Memory observed: Remembering in natural contexts*. New York: Worth Publishers, 50-65.

Davis, F. (1977). Nostalgia, identity and the current nostalgia wave. *The Journal of Popular Culture, 11*(2), 414-424. doi:10.1111/j.0022-3840.1977.00414.x

Davis, J., & Bauman, K. (2008). School enrollment in the United States 2006. Retrieved from United States Census Bureau website: http://www.census.gov/population /www/socdemo/school.html

Department of Education High Priority Performance Goals. (2010) Reports. Retrieved from http://www2.ed.gov/about/overview/focus/goals.html

Dudden, A. P. (1961). Nostalgia and the American. *Journal of the History of Ideas, 22*(4), 515-530. doi:10.2307/2708028

Klein, K.L. (2000, Winter). On the emergence of memory in historical discourse. *Representations, 127*–150.

Klein, K.L. (December 1995). In search of narrative mastery: Postmodernism and the people without history. *History and Theory, 34*(4), 275-298.

Kliebard, H. M. (2004). *The struggle for the American curriculum, 1893-1958*. New York: Routledge.

Maier, C. (1993, Fall/Winter). "A surfeit of memory? Reflections on history, melancholy, and denial. *History and Memory, 143*.

Nickersen, R.S., and Adams, M.J. (2000). Long term memory for a common object. In Neisser, U., and Hyman, I.E., eds. *Memory observed: Remembering in natural contexts*. New York: Worth Publishers, 125-136.

Otto, S. (2005). Nostalgic for what? The epidemic of images of the mid 20th century classroom in American media culture and what it means. *Discourse: Studies in the Cultural Politics of Education, 26*(4), 459-475. doi:10.1080/01596300500319738

Perkinson, H.J. (1991). *The imperfect panacea: American faith in education, 1865-1990*. New York: McGraw-Hill, Inc.

Petersson, K., Olsson, U., & Popkewitz, T. S. (2007). Nostalgia, the future, and the past as pedagogical technologies. *Discourse: Studies in the Cultural Politics of Education, 28*(1), 49-67. doi:10.1080/01596300601073598

Pinar, W. F., Reynolds, W. M., Slattery, P., & Taubman, P. M. (2006). *Understanding curriculum: An introduction to the study of historical and contemporary curriculum discourses*. New York: Peter Lang.

Remarks by the President in State of Union Address. White House.gov. (2011). Retrieved from http://www.whitehouse.gov/the-press-office/2011/01/25/remarks-president-state-union-address.

Rosenfeld, G.D. (2009, March). A looming crash or a soft landing? Forecasting the future of the memory "industry." *The Journal of Modern History*, 81, 122-158.

Shapiro, S. (1993). Back to basics: A politics of meaning for education. *Tikkun, 8*(1), 46-50.

Toppo, G. (2004, February 25). 2.5 million reissued books sold. *USA Today*. Retrieved from http://www.usatoday.com/life/books/news/2004-02-25-dick-janesidebar_x.htm ?loc=interstitialskip#

Tyack, D., and Cuban, L. (1995). *Tinkering toward utopia: A century of public school reform*. Cambridge, MA: Harvard University Press.

Wildschut, T., Sedikides, C., Arndt, J., & Routledge, C. (2006). Nostalgia: Content, triggers, functions. *Journal of Personality and Social Psychology, 91*(5), 975-993. doi:10.1037/0022-3514.91.5.975

Chapter Two

Professional Paradox: Teachers in Film and Television

Sheila Delony and Mikee Delony

A gathering of men at the 1853 state teachers' convention in Albany, New York, engaged in a discussion of the status of the teaching profession. They wondered why they, as teachers, were not given as much respect and reverence as men who were doctors or lawyers. As the board members and other men discussed the issue, more than three hundred women, also teachers, sat in the back and listened in silence. Although they represented two thirds of the convention attendees, women were not invited to be committee members, nor did they speak up during the proceedings. Growing weary of their ignorant discourse, Susan B. Anthony stood up and spoke out, provoking a debate of whether or not she should be allowed to address the men. When finally granted permission to speak, she stated,

> None of you quite comprehend the cause of the disrespect of which you complain. Do you not see that so long as society says woman is incompetent to be a lawyer, minister, or doctor, but has ample ability to be a teacher, every man of you who chooses this profession tacitly acknowledges that he has no more brains than a woman? And this, too, is the reason that teaching is a less lucrative profession; as here men must compete with the cheap labor of woman. Would you exalt your profession, exalt those who labor with you. Would you make it more lucrative, increase the salaries of the women engaged in the noble work of educating our future Presidents, Senators, and Congressmen. (Lutz, 1959, p. 58)

In her brief, historic remarks, Anthony summed up the feminization of the teaching profession, the challenges of public perceptions of teaching, and paradoxical position of women in the profession. More than 150 years later, her words still resonate.

Cinema and television have produced many representations of the inspirational and life-changing teacher, and most of these well-known, idealized teacher figures are male. Female teachers often play secondary roles rather than lead characters such as Miss Crump in the *Andy Griffith Show* (Whedon & Sweeney, 1963), and are more likely to be conflicted such as Mrs. Gruwell in *Freedom Writers* (DeVito & LaGravenese, 2007), lonely such as Miss Wilder in *Little House on the Prairie* (Landon, 1980), sexualized such as Ms. Holiday in *Glee* (Falchuk & Murphy, 2011), and all-around awful as Ms. Halsey in *Bad Teacher* (Miller & Kasden, 2011). Since, as Dalton and Linder (2008) argue, "visual texts with moving images have become the dominant textual forms of contemporary global culture" (p. 2), we have chosen to examine a sample representation of primarily female teachers in television and film since the 1950s, decades which precede and coincide with the second and third waves of feminist theory and practice, in order to understand how media constructions have contributed to contemporary assumptions about the teaching profession.

Using the lenses of feminist theory, critical media literacy, and cultural theory, the current examination of teacher portrayals in television and movies initially focused on cinematic and televised representations of female elementary school teachers in the United States. However, we soon discovered that although there are more than three times as many women as men teaching in public schools, male characters dominate television and movie depictions of teaching. Therefore, to obtain a broader sample, the examination included male and female elementary teachers as well as a sampling of women teaching at other levels. Although we will pay some attention to the few male elementary teachers featured in popular visual media, we focus on the ways in which the construction of the female teacher builds on at the same time it reflects cultural stereotypes about the teaching profession in general and the female educator in particular. The examples provided are intended to be a representative selection rather than an exhaustive review. For extensive reviews of television and movie teachers, see *The Hollywood Curriculum* (Dalton, 2007) and *Teacher TV* (Dalton & Linder, 2008).

The cross-disciplinary nature of cultural theory and cultural studies provides an ideal grounding for a study of the symbiotic interchange between entertainment media (for our purposes, film and television) and cultural practices. Contemporary wisdom as well as research (Fiske, J., 1989; Bourdieu, P., 1984; Hall, S., 1997; Storey, J., 2003; Rose, G., 2007) proposes that cultural assumptions influence media representations, which in turn influence cultural assumptions. Likewise, Sholle and Denski's (1993) critical media literacy suggests, "the structures of media production . . . may be approached as sets of complex social practices which to varying degrees either serve to reproduce . . . or overcome" (p. 297) social constructions of the teaching profession. They suggest praxis, the enactment of theory, as "an element of possibility for reworking these conditions" (p. 301). Likewise, "our understanding that feminism fuses theory and practice and, in terms of education, yields both praxis and pedagogy" (Coffey & Delamont, 2000, p. 13). Thus, we base our feminist analyses of these representations on the definition of feminism articulated by Donna Haraway (1989): "'Feminist theory and practice . . . seek to explain and change historical systems of sexual difference, whereby 'men' and 'women' are socially constituted and positioned in relations of hierarchy and antagonism" (p. 290). Additionally, in our cultural studies approach to these representations, Coffey and Delamont's (2000) assertion that "as a contribution to the body of work on gender and education, we are concerned with the educational discourses of gender–that is, how gender is constructed and performed through discursive and material practices" (p. 2), forms a basis for our argument. In this chapter, we argue that rather than *raising* the cultural status of teachers, particularly elementary teachers, the media representation of the teaching profession has become increasingly feminized and devalued during the last six decades, a move that perhaps contributes to the current image of the teacher as unprofessional, rebellious, and only accidentally heroic.

In many cases, the classroom experiences of one generation of creators become the cultural constructions of classroom teachers for the following generation of media consumers. When discussing the impact of models of teaching, both real and constructed, on current classroom teachers as well as those planning to enter the profession, Linda Darling-Hammond (2006) describes a "dilemma of apprenticeship" (p. 41), a process by which students are influenced by watching their own teachers in their own classrooms, both effective and ineffective, for twelve or more years before becoming teachers themselves. They carry these images, as well as the teacher exemplars that they see on television and in movies, into their classrooms, often without critical examination of their models. In fact, Sholle and Denski (1993) call television, in particular, "a *pedagogical machine*" (p. 309). Studies reveal that children, especially girls, spend a tremendous amount of time watching television shows about school (Weber & Mitchell, 1995), and, in the process, the countless characters, scenes, and scripts featuring teachers become part of the teaching profession's unacknowledged pedagogy. According to Dalton and Linder (2008) "we, individually and collectively, draw on the narratives we encounter 'as scripts'" filled with both limitations and possibilities for our lives" (p. 3). Current teachers were once shaped by media portrayals of teachers, and they will in turn play a role in shaping the next generation of teachers.

As media becomes more ubiquitous, examination of its impact on the teaching profession becomes more crucial. As Sholle and Denski (1993) assert, "educational theory must engage with the popular as the background that informs students' engagement with any pedagogical encounter" (p. 307). In order to understand on-screen portrayals of teachers, it is necessary to explore the history of women in teaching. Only through such critical examination can teacher educators begin reprogramming the next generation of educators, freeing them from limitations that were put in place by history and are held there by popular media.

"A Sort of Career"[1]: The Paradox of Teaching

While men have more often been featured as classroom heroes on the screen, children's play involving school scenarios has occupied a "particularized, gendered space in the play and popular culture of girls" (Weber & Mitchell, 1995, p.10). This is not unexpected, considering that in North America, Europe, and Australia, most elementary school teachers are women. It may be surprising to realize that this was not always the case. The feminization of the teaching profession began in the early nineteenth century with an economic shift from agriculture to industry. Within the span of two generations following the War of 1812, industrialization replaced many self-sufficient homesteads. The home farm was no longer the primary source of food, clothing, and tools (Grumet, 1988). The American household was almost emptied out. Men went to work in town, children went to common school, and women remained at home. The Cult of Domesticity (Strober & Tyack, 1980) perpetuated the notion that women were innately more pure and virtuous, therefore, limiting their vocation to matters of matrimony and maternity. By extension, teaching was a suitable place for unmarried or widowed women to fulfill their divinely designated roles. Women's innate virtuousness and nurturing spirit were appropriate in the schools, which were viewed as extensions of home and church. As in the home, school-teachers were responsible for the same group of children year after year as they progressed through their studies. Over time, these women could become intimately connected to their pupils. Women were expected to bring maternal nurturance to the *surrogate family* of the common school, and it wasn't long before the mother figure became the only resemblance between the common school and family structure. The school structure eventually transitioned to graded schools; working with one age group for one year at a time. Grumet (1988) explains, "Rather than demand the extended relation that would bind (women) over time to individual children, they agreed to large group instruction where the power of the peer collective was at least as powerful as the mother/child bond" (p. 55).

Single young women had been teaching intermittently prior to the feminization of the profession, often filling in for men who were farming. Men who taught were generally on a path toward other careers. Teaching allowed them to save for college or make other preparations for their chosen professions. As schools became more organized and school governance shifted from local to state-level, accreditation became an expectation. Men did not consider it worthwhile to become credentialed for a temporary position, but women, who had few other options, were willing to earn the required credentials to be teachers (Grumet, 1988). Normal schools were given the charge of preparing teachers and issuing certificates. Preparation of teachers included both academic and moral development (Grant & Murray, 1999) as exemplified by Laura Ingalls's announcement in the opening episode of the 1980-81 season of *Little House on the Prairie* (Landon & Landon, 1980), "I worked hard for my teaching certificate. Who knows, maybe someday it will come in handy." Paradoxically, as the profession became increasingly feminized, the perceived standard for professionalism diminished, as did the value of formal certification.

Popular films such as *Dangerous Minds* (Bruckheimer & Smith, 1995), featuring Michelle Pfeiffer as LouAnn Johnson, an ex-marine; *Kindergarten Cop* (Reitman & Reitman, 1990), in which undercover police officer John Kimble, played by Arnold Schwarzenegger, becomes a teacher; and *School of Rock* (Rudin & Linklater, 2003), with Jack Black as Dewey Finn, a failed musician-cum-teacher, suggest that teaching certification is really not necessary and indeed may inhibit a teacher's success in the classroom. The protagonists of these films imply that good teaching requires little more than Johnson's leather jacket, Kimble's police whistle, and Finn's electric guitar. Perhaps the most publically egregious dismissal of the value of teacher education and certification occurred in the September 27, 2008, Presidential Debate between Senators John McCain and Barack Obama. In this public forum, McCain, while speaking of opportunities for returning Iraq and Afghanistan war veterans, stated, "We need to encourage programs such as Teach for America and Troops to Teachers where people, after having served in the military, can go right to teaching and *not have to take these examinations . . . or have the certifications that are . . .* required in some states" [emphasis added]. Raising the debate over the necessity of certificated and qualified teachers to the political level, McCain's remarks reflect an ongoing public perception of the certified teacher as unnecessary and certainly not a viable and respected profession requiring rigorous and professional training.

By 1900, three-quarters of all teachers were women (Grant & Murray, 1999). Grumet (1988) suggests, "women entered teaching in order to gain access to the power and prerogatives of their fathers" (p. 54). As classroom teaching positions were increasingly filled by women and male teachers moved into administrative positions, maternal instincts "collapsed into strategies for control," trapping female teachers into yet another educational paradox: "The ideal teacher was one who could control the children and be controlled by her superiors" (p. 43). From a 1953 Disney cartoon, "Teachers Are People," which features Goofy as a teacher who is oblivious to the out-of-control children to Opie's teacher, Miss Crump's, outrage in the 1963 episode, "Andy Discovers America" of the *Andy Griffith Show* (Whedon and Sweeney) when Andy's folksy advice to Opie and his friends undermines her authority in the classroom, to Kendle's shouts of "Shut-up" to his out-of-control kindergarten class (Reitman, et al., and Reitman, 1990), and Johnson's description of her students as "Rejects from hell" (Bruckheimer & Smith, 1995), the teacher's ability or inability to keep order in the classroom has been a mainstay of media representation of teachers. Likewise, Hogwarts School of Magic and Wizardry's overbearing Professor Umbridge, played by Imelda Staunton (Heyman and Columbus, 2002), also focuses specifically on rules, regulations, and consequences, and the unnamed teacher in *Phoebe in Wonderland* (Day and Barnz, 2008) frustrates the children with her list of rules which includes the regulation that students many only "ask questions when it's time to ask questions."

Administrative assessment of teachers also focuses on classroom management. In *Dangerous Minds* (Bruckheimer and Smith, 1995), Johnson, struggling to manage the behavior of her out-of-control at-risk students, is told to "get their attention," Finn's principal is relieved to see that his class seems to be well-behaved, and in *Freedom Writers* (DeVito and Lagravenese, 2007), Gruwell's Department Chair, Ms. Anderson, also played by Imelda Staunton, advises that "the best thing you can do is get them to obey." *Doubt* (Rudin, Roybal, and Shanley, 2008), features two nuns, Sister James played by Amy Adams and Sister Aloysius played by Meryl Streep, who embody the teacher/administrator paradox. Sister James's love of teaching and classroom autonomy is severely damaged by Sister Aloysius's insistence on invading her classroom, going through Sister James's desk drawers, and demanding that she control students above all else. As she sits at Sister James's desk, Sister Aloysius reinforces her focus on student behavior by asking, "Are you in control of your class?"

As female teachers learned to control the students in their classrooms, they also tested administrative boundaries. In yet another paradox, "male educators invited women into the school expecting to reclaim their mothers, and the women accepted the invitation and came so that they might identify with their fathers" (Grumet, 1988, p. 55). Although, for many women, teaching represented more independence than they had known up to that point, neither expectation proved accurate. As explained by Coffey and Delamont (2000), "while teachers may have considerable autonomy in the classroom, women teachers, particularly, do not experience the same power within the school and education system generally" (p. 16). In *Doubt*, Sister James answers a query from Sister Aloysius (Rudin, Roybal, and Shanley, 2008) with, "I try to take care of things myself," to which Sister Aloysius replies, "That can be an error. You are answerable to me, I to the Monsignor, . . . There is a chain. Make use of it." Although James's immediate supervisor, like Mrs. Gruwell's in *Freedom Writers* (DeVito and Lagravenese, 2007), is a female, the chain of command almost always leads to control by out-of-touch male superiors. The structure of the school system assumes male leadership and female compliance; however, in their determination to maintain a measure of their autonomy, women feigned compliance in the face of their superiors, and then delighted in the command they held in the classroom. They became proficient at seemingly "accept(ing) the curriculum as bestowed," while asserting their own independence behind closed doors (Grumet, 1983, p. 55).

Perhaps reflecting decades of subversive rebellion, on-screen portrayals of teachers suggest that a good teacher is noncompliant or in conflict with administrators, both male and female. Ms. Johnson in *Dangerous Minds* and Mrs. Gruwell in *Freedom Writers* are examples of teachers who choose noncompliance in order to teach difficult classes and who face skeptical inquiry by their supervisors when their teaching is successful. In *Doubt,* Sister Aloysius demands complete compliance from her teachers at the same time she pushes the limits of her authority by accusing her male superior of misconduct and successfully forcing him out of the school.

Although the infusion of women into the profession had feminized the classroom, this did little to introduce the atmosphere of the home or the mother/child relationship into schools. Female teachers were expected to provide a nurturing atmosphere for their students at the same time the factory model of school systems, increasingly mechanized and impersonal, often failed to "sustain human relationships of sufficient intimacy to support the risks, the trust and the expression that learning requires" (Grumet, 1988, p. 56). This paradox is often modeled in popular representations of female teachers. For example, in *Freedom Writers* (DeVito and Lagravenese, 2007), based on the experiences of a teacher in an inner-city high school, Mrs. Gruwell describes her very successful class as "family," saying, "Room 203 is a kind of home for them. Their trust is all wrapped in us being together as a group." Nonetheless, Ms. Anderson questions her success with this group of students by asking, "What about the new students that come in next year? Can [you] repeat the process every year?"

This film, as well as others, highlights the difficulty of meeting educational goals and criteria at the same time the female teacher creates a "family" atmosphere in the classroom. Furthermore, according to Grumet (1988), "the gender contradictions, the simultaneous assertion and denial of femininity, have served to estrange teachers of children from the mothers of those children. Instead of being allied, mothers and teachers distrust each other" (p. 56). This distrust is revealed in the 2008 film, *Phoebe in Wonderland* (Day and Barnz, 2008), which focuses Phoebe Lichten, played by Elle Fanning, an elementary child with Tourette Syndrome. Phoebe's mother, played by Felicity Huffman has a difficult conference with Phoebe's teacher in which the teacher implies that Elle's difference is the result of "difficulties at home." Later in the evening Mrs. Lichten responds to her husband's comment, "She wasn't accusing you of anything," by saying, "Of course she was." Clearly, Phoebe's mother feels threatened by the intrusion of the surrogate mother into her domestic domain.

The reduction in teacher salaries is further evidence of the devaluing of teaching as women entered the profession. Early nineteenth century women made 60 percent less than their male counterparts. The lower salaries were justified by explanations that female teachers would not be in the classroom long. They would eventually choose to get married or start families, so they really were not worth the investment. At the same time, large numbers of newly arriving immigrant children entering the classroom increased the demand for teachers, a cheap labor force of women teachers was an easy solution to the problem of education funding. In 1853 Catherine Beecher, explained the paltry salaries by noting that "women (could) afford to teach for one half, or even less the salary which men would ask, because the female teacher has only to sustain herself" (as cited in Grumet, 1988, p. 39). Unfortunately, while the circumstances of women's lives have changed dramatically in the last 150 years since Beecher's justification of substandard salaries, the spirit of the justification has persisted: "No matter how successful, teaching is portrayed as a failure to do something else more meaningful . . . The unspoken assumption is that teaching really doesn't pay" (Bauer, 1998, p. 312). This concept is poignantly portrayed in *Freedom Writers* (DeVito and Lagravenese, 2007) when Mrs. Gruwell endures reproach from her father because of the low salary she accepts for her teaching job and condemnation from her husband for taking a second job in order to earn extra money to buy supplies for her classes. Her husband, played by Patrick Dempsey, asks incredulously, "You're gonna get an extra job to pay for your job." Although still saddled with the century-old low pay structure for teachers, twenty-first century teachers also face criticism from family members for choosing a low-paying career.

Representative of the feminization of the profession, movie and television definitions of "good teachers" exemplify service and altruism (Dalton, 2007), and questioning paltry salaries risks having one's dedication questioned. Like nurses, another professional group dominated by women, teachers, although sentimentalized and overvalued symbolically for their impact and community status, are undervalued economically and structurally (Grant and Murray, 1999) and are criticized for questioning the status quo. However, in August 2011, actor Matt Damon publically defended the integrity and dedication of his mother and other teachers against the assumption that teacher job security promotes teacher laziness and ineptitude:

> See, you take this MBA-style thinking, right? It's the problem with ed policy right now, this intrinsically paternalistic view of problems that are much more complex than that. It's like saying a teacher is going to get lazy when they have tenure. A teacher wants to teach. I mean, why else would you take a shitty salary and really long hours and do that job unless you really love to do it? (Damon, 2011).

From Chaste to Promiscuous: Personal Relationships and Sexuality

Healthy romantic relationships are among the sacrifices demanded of most on-screen teachers. Female teachers in early television shows were either unmarried and childless or their lives outside of school were never mentioned (Dalton & Linder, 2008). Historically speaking, the first women teachers experienced strictures against marriage. Their contracts dictated standards for recreation, hygiene, religion, and of course, romance. The teachers typically boarded at the school or with the family of a school board member or one of her pupils. Grumet (1988) explains, "The cult of maternal nurturance ignored female sexuality, oblivious to the erotic gratifications of maternity and the sensual and sexual life of the young women it kept under constant surveillance. The teacher was expected to banish sensuality from the classroom and from her life" (p. 53). Even for modern teachers in the media, "there is never a clear boundary between private and public life" (Bauer, 1998, p. 303). Most teachers on-screen either enter the profession due to romantic failure or are forced to choose between a romantic relationship and a career in teaching. Miss Brooks, played by Eve Arden in the popular 1950s television series, *Our Miss Brooks* (Lewis & Quillan, 1955), is a high school English teacher who is seemingly marking time in the classroom until she can capture a husband. In the 1955 episode, "Home Cooked Meal," she pretends to cook dinner for Mr. Boynton and is advised by her elderly landlady, the real cook that "once a girl gets married, all she needs is lipstick and a can opener." However, Dalton and Linder (2008) suggest that while Miss Brooks appears "ready for a day of domestic chores in the rose-covered cottage . . . her overall performance suggest[s] that Brooks prefers the independence of making her own money and her own decisions " (Dalton & Linder, 2008, p. 26). Miss Brooks's failure to get her man prevents her from " . . . disappearing into the domestic sphere," where "it is hard to imagine that Brooks' strength, independence, and individuality would have thrived, or even survived" (Dalton & Linder, 2008, p. 29).

A quarter century later the producers of *Grease* (Carr, Stigwood, and Kleiser, 1978) provide an intertextual nod to Miss Brooks by casting Eve Arden as the principal of Rydell High. Dalton and Linder note that "by reprising her earlier iconic role, she is simultaneously evoking the nostalgia for and satirizing the 1950s" construction of the unmarried teacher (p. 30). Other well-known film and television teachers representing the tension between romance and teaching include Laura Ingalls Wilder, played by Melissa Gilbert, who is determined to teach after her marriage to Almonzo in the *Little House* series (Landon and Landon, 1980), "Old Lady" Crump, played by Aneta Corsaut, who chooses to teach rather than marry in the *Andy Griffith* Series (Whedon and Sweeney, 1963-1968), and LouAnn Johnson in *Dangerous Minds,* who needs a teaching job because she is divorcing. The dilemma comes full circle from the expectation that nineteenth-century teachers would be single to Mrs. Gruwell's difficult choice in *Freedom Writers* (DeVito and Lagravenese, 2007). Over a century after women were expected to choose between marriage and teaching, she finds herself in a similar dilemma when her husband complains that he cannot remain in the marriage because he cannot be her *wife.* Erin Gruwell is caught between the heavy demands of a teaching career and the impossible requirements of a husband who *allows* her to fulfill her calling to teach as long as it does not interfere with her *duty* to be a self-sacrificing partner who puts his career and his needs before her own.

At the opposite end of the spectrum from the chaste schoolmarm is the over-sexualized image of the teacher seductress. The inclusion of a female teacher's personal life into storylines has been accompanied by an unmistakable focus on her body. This shift from what Weber and Mitchell (1995) call the "teacher's familiar blandness," and Gallop (Gallop as cited in Bauer 1998, p. 301) calls the "breast—singular, symbolic, and maternal," in the second half of the twentieth century has increasingly moved to the female teacher's sexuality, "not the breast, which is already appropriately there, but the [sexualized] breasts" (p. 301). Perhaps, beginning in 1963 when wholesome, homespun Andy Taylor meets "Old Lady" Crump (Whedon and Sweeney) in "Andy Discovers America" (Whedon and Sweeney, 1963), the asexual teacher begins to transform into a woman with a sexual dimension. The audience sees the introduction of Opie's young, unmarried teacher to the series through the admiring eyes of Andy Taylor. As she enters the police station primly dressed in a long-sleeved, shirtwaist dress and heels, the camera shifts from Andy's gaze to his admiring smile as he stands and stammers, "You ain't Old Lady Crump?" In this moment the audience, and Andy, see Miss Crump as not only the authoritative teacher that Opie fears but as the desirable young woman who catches Sheriff Taylor's eye and later his heart.

Bauer (1995) writes that "Hollywood eventually misrepresents all professions, and all vocations are ultimately sexualized" (p. 301), and he laments that "teaching, once represented as a profound class is now represented as a sexual proposition—a shift that should give us pause" (p. 302). In a larger, more disturbing shift in the sexualization of the female teacher the 1984 release of Van Halen's music video, *Hot for Teacher* [Kramer, Angelus and Roth] marks a shift from an appropriate adult teacher relationship to the teacher as *object* of adolescent sexual fantasy. This video features a blond "teacher" wearing only a blue bikini, bursting through the doorway of the classroom and dancing on the teacher's desk, to the delight and enthusiastic approval of her adolescent male students. This sexualization of the female teacher that began nearly thirty years ago and continued with the recent film *Bad Teacher* (Miller and Kasden, 2011) has created "a misleading eroticized pedagogy" (Bauer, 1998, p. 315). Films such as *Dangerous Minds* (Bruckheimer & Smith, 1995) and *Notes on a Scandal* (Fox & Rudin, 2006), which feature attractive female teachers, continue to promote the sexuality of previously non-sexualized role. One of the early scenes in *Dangerous Minds* features LouAnn Johnson's frightening encounter with a male student, Emilio, who responds to her demand for order in the classroom by leering as he vocalizes his interest in "eat [ing]" Johnson. Bauer (1998) describes this classroom as an "eroticized zone, supercharged with violence, disrespect for authority and moral chaos" (p. 307).

Although Johnson finds this situation dangerous and upsetting, fictional teachers in later years at times not only contribute to, but also create, eroticized classroom environments. In the popular television series about a high school chorus group, *Glee* (Falchuk and Murphy, 2009), the love life of chorus director Will Schuester, played by Matthew Morrison, is an important aspect of the story line. In the first season Mr. Schuester's marriage dissolves, leaving him free to pursue his love interest, the school guidance counselor Emma Pillsbury, played by Jayma Mays. In the fifth episode of season two, "The Rocky Horror Glee Show" (2010), Will and Emma rehearse a sexually charged song, "Touch-a, Touch-a, Touch-a Me." During the eroticized song and dance, Emma removes Will's shirt, and they dance suggestively as two female members of the chorus watch through a classroom window. The teacher sexuality quotient is increased with the addition of a substitute teacher and occasional love interest for Will, Holly Holiday, played by Gwyneth Paltrow in a recurring role (Falchuk & Murphy, 2011). In the season two episode, "Sexy," Holiday substitutes for the sex education teacher and acts out her class lesson on "safe sex" by singing "Do You Wanna Touch Me (Oh Yeah)" with the glee club. Dressed in black leather pants, jacket, and bustier, Holiday suggestively sings the lyrics and invites the club members to join her, asking each student, male and female, "do you wanna touch me." In addition to leading the group in the seductive song and dance, in her role as sex education teacher, Holiday shares a kiss with Schuester and provides both hetero- and homosexual counseling to the glee club members.

In the 2011 feature film, *Bad Teacher* (Miller and Kasden), middle school teacher Elizabeth Halsey played by Cameron Diaz, embodies the antithesis of the virtuous teacher model, spending much of the school year drunk and sleeping at her desk while, ironically, her students watch movies about inspirational teachers. However, Jane Gallop's (as cited in Bauer 1998, p. 301) premise that the eroticism of the classroom is focused on the teacher's breasts becomes reality in this film when Halsey decides that surgical breast augmentation will help her attract a man. Her personal fundraising efforts include Halsey increasing profits from the student fundraiser by performing a sudsy, Daisy Duke-clad car wash on the hood of a car, and then stealing the money. She cheats, lies, asks a fellow teacher, "what went so wrong in your life that you ended up educating children," yet ultimately wins the teaching prize, and gets away with all her misdeeds. It may seem that Halsey represents a progressive, new image of the American schoolteacher. However, although she is sexually charged and morally bankrupt, Halsey only teaches because she cannot find a man to support her. Ironically, larger breasts in 2011 and domestic know-how in 1955 are both women's means to the same end: escaping the classroom to return to their culturally assigned place in the home. In the end, teaching is still portrayed as a temporary, "sort of career" (Burgess, 1989, p. 79) suitable for ladies in waiting.

Conclusion

The feminization of the teaching profession began over 150 years ago, and even though "many of the economic and social conditions" no longer exist, "pedagogy and curriculum still bear the character of this era, and we carry in our bodies, in our smiles, our spasms, our dreams, responses to a world that is no longer ours" (Grumet, 1988, p. 47). Analysis of teacher portrayals on television and in movies can encourage consumers of visual media to construct a critical perspective for how these images continue to influence the profession. Rather than remaining passive in consumption and complicit to propagation, perhaps viewers can heed Grumet's (1988) charge: "Stigmatized as 'women's work,' teaching rests waiting for us to reclaim it and transform it into the work of women" (p. 58). Teachers need not be limited to the roles in which television and movies have cast them. Just as visual media influences public perception, real-life teachers have potential to shape the next generation of popular culture production, but "this pedagogical transformation means redeeming our own images from the trivialization they suffer on film" (Bauer, 1998, p. 315). Unlike the hundreds of women sitting silently in the back rows in Amherst, twenty-first century teachers have a responsibility to use their collective voice to increase professional expectations and in turn, improve media representations and public perceptions of the professional educator.

Notes

1. We borrow this section title from Hilary Burgess (1989).

References

Bauer, D. M. (1998). Indecent proposals: Teachers in the movies. *College English, 60,* (3), 301-317.

Barron, D., and Heyman, D. (Producers), & Yates, D. (Director). (2007). *Harry Potter and the Order of the Phoenix* [Motion picture]. Burbank: Warner Home Video.

Bourdieu, P. (1984). *Distinction: A social critique of the judgment of taste.* R. Nice, Trans. Stanford: Stanford University Press.

Bruckheimer, J. (Producer), & Smith, J. (Director). (1995). *Dangerous minds* [Motion picture]. Burbank: Buena Vista Home Entertainment.

Burgess, H. (1989). 'A sort of career': Women in primary schools. In C. Skelton (Ed.), *Whatever Happens to Little Women?* (pp. 79-91). Bristol, PA: Open University Press.

Carr, A., and Stigwood, R. (Producers), & Kleiser, R. (Director). (1978). *Grease.* [Motion picture]. Hollywood: Paramount Pictures.

Coffey, A., and Delamont, S. (2000). *Feminism and the classroom teacher: Research, praxis, and pedagogy.* London: Routledge.

Dalton, M. M. (2007). *The Hollywood curriculum: Teachers in the movies* (revised ed.). New York: Peter Lang.

Dalton, M. M., and Linder, L.R. (2008). *Teacher TV: Sixty years of teachers on television*. New York: Peter Lang.

Damon, M. (2011, August 2). Matt Damon at a rally for teachers in Washington, DC, with his Mom, also a teacher [Video file]. Retrieved from http://www.youtube.com/watch?v=Qaw5wbOsN7w.

Day, D. (Producer), & Barnz, D. (Director). (2008). *Phoebe in wonderland*. [Motion picture]. Albany, GA: Sherwood Films.

Darling-Hammond, L. (2006). *Powerful teacher education: Lessons from exemplary programs*. San Francisco, CA: Joessy-Bass.

DeVito, D. (Producer), & LaGravenese, R. (Director). (2007). *Freedom writers*. [Motion picture]. Hollywood: Paramount Home Entertainment.

Disney, W. (Producer), & Kinney, J. (Director). (1952). *Teachers are people*. (7 July 2009). Video posted to youtube.com. http://www.youtube.com/watch?v=dMdTB ep3W9c.

Falchuk, B. (Writer), & Murphy, R. (Director). (2010). Rocky horror glee show [Television series episode]. In B. Falchuk (Producer), *Glee*. Los Angeles: Fox Studios.

————. (2011). Sexy [Television series episode]. In B. Falchuck (Producer), *Glee*. Los Angeles: Fox Studios.

Fiske, J. (1989). *Understanding popular culture*. Boston: Unwin Hyman.

Fox, R., and Rudin, S. (Producers), & Eric, R. (Director). (2006). *Notes on a scandal* [Motion picture]. Los Angeles: Fox Searchlight.

Grant, G., and Murray, C. (1999). *Teaching in America: The slow revolution*. London: Harvard University Press.

Grumet, M. R. (1988). *Bitter milk: Women and teaching*. Amherst: University of Massachusetts Press.

Hall, S. (1997). Introduction. In S. Hall (Ed.), *Representation: Cultural representations and signifying practices* (pp. 1-11). London: Sage.

Haraway, D. (1989). *Primate visions: Gender, race and nature in the world of modern science*. New York: Routledge.

Heyman, D. (Producer), and Columbus, C. (Director). (2002). *Harry Potter and the Chamber of Secrets*. [Motion picture]. Burbank: Warner Home Video.

Kramer, J. (Producer), and Angelus, P. & Roth, D.L. (Directors). (1984). *Hot for teacher*. Retrieved from http://www.youtube.com/watch?v=g0XLKcMoXRE&feature=fvst

Landon, M. (Writer), & Landon, M. (Director). (1980). Laura Ingalls Wilder: Part I. In M. Landon (Producer), *Little House on the Prairie* [Television series]. Burbank: NBC.

————. (1980). Laura Ingalls Wilder: Part II. In M. Landon (Producer), *Little House on the Prairie*. [Television series]. Burbank: NBC.

Lewis, A., & Quillan, J. (Writers), & Lewis, A. (Director). (1955). Home cooked meal [Television series episode]. In D. Weisbart (Producer), *Our Miss Brooks*. Studio City: CBS.

Lutz, A. (1959). *Susan B. Anthony: Rebel, crusader, humanitarian*. Washington, DC: Zenger Publishing Co.

Miller, J. (Producer), & Kasden, J. (Director). (2011). *Bad teacher*. [Motion picture]. Culver City: Columbia Pictures.

Reitman, I. (Producer), & Reitman, I (Director). (1990). *Kindergarten cop* [Motion picture]. Universal City: Universal DVD. (2009, July 30). Video posted to http://www.youtube.com/watch?v=VziODpQuJFA.

Rose, G. (2007). *Visual methodologies: An introduction to the interpretation of visual materials.* 2nd ed. London: Sage.

Rudin, S. (Producer), & Linklater, R. (Director). (2003). *School of rock.* [Motion picture]. Hollywood: Paramount Home Video.

Rudin, S., and Roybal, M. (Producers), Shanley, J. P. (Director). (2008). *Doubt.* [Motion picture]. Burbank: Miramax Films.

Sholle, D., and Denske, S. (1993). Reading and writing the media: Critical media literacy and postmodernism. In C. Lankshear & P.L. McLaren (Eds.), *Critical Literacy: Politics, Praxis and the Postmodern* (pp. 297-321). New York: State University of New York Press.

Storey, J. (2003). *Cultural studies and the study of popular culture.* 2nd ed. Athens: University of Georgia Press.

Strober, M. H., and Tyack, D. (1980). Why do women teach and men manage?: A report on research on schools. *Signs, 5*(3), 494-503.

Weber, S., and Mitchell, C. (1995). *'That's funny, you don't look like a teacher': Interrogating images and identity in popular culture.* London: The Falmer Press.

Whedon, J. (Writer), and Sweeney B. (Director). (1963). Andy Discovers America [Television series episode]. In A. Ruben (Producer), *The Andy Griffith Show.* Hollywood: Mayberry Enterprises/Paramount.

Part I: Theoretical Analyses of Popular Culture

Having looked historically at some issues, this work begins in the realm of theory. That said, the chapters presented in the first part are not intended to be read as purely theoretical works; indeed, they often offer concrete suggestions on how to apply the theory and/or examples of how the authors have successfully applied them in their own teaching. Ultimately, the editors hope these chapters will prove to be both thought-provoking for the reader and suitable discussion starters in a classroom context.

Many of the chapters in this part are intended to provide background information for students and teachers alike. For example, Geiger's discussion of the intersections of Howard Zinn and Pete Seeger provides new information to historians and musicologists alike. Similarly, McElligatt and Roth's fascinating study of *Finding Forrester* provides solid background on a wide variety of topics sociological and literary that can serve as a starting point for students even as they debate the conclusions of the authors.

Others are meant to be more provocative. After reading Prieto's piece on Disney and South America, for example, questions such as does the government still engage in this kind of propaganda arise and, more importantly, *should* it arise. After reading Duchaney's piece, debates on the meaning of family and the role it plays in identity formation can easily emerge.

Finally, Neeman and Newman's chapter serves and a transition point. It contains points that should elicit strong discussion, such as the various representations of family on current television and whether they should exist in such a fashion. It also contains points of pedagogical practice, leading the reader to think in the more practical terms in which Part II will engage.

Chapter Three

Making a Modern Man: Disney's Literacy and Health Education Campaigns in Latin and South America during WWII

Julie Prieto

In August 1941, Walt Disney spoke to a group of citizens in Atlanta on his way to start a ten-week tour of South America as research for a series of government-sponsored films. In describing the purpose these war-time films, Disney bluntly said to the assembled crowd, "Give kids nothing but sugar-coated stuff and they'll grow up to be cream puffs." Disney went on to explain his new focus on the "cream puffs" of South America in equally blunt terms deadpanning, "Europe's shot, so all that's left is South America and my staff and I are just doing our bit for better relations between the United States and South America" (N.A., p. 9). Disney and his animators undertook this fact-finding trip to South America as the first public act of their contract with the Office of Inter-American Affairs, headed by the young and dynamic Republican scion Nelson Rockefeller. As part of this contract, the Walt Disney Studios agreed to produce a series of commercial films set in and about Latin and South America in order to increase goodwill throughout the hemisphere to be followed by a series of educational films for distribution to the United States's Spanish and Portuguese-speaking neighbors to the south. The result was two full-length animated motion pictures, *Saludos Amigos* and *The Three Caballeros*, fourteen short health films, and a multimedia adult literacy education program. While Disney Studios also produced films during WWII for a number of other government agencies, most notably the Navy, the Treasury Department, and the Office of War Information, as well as films for the Canadian government, these Office of Inter-American

Affairs-funded films remain the most widely distributed and enduring pieces of the studio's war-time catalogue.

This discussion of Disney's war-time production will focus on the most purely pedagogical of the materials produced under contract with the Office of Inter-American Affairs, the short health films and adult literacy program for Latin and South America. Part of the reason for this is historiographical. As Disney's only entries in to the commercial realm for the duration of the war, *Saludos Amigos* and *The Three Caballeros* have received detailed attention from historians and cultural theorists.[1] The health films have received less attention than the commercial products, and the adult literacy program even less. When they are discussed, scholars have tended to cordon off discussion of Disney's cultural production by medium, leading to the separation of discussions of the multimedia literacy program from analysis of the short films comprising the health education program.[2] Medium certainly matters in the analysis of popular cultural forms, but Disney's health and literacy programs were produced to complement each other and together form an integrated pedagogical plan of action for the Americas. Viewing them as two halves of a single program allows us to better understand both what Disney and the Office of Inter-American Affairs aimed to accomplish with the program and what the impact of this war-time attempt at information and education had on the various American allies of the United States during the war.

Disney's health and literacy productions are also crucial and unique in that they were directed almost exclusively towards Latin and South American audiences. Disney Studios and the Office of Inter-American Affairs certainly hoped that their neighbors to the south would see *Saludos Amigos* and *The Three Caballeros*, but these films were produced primarily for U.S. audiences. The commercial films presented U.S. viewers with a positive vision of their hemispheric allies by making its culture seem less strange and by recasting the exotic into a source of fun rather than danger. The health and literacy programs, on the other hand, were meant exclusively for relatively poor, uneducated, and rural audiences in Latin and South America that had little access to regular schooling from their governments. Disney used popular cultural forms not only to teach health, hygiene, and literacy to these people, but to present them with an alternate vision of their long-term future.

The films and pedagogical programs were meant to inspire in Latin and South Americans a desire for further educational instruction and to support their government's attempts to improve infrastructure and reforms that would improve public health. For Disney and the OIAA, it was not enough to instill in rural people a desire for positive goods like clean water; they had to want the dam and the plumbing that would pump clean water into their homes. Disney's films aimed to awaken people, who were imagined to be in a sort of state of nature, to the possibility of inclusion within a modern, hemispheric system that would follow from the adoption of U.S.-style values and aspirations. The health and literacy programs did this by targeting what they imagined to be the most important unit of Latin and South American life: the family. By appealing to Latin and South American ideals of family, Disney hoped to shape collective desires and forms to meet OIAA goals.

While the use of popular culture and the family unit certainly appealed to some rural Latin and South Americans, the campaign disturbed reformers and educators among the elite in a number of countries. Particularly in Mexico, educators who had been involved in creating the materials for Disney's pedagogical programs were often resistant to U.S. attempts to intervene in what they saw as internal debates over the course of social reform in their countries. These concerns among urban elites in Mexico and other countries caused a backlash against Disney's health and literacy campaigns that led to their termination and seeded discontent with U.S. popular culture.

Disney, Popular Culture, and the Pedagogical Push

Disney's literacy and health campaign was constructed in the context of a larger push by the U.S. government to improve its relations within the hemisphere. In August 1940, President Franklin Roosevelt established by executive order the new Office for the Coordination of Commercial and Cultural Relations between the American Republics, later renamed the Office of Inter-American Affairs (OIAA). Placing the new organization under a youthful Nelson Rockefeller, FDR gave the agency the broad mission of increasing ties and improving goodwill between the United States and its neighbors to the South in anticipation of general war, while squelching any nascent fascist sympathies.[3] The administration was concerned in particular with the potential collapse of traditional markets for selling raw materials in wartime, which would mean that the privations of war would spread disproportionately to Latin and South American countries, creating a window for pro-Axis forces to gain traction with certain political factions and governments.[4] Though it began with a focus on purchasing power and loans, the OIAA's mission quickly expanded to encompass more long-range economic and commercial development projects. These projects focused on systemic transformations of Latin and South American economies to address some of the underlying causes of economic inequality in these nations and ultimately covered a wide range of projects geared towards "modernization." Most of this money went towards massive infrastructure projects, such as the rehabilitation of the Mexican national railway system and a large-scale industrial development program that concentrated on dam building and irrigation initiatives, but a significant amount of the OIAA's money and personnel worked on what could be termed "cultural projects." Much of this work was justified in terms of its importance to the war effort, but Rockefeller was determined that his programs become permanent fixtures of hemispheric relations, and he imagined that cultural change was a necessary precursor to lasting economic and social change in the hemisphere (State Department, p. 183-210).

Rockefeller turned to Disney in early 1941 to help him with his cultural modernization program despite substantial opposition within his own organization. For the newly empowered Rockefeller, contracting with Disney studios offered an incomparable push for his envisioned program of cultural modernization (Reich, p. 210-55). Disney characters were already popular in Latin and South America, and any programs the studio worked on were sure to attract attention. The studio was also one of the few that had the resources to produce original programming quickly and on a relatively large scale.[5] Still, the organization in the summer of 1941 was plagued by a studio-wide animators strike, which started on May 29, 1941, after Walt Disney's firing of union organizers and after months in which the company flouted recommendations from the National Labor Relations Board. In a July 7 meeting, Kenneth Thomson of the OIAA criticized Rockefeller's decision to hire Disney, warning that "labor is of course international and the committee would be in the position of sending as a good will emissary to the other American republics a man who will not deal with labor" (Thomson, p. 1). Thomson and others in the OIAA were concerned that not only would Latin and South Americans reject Disney films in the future for the company's anti-labor stance, the rest of the U.S. government would look down on the upstart OIAA and its support for the studio.

Rockefeller ignored these criticisms and hired Disney to make films for Latin and South America despite the controversy. Although there seems to have been no official quid pro quo, Disney in turn quietly solved his labor problem while away on his August 1941 trip to South America. The company accepted the union, and the strike ended, though soon after, Disney purged around half of his staff (Smith, p. 1). This was clearly not a satisfactory ending to the labor problem for the OIAA officials like Thomson, but it allowed Disney to refocus his remaining animators to OIAA projects and stay out of the news. It also allowed the OIAA to largely escape criticisms that it was openly dealing with a company that had so recently defied the Roosevelt administration.

When Walt Disney returned from his tour of South America, the studio began work on the first four films of what was to be fourteen short films for distribution in Latin and South America. These four films were intended to be a trial for Disney to show what they could accomplish with health instruction in Latin and South America. Befitting their position as models of Disney animation, they were slick and well-produced, making use of the signature Disney style and occasionally of characters that would be recognizable to general audiences throughout the Americas. The final film even made use of mixtures of live-action and animation in a way that hearkened back to the recently released *Saludos Amigos*. The studio was clearly trying to capture the attention of rural Latin and South Americans by capitalizing on its very recognizable worldwide brand and by associating its educational offerings with its entertainment films. The line between entertaining and informing was purposefully blurred, with animators trying to draw in Latin and South Americans by offering a popular cultural experience that they were hopefully already familiar with in order to present new information in a congenial setting. These films are also unified by their emphasis on placing Latin and South America within a framework of modernity and of hemispheric social change. While the films do not completely ignore health and nutritional lessons that could be adopted by the average rural farmer in the short term, they tended to emphasize the promised health and nutritional improvements that would come with the adoption of modern technological improvements. While the films were originally written and produced in English, they were each translated and dubbed into Spanish before general release.

The first of these films, *The Grain That Built a Hemisphere*, completed in January 1943, is emblematic of this initial approach to instruction. Told in documentary style, the ten-minute film presents a history of the hemisphere centered on the domestication and consumption of corn. It opens with animated hunter-gatherers tracking and shooting a Bambi-like deer until they discover a complementary food source, the seeds of a grass plant that they will eventually domesticate, the ancestor of today's corn plant. The narrator confirms that corn allows these people to settle in villages but warns that it also becomes their god. The film takes pains to show religious rituals around corn, including human sacrifices portrayed in relief, that presumably are meant both to distance the viewer from the film's "primitive" subjects and also titillate the audience. Beauty and barbarity are further juxtaposed through images of terraced farms and villages similar to those that appeared in *Saludos Amigos* with monuments to corn gods and in the lengthy repetition of images of a hunched over indigenous man grinding corn by hand over brightly animated pictures of corn-based foods. In the film, these images of superstition and toil are only erased when tractors and modern hybridization come to the corn fields, allowing the indigenous farmer to leave his backbreaking hoeing in favor of a life of relative leisure in one of his "buildings of the future, monuments to corn" (*Grain*, January 1943).

The film is visually stunning, bright, colorful, and identifiably Disney. There could be no mistake about its provenance. Equally, there could be no mistake that Disney was bypassing practical lessons in food, eating, and agricultural practice in favor of presenting a sweeping vision of the American future. This new world would build on the Latin American past, but it was based on a vision for revolution as broad as the portrayed transition from family-bands of hunter-gatherers to the growth of agricultural communities set in neat villages. That this revolution depended on technology from the United States was deemphasized in favor of a more benign story of hemispheric cooperation.

The three health films released soon after—*The Winged Scourge*; *Water, Friend or Enemy;* and *Defense Against Invasion*—repeated the pattern. *The Winged Scourge* follows "public enemy number one," the mosquito, bringer of malaria (*Winged*, January 1943). In the film, a family farm, looking decidedly Anglo-American, falls to ruin because the father of the family has contracted malaria due to a failure to prevent the sickness in his home. In response, the dwarves from *Snow White* are called to spray oil and Paris Green on pools of standing water in order to kill mosquito larvae around their home, thereby demonstrating what the father should have done to spare his family from poverty and sickness. Of the four initial films done by Disney, this is the one that most directly uses previously established animated characters in order to introduce health messages to Latin American audiences. Not only is the Disney style evident and the representations of people, which are reminiscent of those in the studio's most recent films, the use of the dwarves hearkens back to previous animation in a way that assumes audiences will be familiar enough with the studio's back catalogue to identify with the characters and with their health message.

Water, Friend or Enemy is the most complicated of the films, presenting an antidote to *The Winged Scourge* by contrasting its determined silliness with dark imagery and vaguely sinister magical elements. Told from the point of view of water itself, the film opens with scenes of refuse slinking into rivers, turning them into red pools with floating skulls. The red, skull-filled water is then poured into glasses for families to consume before being replaced by images of empty chairs around a table, presumably once inhabited by the dead lost to waterborne illness. The solution given by the film is to make a well. What follows is a relatively complex to-do for how to build a basic well, followed by a short reminder that water can be decontaminated by boiling, a far simpler fix for people with limited access to untapped sources of clean water (Wilson, *Memorandum*, p. 1).

The final film, *Defense Against Invasion*, mixes live action elements with animation. In *Defense*, a group of real children and a dog enter a doctor's office to get a vaccine. After they express dismay at having to receive a shot, the doctor explains the way the vaccine works using animation, which likens the body to a city and the vaccine to an army that protects the city against foreign invaders. This is a modern, mechanized army that fights the invader with microscopic tanks and formidable looking "vaccine guns" (*Defense*, August 1943). Everywhere the modern is emphasized. The message is that just as the city can be a site of modernity so too can bodies that are protected by the latest medical advances. The film is also notable in that it is the only one that could be said to make even an oblique reference to the World War and to the United States's rapid production of armaments using Latin and South American raw materials.

While the films represented a large output for the studio considering its reduced workforce, comprising almost as much new animation as *Saludos Amigos*, the Office of Inter-American Affairs was critical of Disney's first attempts at promoting health in the Americas. Thompson, Rockefeller, and other officers tended to recognize that the films were gorgeously animated and visually striking, but there was wide concern that they were too complicated for rural Latin American audiences. On *Defense Against Invasion*, Charles Wilson of the OIAA wrote that the whole message "would go way over the heads of the Latin American people" (Wilson, *Memorandum*, p. 1). They were simply too rural, and isolated, in many cases to understand how a city works, much less to comprehend how the city could map on to their own physiology. Of *Water, Friend or Enemy* the same report noted that the suggestion that people take samples of drinking water to their local health officials to be tested was ludicrous given the primitive conditions experienced by many farmers, and it worried that the red water would be seen as festive, not dangerous. It suggested that the water be made black to match the Spanish phrase for contaminated waters, *aguas negras* (Wilson, *Memorandum*, p. 3-4).

Many of these concerns were rooted in prejudices and racialized readings of events that relegated Latin Americans to the category of primitives who could not understand basic messages and metaphors even if presented in cartoon form, a medium characterized at the time as having special appeal to children. However, some of these concerns were clearly justified. Advice for making wells and spraying Paris Green clearly ignored the real difficulties of the poor in obtaining chemicals and materials that comprised part of the standard practice for farmers in the United States OIAA officials were rightfully concerned that when it came to these materials, it was not lack of knowledge that kept Latin Americans from adopting certain technologies in their fields: it was lack of material resources. The OIAA was also concerned about the possibility of a backlash in the hemisphere against Disney films due to these shortcomings. While most advance word on the films was positive, in the words of one Mexican newspaper, the films "were an insult to pedagogy" (Rowland, p. 2-4).

Planning for a Healthy Hemisphere

As a result of Disney's shortcomings in the first four trial health films, the OIAA convened a week-long conference in Los Angeles for both its officials and Disney animators to discuss the future of the program. Called to order on May 25, 1943, the Seminar on Adult Education provided the framework for the rest of Disney's health campaign, established a new set of standards and goals for the films, and put into place the agreement for Disney to begin work on a literacy education program for Latin and South America. This series of meetings was considered of the highest priority on both sides, and Nelson Rockefeller,

Charles Thomson, and Kenneth Holland all flew in to Los Angeles for the event. Along with them were several Latin and South American educators including Enrique de Lozada, who had worked with the Rockefeller Foundation and was a well-recognized expert in education and indigenous peoples; Luis Martinez Mont, of the Guatemalan Department of Education; and representatives from Brazil (Rockefeller, *Memorandum*, p. 1-2). These officials met with Walt Disney and with the animators assigned to OIAA projects. This was a chance not only for OIAA officers to see the studios and to learn more about the processes used to make the health films but for the animators to better understand what OIAA officials wanted the films to accomplish. Sessions were held at the Walt Disney Studios and in a series of "field trips" to a number of classrooms around Los Angeles County, where the group saw health classes being implemented in a variety of grade levels, traveling units of domestic animals for schools, and teacher education courses in the use of visual technology (OIAA, *Seminar on Visual Education*, p. 1-5).

While the conference events were wide ranging, the centerpiece was clearly the long discussion meetings held to negotiate the content of the next round of pedagogical materials. Rockefeller, Thomson, and Holland provided input and worked closely with Disney's writers and animators to form the basic stories that would comprise the next series of health films and the literacy campaign, developing short summaries of plots (Disney and Hyland, p. 1-7). Animators were also coached on the kind of elements they should and should not use in their materials. Particular symbols, such as religious imagery, present in *Water, Friend or Enemy*, were banned, and the use of identifiably Latin American characters was emphasized (Cutting, p. 1). Disney was given guidelines about how much knowledge to assume on the part of the audience and how much humor to use. For the most part, the animators seemed to welcome the input, expressing concerns that they did not know enough about the situation on the ground in Latin America to know what to teach. These kinds of questions persisted more than a year in to making the second batch of films, as Disney employees were still sending memos to OIAA officials asking for more basic information on Latin Americans:

> The question in my mind now seeks information regarding the everyday life of the common farmer or factory worker, or people of a similar social class. I would like to know the average mentality—what such people wear—the jobs they do and the tools they work with—the foods they eat and where and how they prepare them—where they dispose of garbage, human excrement—the games they play etc. (Wilson, *Cleanliness in Health Planning*, p. 8-9)

Even so, it is important to note that Disney animators were now asking these crucial questions, presumably with the expectation that they would receive guidance. The Latin and South American educators at the conference helped provide some needed insight early on, while Disney's planned outings to Los

Angeles classrooms probably served to temper some of the OIAA's expectations for the immediate success of the visual education program (OIAA, *Seminar on Visual Education*, p. 4-5).

Coming out of the conference, the decision was made that elements from the first four films would be retained, but the overall content would be markedly different from what came before both visually and in message. The key change in both the visual realm and in content was a renewed emphasis on simplicity (OIAA, *Memo on Tuberculosis*, p. 1). Gone were pronouncements that rural farmers purchase or set aside the time to produce complex apparatuses on their farms in favor of suggestions that would represent much smaller outlays of energy and resources. Even when farmers were encouraged to make real technological improvements to their farms, these were offset by more practical suggestions. The animation style too was radically simplified as Disney was encouraged to increase their output rather than pour money into creating an innovative visual style. This was true of both the new health films that Disney was charged with producing and with the new materials for the literacy curricula. While the recognizable Disney style was to remain visible in the new productions, there would be no more funding for complex backdrops, mixtures of live action and animation, or recognizable characters, which required more attention to detail. Instead, the characters of the new films would be a "universal Latin American type," often just a darker-skinned version of a stylized man, that could be animated quickly (OIAA, *Seminar on Visual Education*, p. 8). Disney animators were also commended for their previous attempts to appeal to Latin American families, and the group together decided to adopt as a guiding principle that "the family should be the social unit for illustrating group living. Through problems of the family we can show how people can live together better" (OIAA, *Seminar on Visual Education*, p. 8-9). Latin and South American people would be defined in terms of their family connections, and people would be implored to make changes for the sake of their family's health.

These new guidelines are evident in the ten health films produced by Disney for the OIAA after the Seminar for Adult Education. Films produced after May 1943 fell into two basic categories, but together they formed a unified set of basic health lessons focused on problems impacting rural places or cities with poor infrastructure. Again, films were produced first in English and then translated after they were approved by the OIAA. The first category of film treats the issue of disease. In films such as *Hookworm, How Disease Travels, What Is Disease?* (also called *"The Unseen Enemy"*), *Tuberculosis*, and *Insects as Carriers of Disease*, Latin and South Americans are introduced to a farmer who through his carelessness is struck ill by a disease. Through this man, the audience sees what microbes look like up close and how they operate in the body. Once the character is well, the film then outlines some basic precautions that the main character could have taken to prevent the illness. While the main character was meant to be universal, several reuse a new character designed for the series named "Careless Charlie," who serves as a classic cartoon buffoon-type focal point for the lessons. The film *Insects as Carriers of Disease* is emblematic of this type. In the cartoon, Careless Charlie is shown rejecting human company in favor of making friends with the lice, flies, and mosquitoes in his home. When he contracts an illness, a narrator magnifies the size of each of Charlie's "friends" to show him that they are in fact monsters that carry invisible "filth" not only to every surface of his home but to his body. Charlie is then shrunk down so that he can be attacked by the now monstrous giants living in his home before he is taught how to drain pools around his home and cover his food. While comical, the film breaks down insect disease transmission in the simplest possible terms (*Insects*, June 1945).

While these films generally star Careless Charlie, or a more robust character created to provide a counterpoint to Charlie, "Ramon," Disney and OIAA officials thought of the disease films as being directed towards families. Collective action was seen as the proper way to fight disease. In the planning of *Tuberculosis*, Disney animators wrote to Charles Wilson in the OIAA:

> The Latin American is fatalistic about it. It is definitely an economic disease. It can't be improved until you let people earn a better living. Some effort has been made in Latin America to fight Tuberculosis, but it hasn't been enough. There are two things to consider 1) preventative and 2) curative measures. Is Latin America yet in the preventative stage? I am afraid that for the next ten or twenty years we will have to take curative measures but we can begin now to take preventative measures. It seems the family unit is the way to approach this subject. Tuberculosis spreads and thrives very much as leprosy. I would suggest that the family theme and their interdependence be stressed. We should show that the disease may make invalids of the father or mother or kill them. The Latin American mind, because of its religiousness, fears invalidism and misery more than it does death. I think it would be a good idea to show the breaking up of the family unit, the loss of happiness and wholesomeness (Wilson, *In Planning*, p.1-2).

Officials on both sides imagined Latin American people as primitives who valued superstition and collectivism over modernity, and they believed that their audience would listen to health messages only if they fit in with their cultural framework. Disney officials saw these racialized differences not as innate but as a developmental stage that would eventually be superseded by future development.

The second class of health films are more direct in their hearkening to this imagined future of development and progress. These films—*Cleanliness Brings Health, Infant Care and Feeding, The Human Body, Planning for Good Eating*, and *Environmental Sanitation*—focus on nutrition, sanitation, and basic hygiene. They stress in particular child nutrition and provide guidelines for eating a variety of foods, including fresh fruits, vegetables, dairy, and meats. Still, in films such as *Infant Care and Feeding*, little mention is made of what to do if foods are unavailable due to poverty and not lack of knowledge. The only solution comes in the form of help from local medical officials, presumably working for an abstracted public health service. Sanitation is treated even more as a collective problem to be dealt with by government services, offered in the context of families, towns, and cities. In *Environmental Sanitation*, Disney presents a vision of a future Latin American city that has solved the problem of sickness by providing for reservoirs and pipes to serve the poorer districts, ending with a call for "pure clean water available at last in every home!" (*Environmental Sanitation*, April 1946). For Disney and the OIAA, even if some problems in Latin America could not be solved given the current state of development, there was still a benefit in informing people that more was possible. Even if this vision for future sanitation and government support seemed misguided, Disney and the OIAA imbued the films with this optimistic vision for a healthy and modern hemisphere looking to the future rather than the unhealthy present.

Reducing "Illiteracy of Character"

Along with the ten new health films, Disney produced four literacy films and ten initial lessons for teaching adults to read Spanish (Wallace, p. 5-6). The plan for this program was approved during the Seminar for Adult Education, and the program was developed to complement the ten later health films (OIAA, *Report*, 1-2). Teaching people to read was seen as an essential step by the OIAA to creating the conditions that would allow modern economic development to flourish in the region. Learning about health and the body was essential for keeping people alive, but reading was necessary for developing the mind of the Latin American. Educating people in the hemisphere was also seen as essential for creating democratic and economically modern societies. In a written statement read to the Seminar on Adult Education, Vice President Henry Wallace referred to the contemporary state of Latin and South Americans as one of "illiteracy of character," a systemic ignorance that kept people poor even in a state of worldwide technological wealth. Visual education tied to popular forms had the potential to cure the hemisphere not just of disease but of this mental malaise that prevented millions from reaping the benefits of progress.

In countering this malaise, Disney and the OIAA created a program that would not only teach people to read but convince large numbers of people of the utility of reading. The first ten lessons in reading were designed to be centered around, "an inspirational, evangelical, incentive film to open the literacy campaign, intended to bring in both the illiterate students and the volunteer teachers by arousing their interest in the literacy problem and showing them their part in the campaign to eradicate illiteracy" (*Program*, p. 1-6). Materials would be written to complement the films showing simple words that could be learned easily in order to quickly establish the utility of reading. These were to be accompanied by more in-depth lessons covering basic word and sentence structure. Each of these lessons was connected to one of the health films. These were consciously echoed not only because they were considered to be part of the same development scheme, but because Disney's animators believed that rural people would be interested in learning how to read only if they could connect to the content (LeRoy, p.1). Because the health films had been relatively well received in their first few months of showings in a number of Latin American countries, both the OIAA and Disney imagined that people had received and internalized the messages more or less as intended and hoped that the literacy films could ride on the back of these successes.

In order to investigate the effectiveness of the literacy program, Disney funded a test run in various cities in the Southwestern United States, Mexico, Honduras, and Ecuador. Dr. Mildred Wiese, who worked on the development of the program, performed the first round of tests during summer 1944 in Santa Ana, California, Las Vegas, and New Mexico. Even though her report noted the high dropout rate among students who began the classes, she declared them to be a success both in words learned and in terms of encouraging students to continue learning. She noted that they seemed to absorb the health messages less but thought that this was a minor concern (Kilpatrick, p. 1). While Wiese was in the United States, Eleanor Clark and Ismael Rodriquez Bou of the OIAA went to Mexico to establish testing sites in rural Guadalajara, Mexico, meeting along the way with the U.S. Ambassador George Messersmith and the Mexican Secretary of Public Education Jaime Torres Bodet. This attempt to establish courses was met with what they called "passive resistance" as local officials refused to help OIAA employees obtain students. Bou and Clark reported that even the local church forbade students from attending classes and left Mass to go on long enough that it was difficult for women to arrive to the courses on time (OIAA, *Report*, p. 34). When students did attend classroom sessions, the testers read in their pupils a distinct lack of ambition and passivity. Even though exams at the end of the courses did not show much cognitive improvement in the literacy program's students, the testers still deemed the test a success in Mexico because those that did remain in the course seemed enthusiastic by the end of the course. Testing in Honduras and Ecuador was also declared to be a great success (OIAA, *Report*, p. 44).

The congratulatory air was short-lived. By September 1944, a series of editorials by Eulalia Guzman, a Mexican educator who had worked on the films with Disney before becoming critical of their content and methodology, soured the OIAA on continuing to finance the literacy program. Guzman's articles exposed some of the flaws that Disney had merely glossed over in its reports. Writing of program in a September 15 article in *Ultimas Noticias*, Guzman noted:

[T]he films may appear excellent, because they are deceived by the novelty of the teaching and the variety of devices used. But Latin American teachers who really are teachers cannot help noticing the serious errors found in the lessons, both in the way that they are developed and in the language of the narrator. (Guzman, p. 2)

While she noted that novelty could attract pupils, she criticized the English-speakers at Disney for creating a program that seemed distinctly foreign to the structure and rhythms of the Spanish language. Minor errors in grammar could of course be fixed, but she argued that the whole idea of teaching literacy skills with moving pictures was grossly inefficient compared to what able-bodied teachers could do with simpler tools. The OIAA did not find the articles to be particularly threatening to its reputation in Mexico, but U.S. embassy officials worried that in promoting the program the United States was tapping into, "feeling in Mexico against any effort on the part of the United States to teach Mexicans their own language" (Bou, p.1). They were creating a backlash against U.S. cultural intervention in Latin America that the embassy feared would spill over to the OIAA's other programs in the hemisphere and to their own cultural relations work. Though the program was not officially shelved until 1946, these criticisms effectively killed the program and ended Disney's attempts to teach reading in the hemisphere.

Conclusion

The history of Disney's health and literacy campaigns in Latin and South America during WWII present a mixed picture in terms of success. Even so, these programs point to the importance of popular cultural forms in carrying U.S. government-sponsored messages abroad prior to the Cold War. These messages were not always what one would term traditional "propaganda." The Disney films and curricula in fact had little to say directly about the war effort and only obliquely referenced current events. They did, however, serve to promote a long-term U.S. vision for the hemisphere, one in which Latin and South Americans would be educated and would demand improvements in their health and infrastructure. That the United States would be in a good position to offer guidance in pushing forth programs of economic and social reform in the hemisphere was not mere coincidence even if this provided only a long-term possibility for increased influence in the hemisphere. These films also drew on a common visual language in the Americas that at least initially, created goodwill for the project and allowed it to continue even when signs pointed to problems in the project. This common language emphasized the collective over the individual. In most cases this meant family in the literal sense, but zooming outward, this family becomes a family of nations, each connected by a shared popular visual culture.

Notes

1. While the work does focus more on Disney's comic strips than films, Ariel Dorfman and Armand Mattelart's now classic (1984) *How to Read Donald Duck: Imperialist Ideology in the Disney Comic* (New York: International General) provides key insights into the study of Disney's visual products. Gaizka S. de Usabel's (1982) *The High Noon of American Films in Latin America* (Ann Arbor, MI: UMI Research Press) also provides an important guide for understanding not only Disney but U.S. film production during WWII.

2. The health and literacy films have been analyzed in several recent articles, including: Bob Cruz Jr., (2011), Paging Dr. Disney: Health Education Films, 1922-1973 in Van Riper, Bowdoin [Ed.] *Learning from Mickey, Donald and Walt: Essays on Disney's Edutainment Films*, p. 127-144 (Jefferson, NC: McFarland & Co.); Shale, Richard (1982) *Donald Duck Joins Up: The Walt Disney Studio During World War II* (Ann Arbor, MI: UMI Research Press); and Cartwright, Lisa and Goldfarb, Brian (1984) Cultural Contagion: On Disney's Health Education Films in Latin America in Smoodin, Eric [Ed.], *Disney Discourse: Producing the Magic Kingdom* (New York: Routledge). While Cruz's analysis of the films is valuable, he does not use archival sources. Cartwright and Goldfarb do use archives but mostly seem to rely on material from the Rockefeller Foundation Archives, giving them a view of the films that reflects the organization's interests in health education. Because I primarily rely on the records of the Office of Inter-American Affairs, collected at the National Archives, which includes copies of correspondence, memos, and story boards from Disney Studios, my analysis focuses on different aspects of the films, notably their attempts to connect with a vision of Latin American collectivism and future cultural development.

3. Franklin Roosevelt established the Office for Coordination of Commercial and Cultural Relations between the American Republics (OCCCRBAR) in August 1940, with Nelson Rockefeller at the head of the new agency. He signed Executive Order 8840 formally establishing the reorganized Office of Inter-American Affairs on July 31, 1941. Nelson Rockefeller thereafter was known as the Coordinator of Inter-American Affairs (CIAA) until the dissolution of the OIAA in 1946.

4. While there is relatively little literature on the OIAA's organizational history, it is often mentioned in larger histories of cultural and economic relations with Latin America. See Ninkovich, Frank A., (1981), *The Diplomacy of Ideas: U.S. Foreign Policy and Cultural Relations, 1938-1950* (Cambridge, England: Cambridge University Press); Niblo, Stephen R., (1995), *War, Diplomacy, and Development: The United States and Mexico, 1938-1954* (Wilmington: SR Books); Rosenberg, Emily (1982) *Spreading the American Dream: American Economic and Cultural Expansion, 1890–1945* (New York: Hill and Wang). Perhaps the most comprehensive history of the OIAA is an internal organizational history created for the State Department, (April 7, 1967): *A History of the Office of the Coordinator of Inter-American Affairs*, National Archives and Records Administration (NARA), Record Group (RG) 229, Records of the Office of Inter-American Affairs, Box 511, Folders 1-2.

5. It is important to note that many of these resources were greatly augmented by early payments on the OIAA contract. Numbers and payment schedules are available for the health and literacy campaigns in Office of Inter-American Affairs: OIAA, (February

25, 1944), *Project Authorization, Inter-American Educational Foundation, Inc.,* NARA, RG 229, Box 1150.

References

Bou, I.R. (October 16, 1944). *Memorandum.* NARA, RG 229, Box 1151.

Cartwright, L., and Goldfarb, B. (1984). Cultural Contagion: On Disney's Health Education Films in Latin America. In Smoodin, Eric (Ed.), *Disney Discourse: Producing the Magic Kingdom.* New York: Routledge.

Cruz Jr., B. (2011). Paging Dr. Disney: Health Education Films, 1922-1973. In Van Riper, B. (Ed.), *Learning from Mickey, Donald and Walt: Essays on Disney's Edutainment Films.* Jefferson, NC: McFarland & Co.

Cutting, E. (June 16, 1943). *Letter to Francis Alstock.* NARA, RG 229, Box 214, Information, Motion Pictures, Plans-Policy-Procedure, Films.

Defense Against Invasion (Short Film). (August 1943). Los Angeles: Walt Disney Studios.

Disney, W., and Hyland, C.. (January 28, 1944). *The Objectives of the Basic Economy Film Program.* NARA, RG 229, Box 1150, Folder, Adult Literacy Series-Completed Project.

Dorfman, A., and Mattelart, A. (1984). *How to Read Donald Duck: Imperialist Ideology in the Disney Comic.* New York: International General.

Environmental Sanitation (Short Film). (April 1946). Los Angeles: Walt Disney Studios.

The Grain That Built a Hemisphere (Short Film). (January 1943). Los Angeles: Walt Disney Studios.

Guzman, E. (September 15, 1944). *Ultimas Noticias.* p. 2.

Insects as Carriers of Disease (Short Film). (June 1945). Los Angeles: Walt Disney Studios.

Kilpatrick. (June 30, 1944). *Letter to Cutting.* NARA, RG 229, Box 214.

LeRoy, D. (July 15, 1943). *Letter to Nelson Rockefeller.* NARA, RG 229, Box 214.

N.A. (August 13, 1941). Disney seeks to weld ties with Latins: Noted artist pauses here on trip to South America. *Atlanta Constitution,* p. 9.

Niblo, Stephen R. (1995). *War, Diplomacy, and Development: The United States and Mexico, 1938-1954.* Wilmington: SR Books.

Ninkovich, F.A. (1981). *The Diplomacy of Ideas: U.S. Foreign Policy and Cultural Relations, 1938-1950.* Cambridge, England: Cambridge University Press.

OIAA. (1943). *Memo on Tuberculosis.* NARA, RG 229, Box 214.

OIAA. (February 25, 1944). *Project Authorization, Inter-American Educational Foundation, Inc.* NARA, RG 229, Box 1150.

OIAA. (December 1-3, 1945). *Report on an Experiment of the OIAA in the Use of Films for Teaching Health and Literacy.* NARA, RG 229, Box 218.

OIAA. (May 25, 1943). *Seminar on Visual Education at Walt Disney Studio.* NARA, RG 229, Box 218.

Program for the First Ten Lessons in Reading. (1944). NARA, RG 229, Box 214.

Reich, C. (1996). *The Life of Nelson Rockefeller.* New York: Doubleday.

Rockefeller, N. (January 16, 1943). *Memorandum to Enrique de Lozada.* NARA, RG 229, Box 1151, Education Division, Project Files.

Rosenberg, E. (1982). *Spreading the American Dream: American Economic and Cultural Expansion, 1890–1945.* New York: Hill and Wang.

Rowland, E. (September 13, 1944). *Memo to Waring Quoting* Ultimas Noticias. NARA, RG 229, Box 215 Information, Motion Pictures, Disney Activities.

S. de Usabel, G. (1982). *The High Noon of American Films in Latin America.* Ann Arbor, MI: UMI Research Press.

Shale, R. (1982). *Donald Duck Joins Up: The Walt Disney Studio During World War II.* Ann Arbor, MI: UMI Research Press.

Smith, G.G. (May 26, 1942). *Smith, Financial Director to Coordinator of Inter-American Affairs.* NARA, RG 229, Box 215, Information, Motion Pictures, Disney Activities.

State Department. (April 7, 1967). *A History of the Office of the Coordinator of Inter-American Affairs.* National Archives and Records Administration (NARA), Record Group (RG) 229, Records of the Office of Inter-American Affairs, Box 511, Folders 1-2.

Thomson, K. (July 17, 1941). *Letter to John Hay Whitney.* NARA, RG 229, Box 215, Information, Motion Pictures, Disney Activities.

Wallace, H. (May 25, 1943). *Statement Quoted in Seminar on Visual Education at Walt Disney Studio.* NARA, RG 229, Box 218.

Wilson, C. (1943) *Cleanliness Brings Health Treatment.* NARA, RG 229, Box 214, Disney.

———. (July 12, 1943). *In Planning.* NARA, RG 229, Box 214.

———. (July 12, 1943). *Memorandum.* NARA, RG 229, Box 214, Information, Motion Pictures, Plans-Policy-Procedure, Films.

The Winged Scourge (Short Film). (January 1943). Los Angeles: Walt Disney Studios.

Chapter Four

Uncovering Images of Teaching: Towards a Teacher-Activist Ideal

Sylvia Mac and Denise Blum

When discussing "The Noble Profession" (Parkerson & Parkerson, 2008) in an educational foundations-course, pre-service teachers reveal some unsettling yet common perceptions about their role as a teacher. The students most frequently cite "helping children" or "making a difference in a child's life" or "loving children" as the reasons they want to become a teacher. Commonly referred to as the "selfless profession," teaching is deemed to be successful when teachers focus on care and sacrifice, and embrace the saying, "[N]o one does it for the money." While certainly none of these sentiments is ignoble, the emphasis on responses such as these reflects the feminized nature of teaching as nurturing, caring, and sacrificing—a profession that does not necessarily require skills but rather a nurturing personality. Adding to this gendered image, box-office hit films, which include teacher portrayals such as Arthur "Mr. Chips" Chipping, Glenn Holland, LouAnn Johnson, Erin Gruwell, and John Keating, reinforce the notion that personality traits such as passion, caring, and charisma are fundamental teaching prerequisites, not professional preparation.

These cinematic representations also reinforce the messianic archetype of teachers. Students, typically working-class children of color, are posited as lacking and incomplete until the benevolent teacher, typically white middle class, comes in to mold the children of the future and to ensure that the students leave the classroom as better people. Since media and pop culture influences society's understanding of what constitutes a successful teacher, teacher education programs must address society's and pre-service teachers' skewed understandings of the teaching because this positioning of the teacher as healer, molder, and savior and the students as empty vessels negates the possibility for a collaborative community where students have something meaningful to contribute.

Teacher preparation courses focus on competencies, skills, and formal knowledge, yet such curriculum models neglect the centrality of the teacher's professional identity and instead focus on developing the stereotypical maternal characteristics. Whether intentional or not, neglecting the importance of professional skills merely reinforces the status quo, fostering an instrumental approach to teaching that coincides with the neoliberal factory model of schools that has existed since the Common School era: teachers then and now are trained to produce unthinking, unquestioning workers at the expense of developing skills such as critical thinking. This is not an exaggeration, as the Texas GOP rejected the "teaching of higher order teaching skills" (Strauss, 2012, para 3). Using a Marxist lens, teachers become servants of the capitalist state suppressing students' individuality in favor of producing competent workers for the state (Gregory, 2007). As public servants, teachers must teach in an environment of increasing micromanagement and surveillance, whereby their professional identity is repressed, and teachers become simply an arm of the state in producing an unquestioning labor force. This business-factory model of scripted curriculum, standardization, and merit pay with more responsibilities and accountability than ever, has stymied teacher professional identity development beyond anything robotic. Yet the idealized popular notions of a "caring" and charismatic mother-savior persist and teachers are chided, if not given the pink slip, when they do not meet benchmarks, oftentimes told that they do not "care enough."

This chapter seeks to interrogate popular culture stereotypes and to make suggestions as to how teacher educators might address professional identity in teacher education courses. We approach this topic in four steps. First, we provide a framework for teacher identity. Second, we address the pervasive stereotypes. Third, we talk about the confluence of stereotypes with the neoliberal purpose of schooling. Fourth, we propose ways to encourage teacher identity development, noting the possibilities for activism.

Role Versus Identity

In relation to teacher's work, neoliberal policies tend to work with the notion of the teacher's *role* rather than *identity*. Neoliberal policymakers can quantify, measure, and mandate "what teachers do" (role) more easily than "what teachers are" (identity). Professional teacher *identity* links "what I do" with "why I am here." *Role* more comfortably fits the technical-rational conceptualization of teaching that lays at the heart of neoliberal education agendas. In the struggle to define effective teaching using a technical-rational approach, teaching has been reduced to a series of behaviors supported by "scientific" research. Such research has been almost always predicated on didactic methods used in elementary settings, which seem to produce high scores on tests of basic skills. One example of technical rationality is the Florida Performance Measurement System (Darling-Hammond, 1992). The FPMS specifies an extensive list of teaching behaviors to be enacted by a classroom teacher and tallied by an evaluator, thus reducing teaching to a set of technical operations. *Identity* has been typically associated with a static essence; however, it is demonstrably more complex, interwoven among various dimensions of teachers' works. Studying teachers' professional lives, Ball and Goodson (1985, p. 18) have argued that "the ways in which teachers achieve, maintain, and develop their identity, their sense of self, in and through a career, are of vital significance in understanding the actions and commitments of teachers in their work." Identity is dynamic and biographical, developing over time. Accordingly, neoliberal agendas would prefer *role* rather than *identity* because reflexive, politically aware teachers with a strong sense of purpose are likely to prove to be more unwieldy than those fixated on the technical aspects because, in a neoliberal schooling environment, 'good' teaching can be reduced to a list of behaviors with little imagination or craft remaining. Teachers without creativity and skepticism are more manageable as apparatuses of the state.

Professional teacher identity should extend beyond a caring teacher to recognize the importance of teachers as catalysts and activists for societal improvement. The education system has the power to either break or maintain the status quo. Empowered teachers are critical in the realization of broader transformative aims of education. Helping individual students certainly is an important job in its own right, but more importantly teachers have the opportunity to fight against and decrease institutionalized racism, classism, sexism, and ableism. Empowered teachers do not have to feed the meritocratic discourses with success stories of the one student who fought against all odds, who pulled him/herself up by the bootstraps to overcome achievement gaps; they can become teachers who fight for ALL students to have the equal chance to succeed. Herein lies the potency of education and the teaching profession and the threat of emphasizing professional teacher identity rather than the teacher's role: the interaction between the socio-cultural/political and the professional contexts gives rise to identities within which such activism may flourish (Mockler, 2011).

In order to advance a richer, more transformative vision for education, we must understand the processes by which teacher professional identity is formed and mediated. Mockler (2011) argues that the mediation of teachers' professional identities occurs at the confluence of three dimensions: personal experience, professional context, and the external political environment (which includes media and government policy). These three dimensions work in a dynamic, shifting manner that depends on circumstance and context; as any one of those contexts changes, the "unique embodiment" of teacher identity changes as well, leaving teacher identity in constant flux (p. 522).

Both the literature and practitioners emphasize that a moral purpose drives teachers' work. Pre-service and current teachers remain adamant that teaching is the most important job in the world, although not because of the power of education to change the existing social structure but because of the rewarding nature of a job which impacts a child's life. This notion has complex implications for the formation and mediation of teacher professional identity. Fullan (2006) refers to a "moral/spiritual leadership" component of teachers and administrators that has at its heart the desire "to make a difference in the lives of students" (p. 14). Two commonly held assumptions dominate the discussion of moral purpose: one, that moral purpose is a primary driving force for the teaching profession; and two, that driven by this moral purpose, a desire to do good or to make a difference will necessarily be practiced as part of the profession.

Nias (1997), however, has provocatively posed the question, "Would schools improve if teachers cared less?" She suggests that a commitment to moral purpose and care can interfere with what she sees as the school's primary task, that of "equipping students for life" (p. 22) —with meaningful, challenging academic learning. Teachers only have so much time, and Nias argues that it needs to be predominantly channeled into their pedagogical responsibilities, not into "care" construed as altruism and self-sacrifice. This type of "care" perpetuates the quasi-maternal teacher archetype, as a convenient way of exploiting teachers, especially those who are women, and also of conning them into taking on, unpaid, work which would be better done by other trained professionals, namely counselors or social workers (Nias, 1997). This idea definitely has more and more relevance with the development of community schools and the need to address home issues that may influence student achievement. This division of labor would divide the historical moral purpose among other service providers, allowing teachers to focus more on pedagogy.

A moral purpose alone does not ensure that meaningful teaching and learning will occur. Accordingly, Freire (2006) states "my hope is necessary, but it is not enough" (p. 2). Nevertheless, a moral purpose drives claims made by politicians and bureaucrats in support of "fast tracking" teacher certification programs such as alternative certification and the five-week preparation program that prepares those who participate in Teach for America. While individuals who participate in TFA may care a great deal or have the students' best interests at heart, they reify the messianic discourse when they enter low-income, urban schools for a two-year assignment. Indeed, watching films that perpetuate the unrealistic messianic notion of teaching such as *Freedom Writers* or *Dangerous Minds* has become de rigeur for such idealistic teachers.

Despite their noble intentions, however, there is a fundamental question not asked often enough: is their five-week training and idealism enough to address the critical needs in these schools or does it only further perpetuate the problem of uncertified teachers in and perpetuate the stereotypes of low-performing schools? Does TFA promote real, lasting change? Furthermore, the expression of moral purpose can become an impediment to debate and discussion, insofar that it can represent the "moral high ground" to which there is no rebuttal. Who can fault TFA teachers who sacrificially dedicate two years of their lives "in the trenches" to helping students before moving on to their more desired career? Further supporting this troubling notion, Wiggins and McTighe argue that a disconnect exists between what might be considered a teacher's moral purpose and their job reality:

> Over the years, we have observed countless examples of teachers who, though industrious and well meaning, act in ways that suggest that they misunderstand their jobs. It may seem odd or even outrageous to say that many teachers misconceive their obligations. But we believe that this is the case. Nor do we think this is surprising or an aspersion on the character or insight of teachers. We believe that teachers, in good faith, act on an inaccurate understanding of the role of "teacher" because they imitate what they experienced, and their supervisors rarely make clear that the job is to cause understanding, not merely to march through the curriculum and hope that some content will stick. (Wiggins & McTighe, 2007, p. 128)

The articulation of one's professional identity requires teachers to have an "internal conversation" (Archer, 2007) that allows them to construct themselves as teachers in their own minds and also within their community context. Teacher educators assist in helping to draw links between a teacher's own moral purpose and his/her professional practice to ensure that well meaning teachers do not "misconceive their obligations" (Wiggins & McTighe, 2007, p. 128); they are not social workers, counselors, or surrogate mothers, all of which are packaged in the cinematic super teacher portrayals.

Media Messages

The current technological revolution brings to the forefront, more than ever, the role of media like television, popular music, film, and advertising, as the Internet rapidly absorbs these cultural forms and creates ever-evolving cyberspaces and emergent forms of culture and pedagogy. Kellner and Share (2007) have conducted extensive research demonstrating that daily media saturation generates forms of socialization and education. Media construct meanings, influence and educate audiences, and impose their messages and values. Through the ubiquitous nature of media stereotypes, biased information inevitably becomes incorporated into "common knowledge" or schemata that viewers form about stereotyped groups.

From this perspective, media culture takes on the form of pedagogy, which teaches proper and improper behavior, gender roles, values, and knowledge of the world. Media portrayals of teachers, thus, have already begun to shape pre-service teachers' ideas of "good" or "bad" teachers and how they envision themselves as teachers before they even begin coursework. Individuals are often not aware that they are being educated and positioned by media culture, as its pedagogy is frequently invisible and is absorbed unconsciously (Kellner & Share, 2007).

As Mockler (2011) indicates, one of the three dimensions of teacher identity formation is the external political environment, and since media heavily influences this environment, pre-service teachers must understand media culture in order to analyze teacher professional identity. Accordingly, the next sections review the prominent teacher portrayals in media: teacher as mother, teacher as savior, and teacher as villain. In doing so, the sections reveal what these portrayals reinforce, as well as what is purposely absent in these depictions, and the reasons behind that agenda. Additionally, they illustrate the purposefulness of absence from, and emphasis on, certain character traits and images.

Teachers as Mothers and Saviors

The teacher as mother and teacher as savior epitomize popular metaphors in media and tend to be conflated into one. The teacher as mother image incorporates sacrifice and care beyond all else. The savior images portrays the miracle worker who finds a creative way, that happens to also involve a tremendous amount of care and sacrifice, to enable students to beat the odds and succeed despite the system's unfair policies or treatment of students' ability and culture. This "higher calling" and moral purpose draws attention away from a system marked with inequity and focuses instead on the role of the teacher to care, nurture, and mother as the path to success.

The teacher as savior and teacher as mother metaphors are so socially and historically embedded in popular culture that teacher candidates rarely, if ever, enter the teaching profession interrogating the system or with the idea of reforming the system as a teacher activist. Instead, they use these miracle worker portrayals as models for how they would like to teach. While the teachers in films such as *Dead Poets Society* (1989), *Dangerous Minds* (1995), *Stand and Deliver* (1988), *Mr. Holland's Opus* (1995), and *Freedom Writers* (2007) most definitely have a positive impact on students, such films help mainstream America ignore serious problems in the public school system and society. They feed us fantasies that entire school systems could be transformed if the rest of those useless teachers would just care enough. Certainly there is nothing wrong with teachers who care and have a big heart, but it is also important for teachers to see themselves as not just a savior for individual needy students but as activists with the power to affect systemic change. Moreover, white women dominate the teaching profession in reality and in film, thereby reinforcing the maternal savior myth. Teacher educator activists are confronted with undoing these socialized notions in teacher preparation programs.

Baudrillard (1983) argues that the constant repetition of images through the media has effaced the distinction between reality and fiction. These popular images of teachers, composed across time and place from novels, advertisement, and film, form a significant part of what Mitchell and Weber (1999) call the "cumulative cultural text of teaching" (p. 166). The images have a profound effect not only on popular notions of teacher identity and expectations, but also on pre-service teachers and teacher educators. Immersed with popular cultural representations of the individualistic, charismatic teacher, the public frequently compares and judges real teachers as second-class people because, as Gregory (2007, p. 17) notes, "Most of us real teachers simply do not measure up as Titans or goddesses." In the neoliberal school environment, such not measuring up has serious implications: policymakers, media mavens, and society label teachers incompetent and unskilled babysitters.

Teaching for student success does not preclude adopting some of the characteristics of the filmic representations of a good teacher. Even within the neoliberal framework of accountability, there is still a place for the charismatic, passionate, iconoclast teacher. However, Moore (2004) argues against reinforcing this type of personality too much. He notes that this portrayal creates "an unfortunate symbiosis" in the understanding of the role of teacher and the students' expectations of learning as entertainment (p. 69). The teacher also fears that the student will become quickly disillusioned if the entertainment, or pedagogy, is not sufficiently engaging. In the end, students' lack of engagement or achievement becomes the fault of the not-entertaining-enough or not-charismatic-enough teacher. The constant iteration in popular culture of the charismatic teacher can undermine the competent and reflective practitioner (Moore, 2004).

Teacher as Villain

In contrast to the charismatic teacher, pathetic and monstrous teachers also parade through popular culture. Moore (2004) characterizes these teachers as "evil," highlighting social fears of the teacher's power. In the children's book, *Miss Nelson Is Missing*, Miss Viola Swamp is the meanest, most horrifying substitute teacher a child could ever imagine, forcing children to be quiet and do arithmetic. She also cancels story hour and assigns them an insurmountable amount of homework. In the *Harry Potter* series, Professor Dolores Umbridge not only terrorizes Harry Potter to the point of making him bleed (literally) but also uses her authority to make everyone at Hogwarts miserable. In *The Simpsons*, teacher Edna Krabappel lives up to her name as a bitter, loveless loner, describing her job as a "glorified babysitter to a bunch of dead-eyed fourth graders" ("Separate Vocations," *The Simpsons*, 1992). Similarly, Charlie Brown's teacher in *Peanuts*, demonstrates an irrelevant pedagogy, as the class hears a lot of "Wah wah woh wah wah" from their teacher and not much else. In *Glee* Sue Sylvester, high school cheerleading coach, becomes the glee club's most ruthless bully while competing for funds, throwing dirt in students' faces, and shoving them into lockers. Sheba Hart, a teacher in the film *Notes on a Scandal* (2006), initiates a sexual relationship with her fifteen-year-old student.

These melodramatic school scenarios and teacher images may be exciting, as they are created to draw an audience and tap into a general interest that everyone can relate to: schools and teachers. However, these scenarios negatively reflect on what is popularly understood as a professional identity that society has deemed to be the paragon of morality. Unwittingly, these negative teacher stereotypes function to reinforce the blame of poor student achievement on the teachers. Moreover, these portrayals serve to discipline pre-service teachers and veteran teachers into roles of unquestioning deference and submission to an increasingly neoliberal education system and the authorities that maintain it, lest one be mistakenly known as Miss Viola Swamp or Sheba Hart.

The Big Picture

While these dramatic extremes, teacher-as-mother or savior juxtaposed to teacher-as-villain or boring, serve to individually or collectively represent institutional and traditional views, films such as *Waiting for Superman* (2010) reinforce discourses of inept and lazy teachers as the cause for failing schools, ignoring structural inequities and discrimination. Popular films and images of teachers focus on caring and miracle working to achieve the reward of touching the life of one student, not addressing inadequate salaries, resources for the children, and assessments. Media skirts the task of highlighting the system that restricts the majority of children and their families from getting ahead and having a future that is radically different from their past. The teacher is positioned as mother and savior and the students as empty vessels or clay for molding. This dynamic permits those in power to attribute low student scores to the teacher not possessing the miracle gimmick for creative, over-the-top entertaining or pedagogy and to not sacrificing or caring enough to save those who are all but lost in the system.

This belief system—that teachers are to blame because they aren't willing to sacrifice themselves at the altar of public school success—also creates a cycle of blame. There is a continuous accusational volley between society, which blames the teachers, and educators, who blame the children's families or the children themselves, for societal circumstances that give low-income children a different starting line in the race and further hurdles once the race begins. This blaming logic not only distracts the public from the larger issues, but, more importantly, it maintains the status quo. Worse, the short-term systemic "bandaids" continually distract from any national conversation regarding making long-term, systemic changes in the system of schooling.

Teachers have become the most logical scapegoat. The popular statement, "Those who can, do; those who can't, teach," implies that people with practical skills are out doing constructive things, while those who can't make it in the real world find a less demanding refuge in teaching. This pervasive discourse reifies an understanding of teachers as an ignorant, exploitable labor force, and also provides a rationale for treating them as expendable if they do not perform their role of care and entertainment as miracle workers. Keeping teachers overwhelmingly busy with scripted teaching and paperwork and concerned about caring enough diverts their attention and energy from mastering an understanding of the system and organizing for activism and policy reform to improve education and society as a whole.

These teacher portrayals and the rhetoric reinforced by them silence the pivotal role that the U.S. government intends a teacher to play in maintaining status quo in society (Giroux, 2012). Teaching is the only profession that allows one person the possibility of influencing masses of energetic and creative young people. Therefore, the deliberate portrayals of "good" teachers as caring and sacrificing instead of political, to the extent of systematic change, leave the status quo unchallenged, ensuring that systemic change remains out of reach and leaving the burden not on the government but on our individual teachers.

Social justice advocates believe that the understanding and application of systemic change and activism must have a place in teacher training programs (Cochran-Smith, Shakman, Jong, Barnatt, Terrell, and McQuillan, 2009). Common myths that teaching for social justice either neglects subject matter knowledge or indoctrinates pre-service teachers with a certain political ideology need to be dismissed. Teaching is political. The authors argue "that the critiques are largely based on false dichotomies between social justice and knowledge/learning, on one hand, and flawed assumptions about teacher education as a neutral and value-free enterprise on the other" (Cochran-Smith et al., 2009, p. 349).

This discourse can be seen clearly in the *New York Post*'s columnist Michael Goodwin's attack on New York City public school teacher and founding member of the Grassroots Education Movement (GEM) Sam Coleman. On January 18, 2012, in a piece titled "Teacher's Blind to Reality," Goodwin attacks Coleman saying that "[w]e get it that you don't have a clue about the role of your profession. You're a 'social justice' type, too much a community organizer to be stuck in front of bored kids who can't read" (para 12). Goodwin claims that "social justice types" have no place in public education as a neutral, apolitical sphere; teachers would be more helpful by remaining quiet about social inequalities and taking their proper place in the system. Supporting the common myths found by Cochran-Smith et al. (2009), Goodwin equates advocating for social justice and lack of learning and critical thinking. He lays the blame for low-achieving students at Sam's feet, claiming that "his plan to help students learn has precious little to do with the classroom" (para 10) and ignores the well-researched facts Sam cites that point to growing wealth inequality and unequal access to quality public schooling. Sam argues, "[I]t is our responsibility to fight injustice. If we want all of our nation's students to have access to quality education, we must insist on equity in all spheres of education" (para 3). Goodwin ends his rant with "Heaven help New York, and especially the students of teachers like Sam. With 'educators' like that, they don't have a prayer" (para 16).

Why are columnists like Goodwin and those who support his views so angered by teacher advocates like Sam? Why does society blindly support teachers who fit the mold of teacher-as-savior but not teacher-as-advocate? Why is a teacher who fights for equity painted in such a negative manner, his legitimacy as a teacher questioned? In a 2012 article for *Truthout*, Giroux argues that critical education and teacher advocates challenge the neoliberal system which relies on constructing consent that makes inequalities seem like common sense, the only way, maybe even necessary. He states that "the task of educating students to become critical agents who can actively question and negotiate the relationships between individual troubles and public issues" is dangerous to the system because it has the ability to challenge it (Giroux, 2012).

Conclusion

Moving from images of teachers-as-mother or savior to the more productive teacher-as-activist requires teacher educators to lay a critical foundation of the purpose of schooling for future teachers. Pre-service teachers frequently do not consider the socializing mechanisms of the invisible or hidden curricula of popular culture images of heroic teachers and instead adopt the savior role for themselves, positioning themselves as healers and advocates, not activists. Without questioning these images and rhetoric, they can perpetuate an inequitable system and society without meaning to do so. Pre-service teachers must be provided opportunities to examine the socializing power of media on teacher identity and the historical and political underpinnings of the dominant teacher images. Pre-service teachers can then take the first step to acknowledging a teacher's potential to work within the system, while actively educating and working against it, to change and empower teachers in new ways.

It has been argued that public education remains "the one best system" (Tyack, 1974); it is important to concentrate on its potential to foster justice in society. Noguera states:

> it is the only system that turns no child away, regardless of race, status, language, or need. For this reason, public schools are the only institution that are positioned to play a role in addressing the effects of poverty and social marginalization and furthering the goal of equity. Teachers are poised in the trenches of the most powerful and political societal institution in shaping the hearts and minds of the masses. (Noguera, 2008, p. xxvii)

If pre-service teachers model themselves after the teacher-saviors found in popular culture and believe that public schools are broken and in need of a superhero to rescue them, rather than understanding their potential to affect systemic change, public schools and public school teachers will not realize the potential that Noguera describes.

Teaching and education rarely become spaces for issues of social justice or activism, and teachers are rarely seen as strong advocates with high intellectual capacity, which causes us to lose sight of the power of education to be a liberating and equalizing force. When teaching is limited to change on an individual basis, rather than change on local, national, or global levels, we feed into meritocratic rhetoric and ignore societal structures and institutions as causes for social ills. We become complicit in arguments that "bad" and "lazy" teachers are to blame for student underachievement, rather than harmful educational practices. Hegemony is never really challenged despite attempts to incorporate multiculturalism or cultural sensitivity.

Accordingly, we need teachers committed to social justice, not just those interested in ambiguous goals of celebrating diversity and making a difference. Films about teaching illuminate problems about education in a way that professional texts cannot (Trier 2001). Filmic images play a key role in the construction of teacher identity (Fisher, Harris, & Jarvis 2008; Mitchell & Weber 1999; Raimo, Delvin-Schere & Zincola 2002). It is for this reason that Brunner (1994) argues using films "in parity with professional texts" to interrogate students' preconceived notions about teaching. Filmic images of teachers can be a catalyst for discussing the role of the teacher, recognizing that in many cases, these images are more real for students than the professional literature. Therefore, it is imperative for pre-service teacher educators to tap into these films in order to produce teachers that are socially just. With this in mind, the lesson ideas and specific plan provided in this chapter's appendices use pop culture and critical media literacy to encourage pre-service teachers to explore the teaching profession and activism.

Note

1. There is a variety of mixed data regarding the success rates and longevity of Teach for America participants. However, even the most supportive studies note that of the participants that chose to remain in education, many move on to wealthy, white, and/or private schools, or enter school administration after their two-year commitment in high-risk schools ends. Many who argue Teach for America is successful also acknowledge that supporters "don't know how much more effective it would be in tandem with an even more robust training regimen" and acknowledge that "it is hardly the last word on how to train teachers" (Rotherham, 2011, para. 9).

References

Archer, M. (2007). *Making our way through the world: Human reflexivitiy and social mobility.* Cambridge: Cambridge University Press.

Ball, S. & Goodson, I. (Eds). (1985). *Teachers' lives and careers.* London: Falmer Press.

Baudrillard, J. (1983). In the shadows of the silent majorities. New York: Semiotext(e).

Brunner, D. (1994). *Inquiry and reflection: Framing narrative practice in education.* New York: New York Sate University Press.

Cochran-Smith, M., Shakman, K., Jong, C., Barnat, J., Terrell, D., & McQuillan, P. (2009). Good and just teaching: The case for social justice in teacher education. *American Journal of Education* 115 (3), 3347-3377.

Darling-Hammond, L., & Sclan, E. (1992). Policy and Supervision. In C. Glickman (Ed)., *Supervision in Transition* (pp. 7 - 29). Alexandria, VA: Association for Supervision and Curriculum Development.

Fisher, R., Harris, A., & Jarvis, C. (2008). *Education in pop culture: Telling tales on teachers and learners.* London: Routledge Press.

Freire, P. (2006). *Pedagogy of hope: Reliving pedagogy of the oppressed.* London: Continuum Press.

Fullan, M. (2006). *Turnaround leadership.* San Francisco, CA: Jossey Bass.

Giroux, H. (2012, February 22). Why teaching people to think for themselves is repugnant to religious zealots and Rick Santorum. *Truthout.* Retrieved from http://truth-out.org/index.php?option+com_k2&view+item&id=6812:why-teaching-people-to-think-for-themselves-is-repugnant-to-religious-zealotsand-ricksantorum.

Goodwin, M. (2012, January 18). Teachers blind to reality. New York Post. Retrieved from http:www.nypost.com/p/news/local/teacher_blind_to_realityKGf9pTZS!g@178UqfdMOCP/1.

Gregory, M. (2007). Real teaching and real learning vs. narrative myths about education. *Arts and Humanities in Higher Education, 6*(1), 7-27.

Kellner, D., & Share, J. (2007). Critical media literacy, democracy, and the reconstruction of education. In D. Macedo & S.R. Steinberg (Eds.), *Media Literacy: A Reader* (pp. 3-23). New York: Peter Lang Publishing.

Meyer, G. (Writer), & Lynch, J. (Director). (1992). Separate Vocations. *The Simpsons* (Television series episode). Retrieved from http://wtso.net/movie/157-The_Simpsons_318_Separate_Vocations.html.

Mitchell, C., & Weber, S. (1999). *Reinventing ourselves as teachers: Beyond nostalgia.* London: Falmer Press.

Mockler, N. (2011). Beyond 'what works': Understanding teacher identity as a practical and political tool. *Teachers and Teaching: Theory and Practice, 17*(5), 517-528.

Moore, A. (2004). *The good teacher: Dominant discourses in teaching and teacher education.* London: Routledge Press.

Nias, J. (1997). Would schools improve if teachers cared less? *International Journal of Primary, Elementary, and Early Years Education, 39*(5), 11-22.

Noguera, P. (2008). *The trouble with black boys: And other reflections on race, equity, and the future of public education.* Hoboken, NJ: Jossey-Bass Press.

Parkerson, D. H., & Parkerson, J. A. (2008). *The American teacher: Foundations of educ-ation.* New York: Routledge.

Raimo, A., Delvin-Schere, R., & Zincola, D. (2002). Learning about teachers through film. *The Education Forum, 66*(2), 123-143.

Rotherham, A.J. (2011, February 10). Teach for America: 5 myths that persist 20 years on. *Time.* Retrieved from: http://www.time.com/time/nation/article/0, 8599,2047211,00.html.

Strauss, V. (2012, July 9). Texas GOP rejects 'critical thinking' skills: Really. *The Washington Post.* Retrieved from http://www.washingtonpost.com/blogs/answer-sheet/post/texas-gop-rejects-critical-thinking-skillsreally/2012/07/08/gJQAHN pFXW_blog.html.

Trier, J. (2001, Summer). The cinematic representation of the personal and professional lives of teachers. *Teacher Education Quarterly,* 93-108.

Tyack, D. (1974). *The one best system: A history of American urban education.* Cambridge, MA: Harvard University Press.

Wiggins, G., & McTighe, J. (2007). *Schooling by design.* Alexandria, VA: ASCD.

Appendix A:
Preservice Teacher Lesson Plan Ideas

• Have students bring a *Youtube* film clip of a popular teacher movie, prepared to lead a discussion on the traits and skills that the film deems necessary to be a "good teacher."

• Have students bring and discuss a book or advertisement about teaching, prepared to lead a discussion on the traits and skills that the book or advertisement deems necessary to be a "good teacher."

• Have students do a "google image" search for "teacher," noting what type of images emerge and analyzing them in pairs or small groups.

• Have students discuss their images of a "good teacher" and "bad teacher" and the origin of these images.

- Have students write and draw an accompanying picture to any metaphors they may have about teaching. One example: Yeats' "not filling the pail, but the lighting of a fire."

- Have students brainstorm about metaphors that could be used to reflect teacher-as-activist. Have students write and draw an accompanying picture.

Appendix B:
Sample Preservice Teacher Lesson Plan

Materials:
- Computers with Internet access

- Paper

- Crayons / markers / colored pencils

Target Audience:
- Pre-service teachers

Objectives:
- To discover/explore images of teachers in popular media

- To understand how these images affect our perception of the role of the teacher

- To explore other roles / identities for teachers

Steps:
- Ask students to describe characteristics of teachers and their role in the classroom. Write these answers under the heading teacher characteristics and role.

- Ask students to discuss the teacher activism. Does it have a place? Why is activism important? What is the difference between Activist and Savior?

- Ask students to Google images by entering the search term "teachers." Select one image to analyze.

- Ask students to discuss what they saw:

  o Messages and Values

      ▪ What kinds of behaviors and what kinds of consequences are depicted? [i.e., where are teachers positioned in relation to students in the images? What are teachers seen doing? How has this limited our concept of the role of teachers?]

- What social or ideological messages are a part of the message's subtext? [i.e., why are teachers seen as helpers and nurturers, but not as activists? How would the world / our society be different if teachers were seen as advocates? What are the implications of this persistent nurturing, passive image of teachers?]

o Codes and Conventions

- What types of visual and / or verbal symbolism are used to construct the message? [i.e., what are some examples of body language / facial expression of the teachers in the images? What other images are depicted in the image besides the teacher?]

- What kinds of persuasive or emotional appeals are used in this message? [i.e, what emotional appeals are commonly associated with teaching?]

o Producers and Consumers

- Who is the target audience? [i.e., are these images for the public or for teachers? Are the perceptions different? Why?]

- How do different individuals respond emotionally to this message? [i.e, how does the public respond compared to teachers? Do the images spur you to action?]

- Ask students to reflect on the Google images and the teaching profession. What kind of teacher would they like to be? How would they differ from the image they selected?

- Ask students to draw an alternate image of the teacher, one they'd like to be, paying close attention to the positioning in the classroom and to students, facial expressions and gestures, etc. Ask students to include one important issue this teacher would advocate.

- Have the students design a lesson plan to address this issue, relating it to their content area. Possible ideas include: math and wealth inequality; history and gender equity; science and environmentalism; reading and students with disabilities; reading and multiculturalism.

- Ask students to share images and lesson plans with the group.

Chapter Five

"The Words We Write for Ourselves": Confronting the Myths of Race, Education, and American Genius in *Finding Forrester*

Joanna Davis-McElligatt and Forrest Roth

Gus Van Sant's 2000 film *Finding Forrester* was aggressively marketed as an educative document meant to be used by teachers in the classroom. A cursory examination of online instructional materials yields PowerPoint presentations, study guides, and lesson plans; in addition, the film's novelization, written by James Ellison (2000), was picked up by The Scholastic Book Club and sold in schools. The push to place the film in the classroom makes good sense, for *Finding Forrester* focuses on the power of education to simultaneously discourage and motivate students, and the efficacy of learning processes in public, private, and extracurricular settings. However, the film addresses these issues while also arguing that the nurturance of genius is the highest educative goal, and that any educational system, no matter how inspired, will fail to teach a child who is not already gifted. Furthermore the film also makes the case that education and literacy are not social acts, but private ones; that the acquisition of literacy is the domain of the individual, and not society; and that real writers produce their best work in isolation, rather than in conversation with others.

Many of the instructional resources reinforce these perceptions. In an online study guide meant to accompany *Finding Forrester*, published by Film Education for Columbia Pictures and intended for use by "pupils of ... English and Media Studies," students are asked over and over again to consider literary "recluses," and what makes them tick. These types, students are told, "dress eccentrically," are "obsessive," and have, for one reason or another, "decided to cut themselves off from society" (Harris, n.d., pp. 2-5). The title character of the film, William Forrester, clearly fits the definition, as does the film's protagonist, Forrester's young African American protégé, Jamal Wallace—though perhaps less obviously so. Whereas Forrester, a literal recluse, refuses to publish his work, leave his apartment, or forge bonds with other human beings, Jamal declines to produce decent prose for his high school teachers, divulge his love of writing and reading to his closest friends and family, and, in so doing, fails to make deep connections with the people who love him. As Forrester explains to Jamal one afternoon, both prefer "the words we write for ourselves," than "the words we write for others" (Rich, 2000).[1] Both are brilliant writers of near-equal capability who write alone without community support, and both are what the guide refers to as "isolated character[s]" (p. 4). In fact, under a section entitled "A Study of Representation," students are given a list of statements about Forrester, and asked to "fill in the equivalent facts about Jamal," facts which include the following: "does not want to leave his environment," "has made his space his own," "does not want to meet new people," "does not trust people," "is never wrong," and "has no friends" (p. 4).

The American imagination is endlessly captivated by the exceptional and self-motivating individuated mind in need of neither formal education nor communal sustainment—think Will Hunting in Gus Van Sant's 1997 film *Good Will Hunting*, John Nash in Ron Howard's 2001 film *A Beautiful Mind*, or Howard Hughes in Martin Scorsese's 2004 film *The Aviator*. Indeed, the preponderance of this type in popular culture has, in many ways, overdetermined the ways in which subjects have come to understand what it means to educate and be educated, what it means for students to be labeled either gifted and talented or average, and, in the age of genetics, what it means for certain human beings to be regarded as more biologically predisposed to cleverness than others. This representation of the intelligent mind as utterly self-sustaining and therefore capable of thriving in a social vacuum has affected every level of our educational system, and has likewise powerfully affected how we perceive the potential for significant contributions from ourselves and our fellow citizens. *Finding Forrester's* narrative is explicitly focused on exploring and developing the mythos surrounding this archetype in that it explores the connection between a very particular type of white male literary eccentric and his African American counterpart—a diamond in the rough whose environment, socioeconomic status, and racial identity precludes his ability to achieve the full potential of his genius, who is isolated in a world of diminished expectation, oppression, and lack of opportunity, yet who, of his own volition and hard work, overcomes all obstacles. The film accomplishes this by staging a complex pedagogical, psychological, and personal relationship between William Forrester and Jamal Wallace, presumably built on mutual respect and admiration, though in actuality also steeped in troubling power differentials and violent rhetoric.

In this chapter, we argue that *Finding Forrester* stages a confrontation between two mythic American character types, both of which, through the constructions of Jamal and Forrester, fundamentally underscore the myths of the

American Dream, individualism, and the self-made man. These types can be defined as the dead white male author, on the one hand, and the black male autodidact, or the self-taught prodigy, on the other—represented historically by figures such as Frederick Douglass, our example in this essay, an inspired and gifted man who learned to read, write, and speak by sheer force of will in near impossible circumstances. Through a deconstruction of these various "myths," we want to to interrogate the ways in which these types and their connotations directly influence American's conceptions of education, intelligence, and opportunity. Ultimately, as we witness Jamal negotiate three distinct educational environments—his public school in the Bronx, his private school in Manhattan, and Forrester's penthouse living room—we contend that the film tacitly makes the case that real education is not only the result of hard work and opportunity, but also *genius*. In other words, literacy and the ability to write are skills one either preternaturally possesses or does not possess, skills that can be enhanced through the pedagogical experience, but that can be neither taught nor learned. Furthermore, we claim that by pitting these mythic types against one another the political power of Frederick Douglass's narratives, and the historical impact of subjects like him, is diminished, for the film suggests that the black male autodidact comes into being and finds his voice only when vetted by and filtered through the voice of the dead white male author. By way of conclusion, we suggest that the film encourages its viewers to circumvent the real challenges presented to educators in the urban classroom environment, not only by implying that black students in an urban milieu cannot really be taught, but also by encouraging them to take a view of education that rather radically shifts the focus away from the students who need the most help and consideration.

"I didn't write it for them!": The Dead White Male Author Character Type

In describing how William Forrester came into being, Mike Rich, the film's screenwriter, explains that he is merely a trumped-up reflection of a well-known breed of American author: "So many of America's greatest writers, J.D. Salinger or Thomas Pynchon for example, were eccentric, reclusive types. We made him [William Forrester] more reclusive, more eccentric, more compassionate" (Harris, n.d., p. 5). William Forrester is, quite clearly, hopelessly mired in his own idiosyncrasies: he leaves his apartment only at night and only then to squeeze his hulking frame out of his living room window to wash the glass; he employs a yuppie-type to bring him his mail, royalty checks from his publishers, food, alcohol, and sundries once a week; he is fixated on books and baseball; and he is oddly clothed throughout much of the film in an oversized trench coat, ratty pajama bottoms, a scarf, and, as we are pointedly informed, a new pair of socks daily worn inside out because "the seams ... hurt the toes." He is a Scottish émigré, we learn, who has been living in New York City since his teens, and he brings with him a kind of foreignness which adds greatly to his mystique, evident not only in his thick brogue, but in manner and custom. When he was a young man, Forrester published a single novel, *Avalon Landing*, which earned him the Pulitzer Prize. Some forty years after its publication, Forrester's novel is not only taught in schools, but is still wildly popular with the general public—in fact, we learn, that anyone wishing to borrow one of the twenty-five copies in stock at the New York Public Library must first put their name on a waiting list. In addition to his novel, Forrester published short pieces—essays, we are led to believe, and some short stories—in publications such as *The New Yorker*, but as they remain uncollected in a volume they are rarely read by anyone. The reasons for Forrester's seclusion remain a bit murky throughout the film, but we know that he could not tolerate the prying of literary scholars, who wanted to read too much of him into his work—when asked about the reaction of critics to his prose, he angrily exclaims "I didn't write it for them!" We also come to see, however, that the death of Forrester's younger brother, whom he loved deeply and whom he felt he must protect, shattered his sense of security in the world, and, unable to accept that life is unpredictable and carries with it immense risk, he adopted an alias ("Mr. Johannsen"), fled Manhattan, purchased an enormous penthouse apartment in a Bronx slum, invested in heavy locks, and threw away the keys. He never marries, never has children, and for the forty years he is shut up in his apartment, does not have any significant human relationships at all. He unquestionably suffers from severe anxiety, agoraphobia, alcoholism, and depression. At the film's end, upon Forrester's death, we discover that his fear of the outside world prevented him from treating the cancer which had slowly been eating away at his body over the course of his final few years of life.

It is telling that Rich felt the need to add "more" strangeness to Salinger and Pynchon, for neither are as extreme a case as Forrester. J.D. Salinger, the clear inspiration for Forrester, retreated from the publishing world and the public eye in the mid-1960s, yet lived a perfectly normal and functional life in Cornish, New Hampshire, until his death in 2010 at the age of 91. He had a number of relationships with women, and sired two children. According to an interview with *The New York Times* in 1974—one of his only—when journalists attempted to make contact with him, "the author would turn and walk away if approached on the street and was reported to abandon friends if they discussed him with reporters. There have been articles reporting on his mailbox, his shopping, and his reclusive life, but not interviews" (Fosburgh, 1974). Certainly there were other members of Salinger's Cornish community who stuck close to home, who went about their daily business and never traveled far, who had friends and a pleasant simple life, and who valued their privacy—yet we would never think of them as recluses tucked away in their hermitages, eschewing all contact with the outside world.

Writing as he was in the age of literary celebrity, when authors such as Arthur Miller and Norman Mailer were more than willing to submit to the scrutiny of the public eye, opening up their lives and marriages to national publications on a regular basis, Salinger's refusal to publish or submit to interviews for magazines and literary journals was read as slightly mad. Salinger felt, however, that publishing and speaking about his work publically was a profound violation of his privacy, because he wrote, in the main, "just for myself, and my own pleasure" (Fosburgh, 1974). Salinger was nevertheless aware of the ways in which his rejection of the public sphere was read by the media: "I pay for this kind of attitude. I'm known as a strange, aloof kind of man. But all I'm doing is trying to protect myself and my work. I just want all this to stop. It's intrusive" (Fosburgh, 1974). In spite of the fact that Salinger stopped making his work public after the publication of *Raise High the Roof Beam, Carpenter and Seymour, An Introduction* in 1963, he remains one of the most influential American writers of the twentieth century.

The term "dead white male," in literary parlance, emerged from a growing anxiety about the overwhelming influence of the European and white American on the literary canon, prompted in the main by scholars who questioned why J.D. Salinger's *Catcher in the Rye*, for example, should be regularly taught in American classrooms as a representative *Bildungsroman*, or a coming of age novel, instead of, say, Sandra Cisneros's *The House on Mango Street*—in particular considering that the demographics of American classrooms have been shifting radically in favor of minorities since 1965. This push to address the lack of diversity in the literary canon coincided with the Civil Rights Movement and Women's Rights Movement, and the rise of LGBT social movements, as women and minorities began to insist that the canon undergo radical changes in order to accommodate a wider array of perspectives, histories, and voices. Yet despite the fact that there has been tremendous success in including writers such as Toni Morrison and Sherman Alexie to the literary canon, most American high school students will read only the work of writers such as Mark Twain, John Steinbeck, and Ernest Hemingway. The film's construction of William Forrester—a European novelist who is figuratively dead until he is literally dead—represents, then, a very real resistance to the push for changes to the canon.

Though Forrester spends most of every day reading through the thousands of books in his apartment, and writing on one of his many typewriters, we know very little about his formal education. We know absolutely nothing about his life in Scotland, and very little about his early days in America. In fact, we never learn why he immigrated to New York in his early teens, though we do know that he had little money, and was charged with caring for his younger brother while his mother worked long hours. Forrester's whiteness is European, and therefore non-American, which enables the filmmakers to evade some of the historical implications with regard to the inequities between white and black Americans in his dealings with Jamal. Forrester's obsession with baseball troubles his European identifications, though we do not know if Forrester became an American citizen. His uncertain national allegiance does not appear to detract from his ability to write the Great American Novel, so it might be said that he functions as a Vladimir Nabokov, who wrote *Lolita* in English in America, or a T. S. Eliot in reverse.

As a writer, Forrester is inherently contradictory, a quality mistaken for complexity and depth by the screenwriter. He eschews fame and regard, but remains the endless recipient of it. His art form is entirely communicative, yet he refuses to engage with anyone on even the most superficial of levels. Forrester's knowledge of literature appears to be dominated by the Romantics—which seems appropriate, considering that he might be read as a Byronic hero, a misunderstood loner who follows the whims of his own creative impulse rather than those of society. Indeed, beyond his dealings with the lackey who brings him his weekly supplies, Forrester asks for nothing, needs no one, and avoids entanglements of all kinds. To that end, he is also an utterly self-reliant, rugged individualist. Clearly, Forrester shares with conservative Americans their deep-seated distrust for all institutions, educational, social, and health. Forrester is, therefore, a Horatio Alger type, or a conventional "rags to riches" character popularized by the 1868 novel *Ragged Dick* , whose work ethic and individual genius secure for him his obvious wealth, success, and status. In fact, we are meant to assume he had a hard-scrabble youth, though Forrester himself makes it clear that he had some economic advantages—at the very least more than Jamal has. One afternoon, in typical fashion, Forrester demands that Jamal stir his soup to prevent it from "firm[ing] up." When Jamal asks why it is that his own mother's soup never encounters this particular problem, Forrester explains, rather caustically, that it was "probably because your mother was brought up in a house that never wasted milk in soup." Our attention is drawn quite sharply to not only the very real socioeconomic differences between Jamal and Forrester in that moment, but to the historical differences between them—Forrester's grandparents were the sort who had milk to "waste," and Jamal's were not.

In spite of his unwillingness to engage with the outside world, Forrester nevertheless spends a good portion of every day examining the goings-on in his neighborhood through a pair of binoculars, and videotaping his favorite birds with a high-tech camera, though he admits that he is unable to see all of the birds he would like to because many of them "don't stray that far from the park." The film flirts with the viewer's potential anxieties that Forrester's single status, the oddness of his living alone, and his close relationship with a young boy might be read as queer; at one point, while gazing out the window through his binoculars, he tells Jamal that he sees "an adult male, quite pretty, probably strayed from the park." We immediately learn that he is referring to a bird, the Connecticut warbler, and the tension is broken—shortly thereafter, Forrester will inform Jamal that men write mainly "because they want to get laid," and will offer Jamal advice and help in wooing Claire Spence, Jamal's love interest. Forrester's firebrand masculine intellect is likewise an extension of his heterosexuality—he is aggressive, sharp-tongued, and ruthless, and exists in a world in which men are his only competition. His mind and ideas, he feels, do not necessitate a deeper understanding of his self, so he refuses, to the bitter end, to open up about any personal matters. Most importantly, however, even though Forrester is cloistered and hyper-individuated, he also functions as an Everyman, supremely human and powerfully capable of exposing our foibles, excesses, and follies, as he does in his novel. By recusing himself from the world, Forrester makes evident the senselessness and excessiveness of our involvement in it. This is, perhaps, the defining characteristic of the dead white male author character type, that out of the specificity of his being he is coded as a universal figure.

"A black kid from the Bronx can write": The Black Male Autodidact Character Type

The black male autodidact character type, typified by Jamal Wallace in the film, appeared in American literature for the first time in slave narratives, though similarly powerful accounts of self-education and self-reliance have provided much inspiration and consternation for black subjects who, even now, continue to encounter the type in fiction, nonfiction, and film. Autodidactism was not only evidence of individual motivation, but was fundamentally necessary, for most slaves were not formally educated, and many others who learned to read or write were often compelled to keep their abilities secret, under penalty of torture or death. In fact, a good number of Southern states had laws on the books prohibiting the instruction of writing to slaves as a means to prevent communications that might lead to open rebellions. Frederick Douglass is, perhaps, the best known black male autodidact, and he devotes much of his text, *Narrative of the Life of Frederick Douglass, An American Slave, Written By Himself* (1851), to his struggle for literacy. Douglass vividly recalls that his mistress had begun to teach him the alphabet until his master, Mr. Auld, forcefully intervened, "and at once forbade Mrs. Auld to instruct me further, telling her, among other things, that it was unlawful, as well as unsafe, to teach a slave to read" (p. 35). Adding insult to injury, Mr. Auld further argues that "learning would *spoil* the best nigger in the world,"[2] making him unfit for service (p. 35). Writing and reading were, then, special skills regarded by both slaves and masters alike as great equalizers, for an educated slave, aware at last of his worth and able to articulate it as well as any master, would certainly refuse to be subjugated any longer—in fact, Douglass argues that literacy meant for all slaves the difference between "slavery and freedom" (p. 35). Undeterred by his master's admonition, Douglass, "though conscious of the difficulty of learning without a teacher," "set out with high hope, and a fixed purpose, at whatever cost of trouble, to learn how to read" (p. 35-36). Douglass did, indeed, learn to read, by taking the bit of the alphabet he had learned from Mrs. Auld, listening in on lessons for children, and putting to practice his skills whenever he was given anything in print.

Learning to write was even more necessary, for he would be able to forge notes from his master and secure his escape, though he would first need to learn to spell correctly and master the art of penmanship. By copying the letters ship-yard carpenters left on hewn logs intended for various parts of the ship, before long Douglass mastered L, S, A, and F for lee, stern, aft, and fore. In order to learn new words and letters, he challenged fellow workers to writing competitions, and when they successfully wrote a new word he did not recognize, he quickly memorized it. Yet without access to pen, paper, and ink, all the while enduring the hardships of slavery, Douglass explains that:

> During this time my copy-book was the board fence, brick wall, and pavement; my pen and ink was a lump of chalk. With these, I learned mainly how to write. I then commenced and continued copying the italics in Webster's Spelling Book, until I could make them all without looking at the book. By this time, my little Master Thomas had gone to school, and learned how to write, and had written in a number of copy-books. [...] I used to spend the time in writing in the spaces left in Master Thomas's copy book, copying what he had written. I continued to do this, until I could write in a hand very similar to that of Master Thomas. Thus, after a long, tedious effort for years, I finally succeeded in learning how to write. (p. 44)

As we see, through careful acts of subterfuge, incredible determination, and an acutely brilliant mind, Douglass teaches himself to read and write, and in so doing successfully escapes the bonds of slavery. Even though Douglass was absolutely dependent upon a broad community to literate people in order to learn these skills, even if some of them were unaware of the help they were providing him, Douglass consistently represents himself as a paragon of individual progress, rather than social uplift.

Douglass did, of course, acknowledge that the system of slavery functioned as a very real impediment to personal achievement, but he nevertheless urged his fellow black Americans, in his third autobiography, *Life and Times of Frederick Douglass* (1892) to embrace the spirit of "self-reliance, self-respect, industry, perseverance, and economy," and implored them to take more direct control over their own destinies. So characteristically American is this advice, and so steeped in the logics of individualism, that Frederick W. Turner (1969) makes a strong case that *Life and Times*, and other texts like it, "easily lend themselves to interpretation as black variations of the Horatio Alger idea" (p. 343).[3] Eric Sundquist (1991), in an essay on literacy and paternalism in Douglass's narratives, likewise contends that "Douglass's language in his second autobiography [*My Bondage, My Freedom*] is thoroughly 'American,' in political as well as literary terms, as is the versatile language of the self-made man which dominates" (p. 121). Furthermore, as Sundquist explains, in a "typically American gesture, he [Douglass] makes himself his own father" through careful acts of linguistic construction representative of "the Emersonian impulse to liberate the ego from inherited constraints, to seize and aggrandize the power of domineering ancestors, or their surrogates, in order to fashion one's own paternity" (p. 124).

Out of the isolation of oppression and bereft of prospects for betterment, the black male autodidact signifies the power of the high-functioning individual self to overcome all odds, even when utterly isolated. Yet the inherent problem with the construction of the black male autodidact character type rests in the ability, Turner claims, of the "uncritical reader" "[to] see only the achieved success and forget the means by which it was achieved. In this sense, the blueprint is faulty and its followers doomed to frustration and failure" (p. 344). In other words, the millions of other slaves who found themselves unable to educate themselves, wrest free from their masters, and secure their freedom did not fail to do so because of their inability to be sufficiently self-reliant or hard-working.

Jamal Wallace is a twenty-first-century version of the black male autodidact character type. Aged sixteen, on the cusp of adulthood, Jamal lives alone with his mother in a large, clean apartment in the Bronx. They are by no means wealthy, but Jamal has plenty of pocket money, good food to eat, and nice clothing to wear. His mother works long hours, and does not have much time to communicate and care for her son. He has a decent, if not a bit distant, relationship with his older brother, Terrell, who ekes out a living as a parking lot supervisor at Yankee Stadium. Jamal's father was a very real part of his life until the age of eleven, at which point his father abandoned the family for drugs and alcohol. Justifiably broken-hearted, Jamal copes with his father's sudden absence by writing in pocket journals and reading voraciously—in the main work by canonical white authors such as Anton Chekov, Søren Kierkegaard, the Marquis de Sade, James Joyce, René Descartes, and Sam Shepard.[4] It is striking indeed that at no point in time does Jamal read or reference a single work by an African American writer. Jamal refuses to discuss his love of literature and writing with his mother, his brother, and his friends, preferring instead to pretend as though his only interest is playing basketball—here, too, Jamal is exceptionally gifted. Though the average African American male living in a postmodern urban environment must contend with a lack of quality educational opportunities, rising crime rates, few employment prospects, the influence of drug cultures, and diminished expectations, Jamal circumvents these obstacles by being preternaturally intelligent, endowed with the special ability to remember all he reads and recall it effortlessly. Jamal is also a Horatio Alger type, for he is hard-working, and develops his talents by reading several books a week, writing diligently in his journals, and playing basketball for hours every day. Indeed, we are meant to see that whatever Jamal has he deserves, even if he does not have to work very hard to get it.

Jamal is functionally peerless, isolated in the world of his own intellect, completely devoid of like minds—in fact, Forrester explains to him, no one can understand "how a black kid from the Bronx can write the way you do." Yet, unlike Forrester who intentionally disavowed an intellectual community eager to engage with him and his ideas, Jamal's friends, classmates, and mother are fundamentally unable to connect with him on an intellectual level, even if he were to open up with them about his interests. Terrell knows that Jamal is brilliant, and encourages him to do his best in school, though his support is mainly the result of his fear that Jamal will follow in his footsteps by attending college to play basketball only to fail at both. Things are not much better for him at the Mailor-Callow preparatory school. His closest male friend at the school, John Coleridge, is not exceptionally intelligent and advises Jamal that the way to survive is to keep his head down and never speak up. Claire, though obliviously quite clever, is not quite his intellectual equal, and Jamal has qualms about pursuing any deep relationship with her because he perceives that her father would not approve of an interracial and cross-class relationship. Jamal's isolation, then, is both self-imposed, and imposed from without, but completely all-encompassing. Though Jamal's intellect appears to thrive in confinement, we come to see that he is, in fact, eager for constructive feedback—and he would have to be to be willing to withstand Forrester's abuse in exchange for comments on his writing. In the end, after Forrester's death, we are meant to conclude that Jamal, by developing his own literary voice, has found himself, and in so doing has become his own guide, mentor, and father-figure in the absence of any other.

"From your old school to this one": Representations of Public and Private School Education

When we first encounter Jamal in his public high school his English teacher, Ms. Joyce—tellingly the only African American in a position of authority we will encounter the entire film—is trying, in vain, to lead a discussion about Edgar Allen Poe's "The Raven." Jamal's fellow students, who are almost entirely African American, are noisy and irreverent, ceaselessly cracking jokes, high-fiving, and carrying on loud conversations with one another. The students are dressed in street clothes. Many wear coats and hats, and others still wear their backpacks, more accessories than functional objects, as though poised for flight at any moment. The lesson leaves much to be desired. The teacher glibly informs the students that Poe wrote the poem "when he was strung out on coke and obsessed with death," and the students apparently understand exactly what she means. When one of the students loudly exclaims that the Baltimore Ravens are likewise obsessed with death, which is why they "always get they ass kicked," Jamal laughs, clearly amused, though for the most part he looks straight ahead and pays close attention to the teacher. However, when she asks the students if anyone has read the poem, even though we are meant to believe she has assigned it to the class, no one responds—not even Jamal, whom she pointedly addresses because he has obviously read it. Shortly thereafter, having learned only that Poe was a cokehead, the bell rings, the students flee the classroom *en masse*, and the teacher fecklessly reminds them that an essay is due the following Tuesday. In the end, we are left with the profound impression that very little learning, and very little teaching, is actually taking place at Jamal's school. The setting is too informal, the students are too unserious, and the expectations are too low. The casual chaos of the learning environment itself suggests that, though the teacher might try her hardest, she cannot reach the unreachable; indeed, there is something fundamentally unlearned, perhaps autochthonous, about those under her tutelage.

Ms. Joyce, who doubles as the school's guidance counselor—a commentary on the lack of available funds in the American public school system—calls a meeting with Jamal's mother, Mrs. Wallace, because, she explains, he has scored exceptionally high on an assessment examination. This is "unusual," she claims, not only because Jamal maintains a C average, but also because no other student scored anywhere near as high. In fact, all of the students at Jamal's school, every last one, consistently underperforms. Mrs. Wallace very tentatively states in a frightened and bewildered tone that she knew something was up because she had seen "him reading books all the time, books I never read, some I never even heard of," and on numerous occasions had witnessed him "writing in his notebooks"—this is in spite of the fact, she says, that "all he ever talks about is basketball."[5] Jamal's teacher gently informs her that "basketball is where he gets his acceptance," because, at this school, "the kids don't care about what he can put on paper." And, from what the audience has been shown, this sweeping generalization rings true. Very soon after, Jamal will be offered a spot at Mailor-Callow, described in fulsome terms as "not only the best prep school in the city, [but] one of the finest private schools on the East Coast." Mr. Bradley, a representative from the school, along with Jamal's principal, inform Jamal and his mother that Mailor-Callow withholds a few positions, and enough money for full-ride scholarships, for students who get their attention with high scores on their assessment exams. When Jamal understandably balks at making such a radical shift a few weeks into his sophomore year of high school, his principal, while acknowledging that "leaving for another school, especially a private one, won't be easy," nevertheless insists that "this isn't the right place for you anymore. It's not a difficult choice."

In order to get to his new school, Jamal must take the subway and spend the majority of the trip awkwardly mashed between several trench-coated white men reading newspapers and talking on cell phones. The viewer is immediately clued into the fact that as the train moves further into the city—and further away from the Bronx, its northernmost borough—the inhabitants become not only whiter, but more privileged, harder-working, and wealthier. Viewers have also been set up to understand this distinction, for the film's opening pityingly surveys African American and Hispanic Bronxites loitering in barbershops, play-fighting in front of liquor stores, and idly sitting in front of projects. Mailor-Callow is meant to serve as an extension of this contradistinction. The school itself is in an impressive, multistoried limestone building in downtown Manhattan, a clear indication of the schools long-standing wealth and tradition. Each student wears prim, nicely tailored blue uniform—ties for the boys, skirts for the girls. Jamal's clothes are a bit baggier than those of his peers, to help him maintain a somewhat urban look, and, for the first bit of time he wears his coat, backpack, and a stocking cap wherever he goes, perhaps an indication that he is not quite ready to give up his careless public school identity. However, a few weeks later, after Jamal has committed himself to the school, his uniforms fit him more tightly, he takes to storing his items in his locker, and he no longer covers his head.

Jamal's school has amenities his public school quite obviously does not: a fully-stocked computer lab; a restaurant with china, and attendants who serve students meals and clean up after them; a library with thousands of books; a full-size roof-top basketball court; commuter buses for transporting athletes and students to and from away games; well-kept lockers; and, perhaps most importantly, a generous endowment and board peopled with millionaires. The classroom where Jamal takes his English class, the only one we see, is wood-paneled, lined in heavy, expensive books, and the students sit facing forward in neat rows. The walls are covered in oil paintings, each one rendering a well-known author, and every one of them white and male. As fate would have it, the students are assigned Forrester's novel, copies are handed out, and they are told to read it and produce an essay in a week's time—this, too, is different from Jamal's school, where students do not have texts, are not required to follow through on readings, and likely will not complete written assignments.

Though Jamal's Mailor-Callow classmates grumble audibly, they acquiesce more or less immediately. For example, Jamal encounters Claire one afternoon in the quiet lunchroom poring over *Avalon Landing*, even though she has read it "a dozen times." When he asks her why she is reading it yet again, she explains to him that "they take things real serious around here ... serious enough that I end up getting lunch on my books most days." Jamal responds in the affirmative: "It's a serious place." In contrast, Jamal's public school classmates, whom we see in the crowded, noisy cafeteria eating food on plastic trays at metal picnic benches, joke, laugh, and fight through lunch, which is obviously a wasted hour. Most notably, almost all of his classmates are white, and almost all of them male—Jamal feuds with a light-skinned biracial classmate named John Hartwell on the basketball court, and in one scene an African American youth is shown jostling happily with a crowd of white classmates. But there are no other minorities represented at the school, and very few women, though this is because, Claire informs him, Mailor-Callow had been an all-boys school until her father, determined that she should have the very best education, "got on the board and changed the rules." This kind of parental involvement, care, and consideration is clearly meant to offset Jamal's parents' near total lack of interest in his life.

Robert Crawford, Jamal's English teacher and, in a twist of fate, Forrester's nemesis, does not ask the students questions, or attempt to engage with them on their level, as does Jamal's public high school teacher. Instead, he delivers pompous, uninteresting lectures in an accent that is cultured and quasi-European. He is himself a famous scholar, and the students refer to him as "professor." He enjoys challenging and humiliating students, and he immediately doubts Jamal's abilities. In fact, after Jamal hands in his first essay, written quickly the night before under the guidance of Forrester, Crawford informs him that he believes his work is "too good":

> The acceleration in your progress from your old school to this one is unusual to the point that I must draw one of two conclusions: Either you've been blessed with an uncommon gift, which has just kicked in, or you're getting your inspiration from elsewhere. Given your previous education and your background, I'm sure you'll forgive me for coming to my own conclusions.

Though Crawford has at his disposal Jamal's mediocre transcript, his claim is that Jamal cannot write well because he is poor and black. Yet as we have seen, according to the logics of the film, Crawford is not necessarily wrong in coming to this conclusion—indeed, Jamal is the only African American in his entire school who is able to read and write proficiently. Crawford is, however, wrong to assume this about Jamal, who will not only eventually outsmart, but publically shame him. Unlike Jamal's public school teacher, who instantly recognizes Jamal's potential, but is powerless to inspire him to greater things, Crawford, by underestimating Jamal, brings out his best.

The implications are clear: the palpable differences between Jamal's public school and Mailor-Callow are meant to represent not only apparent distinctions in socioeconomic class, but also in work ethic. The students at Mailor-Callow, even the less intelligent ones like John Coleridge, are not only driven, but fully aware of the rules of education; in other words, they know how to study, how to write, how to read, and how to think critically. The students at Jamal's public school are not only struggling with literacy, but also demonstrate a complete lack of awareness of the function of education. Yet at no point in time do any of the administrators or instructors admit that Jamal's school has failed to inspire and challenge him, and likewise failed to adequately inspire and educate his peers. There is no suggestion that, with more funds, Jamal's Bronx high school might fare better. There is no awareness at all of the very difficult circumstances most poor black students face in urban environments. Rather, the tacit assumption is that Jamal's classmates do not deserve to have a world-class education because they are not already gifted and talented, because they are mediocre, underperforming, and flippant. "The kids," all poor, urban, and African American, have no interest in literacy or the arts, and as we have seen cannot be educated into that interest.

The film ultimately maintains that fine educations are the domain of those who are willing and able to work hard, are naturally gifted, and have deep pockets. Furthermore, according to this logic, the students, and their parents, are in possession of their wealth and advantage precisely *because* they work harder than the inhabitants of Jamal's Bronx slum—the Horatio Alger myth in full force. This means, of course, that there is no point in attempting to make Jamal's Bronx high school more efficacious, for the problem is not with the school, but the pupils. The offer to remove Jamal from his Bronx school, then, is an acknowledgment of his hard work and his natural intellect and genius, but it is also an attempt to place him in a socioeconomic class more akin to his abilities.

"You have William Forrester's Permission": The Dead White Male Educates the Black Male Autodidact

If Ms. Joyce does not push Jamal hard enough, but knows that he is capable of more, and Robert Crawford underestimates Jamal while bringing out his best, then William Forrester, in his pedagogical relationship with Jamal, is meant to strike a definitive balance between the two. Yet Forrester, more often than not, duplicates Crawford's repressive tactics, such as surveillance and humiliation, while never fully committing to a personal connection in quite the same way Ms. Joyce does. Forrester and Jamal are well aware of one another for some time before they ever have an occasion to meet, for the basketball court where Jamal shoots hoops with his friends is directly beneath Forrester's penthouse apartment. The young boys refer to Forrester as "The Window," for they often witness him peering at them through binoculars from his panoptic perch; unable to see him through the darkened window, they are nevertheless aware that "he see us." Convinced that he is a serial killer at large, or as one of Jamal's classmates contends, a "white" "ghost, like the ones in our science books," the community has all but abandoned his building, and leaves him to his own devices. One day during lunch, however, Jamal's friends dare him to enter the apartment, and steal away a totem. He readily agrees, and that night, as he wanders silently around the darkened apartment, he is drawn to the chaotic piles of books, newspapers, and typewriters that litter the place. Just as he slips a letter opener into his backpack, Forrester jumps out, and as the panicked Jamal scrambles to flee the apartment, he leaves behind his backpack, and with it all of his journals.

A few days later the backpack is returned to Jamal—dropped from Forrester's famous window to the ground at his feet—and immediately discovers that Forrester has graded his journals, scrawling all over them in bright red ink. Though we are not sure what his journals contain, we are led to believe they are his own personal musings, likely fragmented in the way that diary writing can be, perhaps deeply personal and intimate, and more loosely strung together than polished prose. Yet Forrester has commented on them as though they were meant to be read by a wide audience, and his notes, which follow, belie that emphasis: "words cheap," "this passage fantastic!," "constipated," "where are you taking me?," and "I want to support this writer, but can we get out of the Bronx for the second?" While Forrester's annotations are meant, on the one hand, to goad Jamal into visiting him again, they also suggest, on the other, that the process by which writers and their intended audiences, readers and the object of their critique, and teachers and students connect does not necessarily need to be the result of direct, sustained, or informed engagement. Though Jamal is visibly, and ironically, disturbed by Forrester's violation of his property, he is also intrigued, and so returns in a few days hopeful that The Window will agree to read more of his writing. Forrester does not outright refuse, but instead screams through the peephole of the door that he will only if Jamal produces "5000 words on why you'll stay the fuck out of my home." This is a characteristically pedagogical directive, even if the assignment is ludicrous. Ever the dutiful student, however, Jamal obliges, turns in his essay, and refuses to leave Forrester's stoop unless he relents and lets him in.

Their first face-to-face meeting is tense, largely because Forrester is racist, condescending, and insulting—he tells Jamal his name "sounds like some kind of marmalade," and then expresses shock that anyone black could write the way he does. When Jamal is reasonably outraged, Forrester goads him, and tells him that in order to work with him he will have to put up with "racist bullshit," or leave. Jamal does turn to go, but not before Forrester takes the letter opener, the very one Jamal tried to steal, and thrusts it violently in Jamal's direction. After a bit he does return again to Forrester, who is no less caustic, demanding and bullying, but he does, at the very least, seem more interested in Jamal's presence. When Jamal asks him, very carefully, why he said "all that stuff about me being black," Forrester responds by saying that his behavior "had nothing to do with you being black," but was instead the result of his own personal, sadistic need to see "how much bullshit you'd be willing to put up with." We know that this is not precisely true, because the insult would make no sense at all if Jamal were a white kid from Queens. Rather, the insult was meant to prey upon Jamal's own insecurities, and force him into a position to swallow his own pride and sense of self in the face of Forrester's might and power, and, in so doing, prevent Jamal from establishing his own position of authority in the relationship.

These series of interchanges perhaps best articulate the relationship between Forrester and Jamal. Forrester is cruel, bitter, and violent, and Jamal is kind, patient, and eager. Though Forrester eventually softens in the end, their pedagogical relationship has long since been firmly established as dysfunctional and unbalanced. Forrester takes advantage of Jamal's earnest desire for feedback by requiring him to perform menial tasks for him, and never asking him politely or thanking him for his effort. He is often violent with Jamal, throwing books across the room and brandishing knives without a second thought. He drinks heavily with Jamal in the room, and even once passes out, never appearing to think twice about it. Given his agoraphobia, he never once thinks to introduce himself to Jamal's mother, who never meets him and only enters his apartment after he is already dead, even though he very often spends entire days and nights there. And, even though Crawford is meant to be the one who continuously doubts Jamal's intellect and ability, Forrester often does the same; in fact, both men underestimate Jamal's near encyclopedic knowledge of the canon, and are stunned to discover that he knows as much as they do, though Forrester is arguably less angry about that fact than Crawford. Most importantly, though Forrester is supposedly interested in helping Jamal develop his own voice, he is adamant that Jamal enforce the standard rules of grammar as he sees them, and explodes into rage when Jamal dares to use colloquial Black English, admonishing him to never "talk like you do out there…in here." This will not stop Forrester from drunkenly mocking Jamal in Black English, however, by exclaiming, "You're the man now, dog!," after Jamal overcomes a particularly difficult hurdle in his writing.

Forrester's unnerving responses to Jamal on a personal level certainly bleed over into his engagements with Jamal's writing. One afternoon, Jamal approaches Forrester because he is struggling to begin a piece for a competition at school; we do not know if the piece is meant to be a work of fiction or a personal essay, because Forrester never asks Jamal for clarification. Instead he pulls out a typewriter, and commands Jamal to sit and to begin typing, but to avoid "think[ing]" while doing so. By way of demonstration, while explaining the process to Jamal Forrester's own fingers glide over the keys, and he produces a fully-formed, and we are meant to believe, if Jamal's reaction is any indicator, dazzling paragraph of flawless prose. In his lessons with Jamal, Forrester does the opposite of what most teachers of writing would advise their students to do: to spend some time thinking about the scope of the project, to sketch out an outline, and then begin to sculpt the first of many drafts. Instead, Forrester believes that one writes the first draft "with the heart," and the second "with the head." These vague descriptors are all we, and Jamal, are offered. When Jamal finds it more difficult than he imagined to write from the heart, Forrester selects one of his own pieces, nonsensically entitled "A Season of Faith's Perfection"—again, we do not know if it is an essay or fiction—and tells him to "start typing" it (though he really means "copy"): "Sometimes the simple rhythm of typing gets us from one page to two. When you begin to feel your own words, start typing them." Jamal dutifully begins to copy Forrester's piece a bit slowly, for it is a strange assignment; though writers might read the work of others extensively, and even model their prose after another in telltale ways, Jamal perceives the act of copying the words of another as the duty of a plagiarist, not a serious author.

The next day Jamal will turn the paper in to Crawford without revising it, and neither will he excise the copied portion. He will also adopt Forrester's title, "A Season of Faith's Perfection." This is patently dishonest, for Jamal assumes that Forrester's manuscript has never been published, and hopes, therefore, to win the competition by passing Forrester's words off as his own. Even with Forrester's permission, which he has only so long as he does not remove any writing from the penthouse, which he does, Jamal's refusal to properly cite Forrester is obviously an act of plagiarism—he actively intends to allow the panel to believe that the words are of his own creation. Furthermore, it is also immediately evident that copying Forrester's text was much more than a benign exercise.

Forrester's words have become, for Jamal, an integral part of his own text, so much so that he feels he must allow them to set the stage of his own expression. As a result of taking Forrester's title, it is apparent that Jamal does not feel as though he owns the words on the page, does not believe that they are sufficiently his, even though he is eager to claim them. And he is, of course, correct; by articulating himself through the prose of his mentor, Jamal's own expression is hopelessly muddled, confused, and lost. Indeed, by shuttering Jamal's efforts to develop his own uniquely African American, Bronxite, and youthful style, Forrester directly attempts to create Jamal in his own image. In fact, after reading the manuscript for the first time, Forrester praises Jamal for having "taken something which was mine," and making "it yours." Though he acknowledges Jamal's "accomplishment," he reminds him that "the title's still mine." The dynamics of ownership, as articulated by Forrester, dictate that even if Jamal has effectively transformed his prose into something else altogether, at root they both know the words are still "mine," or the intellectual domain of Forrester. To that end, Forrester undercuts what is ostensibly a social act—the sharing of ideas in a communal space—by reminding Jamal that the primacy of the individual matters more. Jamal will never be able to escape the power of Forrester's influence, and will never, therefore, be able to assert his own identity and authority as a writer in his own right.

Crawford immediately discovers that Jamal has copied Forrester's work, refuses to allow Jamal to read his manuscript at the writing competition, and throws his back into orchestrating his expulsion from the school. Jamal asks Forrester to come to his aid, by contacting the school by letter and explain that he encouraged Jamal to use his own words, but Forrester refuses, unable to overcome his fears of exposure. Yet Forrester will eventually rescue Jamal, by summoning up the energy and capacity at the twenty-fifth hour to ride his rickety bicycle from the Bronx to downtown Manhattan, even though he has not walked further than 100 feet in more than forty years. Once there, he will read one of Jamal's pieces, entitled "Losing Family," in Jamal's stead at the competition—though no one knows that the piece is Jamal's until Forrester says so. When it is revealed, however, that the words are Jamal's, and that he is Forrester's "friend," the audience then recognizes him with a standing ovation. Even though it seems unlikely that an elderly Scottish aesthete could successfully convince people that the words of a sixteen-year-old African American Bronxite are his own, we come to see that Jamal writes the way Forrester speaks. What makes Jamal such a great writer, the film suggests, is not that he has found his own voice, but that he can successfully ape the style of dead white men. Indeed, whereas Jamal initially hides Forrester's words within his own, Forrester will mask Jamal's words behind his persona, and though Jamal's actions earned him near expulsion, Forrester's will earn him near certain fame. In one final gesture of Forrester's largesse, after he has died he will leave Jamal's family his apartment, and a book manuscript, entitled *Sunset*, the introduction to which Jamal is meant to write, and so achieve with it instant literary stardom. Though viewers are meant to be moved by Forrester's gift to Jamal, the film tacitly makes the case that the only way someone like Jamal—a black male autodidact—could ever succeed is with the help, and at the behest, of a dead white male author. Jamal not only finds his voice by copying Forrester's, he learns to master his mentor's manner of speaking and writing, and even though we know it will only ever be metonymic, we are asked to believe that his expression is now utterly his own.

Conclusion

In their 2001 text *The Black Image in the White Mind: Media and Race in America*, Robert M. Entman and Andrew Rojecki explain that, of late, many films

> feature Blacks who get help from Whites, once again because Blacks cannot handle the world of intellect and power. *Jerry Maguire* offered one example, but later instances include *Men of Honor*, *Rules of Engagement*, and *Finding Forrester*. The White stars (Robert DeNiro, Tommy Lee Jones, Sean Connery) assist the Black males (Cuba Gooding Jr., Samuel L. Jackson, and Robert Brown) who might otherwise become more or less helpless victims of power. Again, these films weigh in on the positive side of the ledger, illustrating the possibility of mutual respect and emotional bonds across racial lines. (p. xvii)

Yet, they argue, "exemplifying the continued cultural and economic constraints on the Black image," "studios failed to cast Sidney Portier or James Earl Jones instead of Sean Connery in *Finding Forrester* as the famous old writer tutoring the talented young Black ghetto kid" precisely because films with all-African American casts are almost impossible to market to white audiences, who prefer to see someone who looks like them in the lead role (Entman & Rojecki, 2001, xvii). But we contend that it would have made a significant difference if Sidney Portier or James Earl Jones were assigned to play Jamal's mentor. A well-respected African American actor in Forrester's role would have powerfully counteracted the implicit assumption in the film that most, if not all, African Americans are uninterested in literacy or the arts. The film's references, and cultural register, would necessarily shift with a majority-black cast in favor of African American ethnic and literary expressions, and we might find Jamal reading W.E.B. Du Bois and Malcolm X instead of Kierkegaard and Descartes. An African American instructor who could understand Jamal's experience in the world might not require him to eradicate Black English from his spoken or written vernacular, but instead choose to enhance and make much of it, as did Zora Neale Hurston and Charles Chesnutt. Jamal might not be encouraged to abandon his community, friends, and school, where his mind is obviously thriving, but might instead be inspired to do better, be more, and strive in his own right; in other words, the implication that gifted and talented African American youths must be removed from their own community schools in order to receive an adequate education might be fundamentally challenged. Most importantly, however, an African American mentor might help Jamal develop his own voice in his own time, by refusing to allow misconceptions about black youth and their capabilities to cloud what he sees, and what he knows to be true. By allowing a young African American boy who struggles with poverty, the lack of a father-figure, and his burgeoning identity in a hostile world to be mentored by someone who not only looks like him, but *understands* him, the filmmakers might have encouraged viewers to confront many of their own mistaken beliefs about black life, and correct them. Indeed, though Jamal is often spoken to and about, for the most part he remains silent, passively watching as others deconstruct him, and attempt to remake him. A film with an all-black cast might allow its protagonist to have some say, and to be proud of that articulation.

Instead, *Finding Forrester* reinforces the misperception that the literary arts are primarily the domain of men of European descent. Indeed, there are no shortage of accomplished white male authors in the film—their oil-painted visages line Jamal's English classroom—but there is only one extraordinary African American in the film. The film repeatedly makes the spurious claims that black parents are as not involved in or concerned about their children's futures as white parents are, that black children are ill-mannered and disruptive in the classroom, that urban environments are hostile to education, and that black children are less intelligent than their white counterparts. Rather than offer real insight into the actual problems students and teachers face in urban environments, the film instead circulates the same tired stereotypes, roles, power dynamics, and myths that have long preoccupied American minds. In the end, the film buttresses myths of American individualism and exceptional genius, almost entirely at the expense of at-risk, impoverished communities of America's most vulnerable students.

The authors of this chapter advocate for continued, rigorous interrogation of myths propped up as truth in films such as *Finding Forrester*. We argue that students and scholars alike need to make a commitment to rethinking how, and in what manner, we allow falsehoods and stereotypes to pass as entertainment. And, most importantly, teachers on all levels need to think more critically about the types of material we introduce into the classroom, and about the particular ways in which representations of education can often support dangerous stereotypes, establish impossible goals, and work to disempower students.

Notes

1. All quotations from the film are attributed to this source.
2. Frederick Douglass, *The Narrative of the Life of Frederick Douglass*, 35.
3. See also James Matlack, "The Autobiography of Frederick Douglass," and Eric Sundquist, "Frederick Douglass: Literacy and Paternalism."
4. Books by these authors are stacked on a bed stand in Jamal's bedroom.

5. In the novelization of the film, Jamal's guidance counselor is not an African American woman, but Jewish, and she informs Jamal's mother that, in spite of all the odds "kids sometimes win the gene pool lottery" (Ellison, 2000, p. 19). Mrs. Wallace states directly that she feels "like I've failed him for not being half as intelligent as he is" (p. 20). While Mrs. Wallace seems much more proud than ashamed in the film, the viewers are meant to understand that Jamal is much smarter than her, or his brother.

References

Douglass, F. (1851). *The Narrative of the Life of Frederick Douglass, An American Slave, Written By Himself.* London: H.G. Collins. (Original work published 1851).

Ellison, J. W. (2000). *Finding Forrester.* New York: Newmarket Press.

Entman, M. E., & Rojecki, A. (2001). *The Black Image in the White Mind: Media and Race in America.* University of Chicago Press.

Fosburgh, L. (3 November 1974). J.D. Salinger speaks about his silence. New York Times. Retrieved from http://www.nytimes.com/books/98/09/13/specials/salinger-speaks.html.

Harris, C. (n.d.). Study guide for *Finding Forrester.* Film Education for Columbia Tristar Films (UK) Ltd. Retrieved from http://www.filmeducation.org/pdf/film/finding%20forrester.pdf.

Matlack, J. (1979). The autobiography of Frederick Douglass. *Phylon* 40(1), 15-28.

Rich, M. (2000). Script for film version of *Finding Forrester.* Retrieved from http://www.script-o-rama.com/movie_scripts/f/finding-forrester-script-transcript.html.

Sundquist, E. (1991). Frederick Douglass: Literacy Paternalism. In William Andrew (Ed.), *Critical Essays on Frederick Douglass.* Boston: G.K. Hall.

Turner, F. W. (1969). Black Jazz Artists: The Dark Side of Horatio Alger. *The Massachusetts Review, 10*(2), 343-344.

Van Sant, G. (Director). (2000). *Finding Forrester* [Motion picture]. United States: Columbia Pictures.

Chapter Six

"If You Should Die before You Wake..." Bart Simpson, Family Dynamics, and the Genesis of Rebellion

Brian N. Duchaney

They have yellow skin, four fingers, and live in a pastel world of pinks, purples, and blues. However, the characters of *The Simpsons* exhibit a rare form of reality found on television sitcoms: they smoke cigarettes, drink beer (often excessively), swear, have sex, carry on infidelities, and worry about how to pay bills (although they do have a penchant for rioting). At the center of this world is Bart Simpson—about whom, over the course of episodes, viewers learn the following: he was born on April Fool's Day and is between the ages of nine and eleven, is left-handed, fluent in French and (once) Spanish,[1] and has Double O Negative blood. Additionally, over the course of approximately 430 episodes, viewers watch Bart struggle with growing up.

In today's world, where parents are usually to blame for any transgression of a child, *The Simpsons* is quick to identify that parenting is not the fault of Bart's behavior, but that Bart's behavior is a necessary by-product of parents who are doing their best to provide for their family. The once self-proclaimed boy who was an "under-achiever and proud of it" has developed beyond the role of conventional bad boy into an amalgam of every boy who is beyond the age of ignorance and entering into a world where he recognizes the struggle for independence, despite the wish to remain in the good graces of his parents. In a societal context, Bart has what Hegel (1977) would term as "*Spirit*," or what is now referred to as a representation of "otherness," where Bart defines his sense of self based on the construct of others.[2] In short, Bart exists as the product of those around him, notably the Simpson family. Yet, in a show that capitalizes on characters as individuals, Bart's otherness is particularly looked down upon.[3] So what is it that sets Bart apart from the rest of the characters on the show? It is difficult to identify one moment where Bart turned on the path to deviant behavior. In order to do so, it is necessary to look at the Simpson family as a whole, but we should realize one important fact: even within his family, Bart is an outsider.

So, where did Bart's "otherness" develop? The family dynamic in *The Simpsons* is portrayed as highly dysfunctional. For instance, in the 2002 episode "Brawl in the Family," baby Maggie calls the police on a family rumble by dialing a telephone symbol representing Homer choking Bart. When an assigned social worker shows up at school with Bart, he brags, "This is Gabriel, my *personal* social worker" (Cohen & Nastuk, "Brawl in the Family"). Yet, family style fighting is well ingrained in *The Simpsons*, with extended fighting evident since their first appearance as an animated short on *The Tracy Ullman Show*. However, unique to the show's exploration of characters is that, unlike live-action television, the *Simpsons* family exist as living images—without the image, the character does not exist.[4] Yet, Bart and the rest of the Simpson family *do* exist for viewers outside the perpetual storyline. It is here that we can find the real Bart Simpson. By exploring the show's treatment of Bart's life beyond the ages of "between nine and eleven," we will see that *The Simpsons* is acutely aware of how children respond to sibling and parental relationships and how the stressors of family are acted out in the form of misbehavior.

The Simpsons is built on family. Like Bart, creator Matt Groening's parents are named Homer and Marge. Groening admits, though, that "the character Homer, unlike my real father, is ruled by impulse. We are self-effacing and guilt-ridden and try to do the right thing and fail. Homer, though, doesn't bother. He wants whatever he wants at the moment, with all his heart" (Scheff, 2007, p. 58). This may explain the Homer of Evergreen Terrace and his numerous jobs (188 as of the 400th episode) beyond his regular job at Springfield Nuclear Power Plant. Yet, despite these impulsive behaviors; despite living an existence that, according to Raja Halwani's (2001) examination of his values in "Homer and Aristotle," may not be moral; despite the hardships that he has faced; Homer does love life, as does his wife Marge.

Through Marge's temperance and Homer's often irascible behavior, both parents combine to form a cohesive unit of guidance for the Simpson children. This is remarkable since both Homer and Marge have absentee parents. In this light, it is possible to attribute Homer's lack of attention as a direct correlation to Grandpa Simpson's wish to remain in self-pity. After being abandoned by his activist wife, Grandpa tells young Homer the following: "Homer, you're dumb as a mule and twice as ugly. If a strange man offers you a ride, I say take it!" (Jean & Polcino, 1997, "Lisa's Sax"). On the other hand, Marge's father is only clearly seen in one episode, 1991's "The Way We Was," an episode devoted to Homer and Marge's first realization of feelings toward each other (Jean et al.). This may explain her need for complete acceptance by her children.[5]

Acceptance of character flaws is a recurring theme of *The Simpsons*. There are many episodes featuring Homer trying to win over the affections of his children, and it is true that the focus of the show has been increasingly centered on

Homer as a symbol of ridicule and humor, but at the foreground of all of the characters' nuances and vulnerabilities (and the show's longevity) is family history. More precisely, family is embedded in the dynamic of how Bart, Lisa, and Maggie are presented to the audience. Central to the story of the Simpson children is the story of Homer and Marge. Of the episodes that recall the past, only three recall the Simpson children in its entirety: 1992's "Lisa's First Word" (Martin & Kirkland); 1997's "Lisa's Sax" (Jean & Polcino); and 1995's "And Maggie Makes Three" (Crittenden & Scott). A fourth episode, 2011's "Mom's I'd Like to Forget" (Kelley & Clements) references Bart's childhood friends but is more about Marge. In combination with "I Married Marge" (Martin & Lynch, 1991) these five episodes rely on furthering the story of Bart through his relationships with others.

"The Way We Was" is one of many episodes that focuses on the establishment of the family unit, particularly that Homer and Marge chose each other. *The Simpsons*, in embracing the family dynamic, consequently builds on the relationship between Marge and Homer, and it should be no surprise that it is filled with its troubles. And, though the show often highlights these challenges (time and again, we watch the couple fight and make up), the impression given to viewers is that the marriage, and similarly the family, will be able to withstand any hardship. This is evident in the episode "The Parent Rap" (Meyer et al. 2001). After Bart and Millhouse are taken into custody for tampering with and crashing Police Chief Wiggums's cruiser, we watch the Simpson family walking the halls of the Springfield County Courthouse. Instead of being aggrieved by his juvenile delinquent son, Homer remarks, "I love our court days," to which Marge responds, "It's about the only thing we do as a family anymore." Lisa then offers a hello to a court officer by name. Bart even refers to Judge Schneider by his first name as well. What this shows is not a disturbance of family but a chance to play family where, under the guise of "normal childhood behavior," Marge is able to make the best of ever-present dysfunction. And, despite the trouble caused by Bart being tethered to Homer as a form of "creative punishment," the punishment brings Homer and Bart closer together. Bart, in a touching proclamation of humility, states, "Everyone else might give up on me, but my parents never will" (Meyer et al., 2001).

Despite Bart's continued realizations of self throughout the show's run, Bart has been portrayed as a rebel.[5] The best indications of Bart as a rebel are not his prank calls or his continued harassment of authority; instead, it is the relationship he has with his family. Likewise, the show dramatizes these events where Bart, in the past or in an assumed future, creates increasing tension for the family. For instance, in the episode "Lisa's Sax" (Jean & Polcino, 1997), Homer tells Lisa the origin of her saxophone after Bart destroys it in a tussle; we learn that Bart, as the first child, is the anchor for which the stories of the Simpson children unfold. In order to learn about Lisa's sax, we must understand that the origins are tied in with Bart's first days at school. To Lisa's chagrin, she asks:

Lisa: Mom, can you tell me the story of how I got my saxophone and not have
it turn into a story about Bart?
Marge: Oh, sure honey. Bart had just completed his first day at school, and
Bart...
Lisa: MOM!
Marge: I'm sorry Lisa. That's just how the story goes. (Jean & Polcino, 1997)

Returning to the story of Bart's troubles at school, we learn that Bart's emotional troubles stem from having difficulty adjusting. Bart draws a picture of himself
with knives sticking in his stick figure body, with rain pouring down on him,
labeling the picture "sad" (Jean & Polcino, 1997).

What is most telling about these episodes, and often for Bart, is that he is
not the central figure in the family that he believes he is, echoing the show's
early changes in format.[6] In the episode "Lisa's First Word," Bart initially sees a
new baby as beneficial, someone to place blame on. But, realizing that attention
was being taken away from him, he responds by shaving baby Lisa's head. Also,
as a result of Lisa's birth, Bart must now be moved from his crib. In protest, we
are given a familiar scene of child rebellion, where Bart clings to the crib whin-
ing, "but *I'm* the baby" (Martin & Kirkland, 1992). However, we are then presented with Bart's new, lovingly handmade, grotesquely misshapen clown bed
that Homer built for him. Homer's initial motivation for good often results in
confusion for his child. Thus his children, notably Bart, struggle for recognition,
which is played out in other episodes outside the typical structure of the show's
timeline.

Of the three future episodes, Lisa seems to be the focus, though Bart is a
major figure in Lisa's life. "Lisa's Wedding" (Daniels & Reardon, 1995) is an
exploration of a daughter's faithfulness to family, as Lisa calls off her wedding
to the charming Hugh Parkfield because he refuses to wear a set of pig cufflinks
given to him by Homer. "Future Drama" (Selman & Anderson, 2005) explores
the lives of Bart and Lisa as they are in high school, as shown to them by Professor Frink. Though the episode details Bart's relationship with his girlfriend
Jenda, it simultaneously shows Bart turning down a scholarship to Yale intended
for Lisa.[7] The remaining future episode, 2000's "Bart to the Future" (Greaney &
Marcantel), is a cautionary tale that is told to Bart by an Indian mystic at an Indian gaming casino. Bart is portrayed as a forty-year-old burnout living with
Ralph, whereas Lisa is president. This future is presented conditionally—this
future will become a reality unless Bart changes his ways.

Groening is quick to distance himself from the real life Bart Simpson. He
says, "I worry about Bart. I think he's headed for juvenile delinquency. Bart as a
teenager will probably be pretty sad, drug abuse and all" (Scheff, 2007, p. 58).
And, like any good parent, Groening worries about how his creation will cope
once left to his own devices. This is no different from Homer's reaction to Bart.
In the episode "I Married Marge," Homer reluctantly tells the Simpson children
about the stress babies cause when Homer fears that Marge is again pregnant:

Homer: Yeah, sure, for you a baby is all fun and games; for me its diaper changes and midnight feedings.
Lisa: Doesn't Mom do that stuff?
Homer: Yeah, but I have to hear about it.
Bart: Were you like this when Mom was pregnant with me?
Homer: Actually, I threw up more than your mother. (Martin & Lynch, 1991)

Retelling the story of Bart's birth, Homer tells, in so many words, that he wasn't exactly ready for the birth of a child, shouting a loud "D'oh!" which echoes through the walls of the hospital, prompting a man in a body cast to say, "Man, poor guy." Immediately, Dr. Hibbert hands Marge a pamphlet entitled "So you've ruined your life" (Martin & Lynch, 1991). Seen in this context, the retelling of the early relationship between Marge and Homer is furthered only through Bart, as at the time, they are unmarried. For the Simpson family, Bart specifically is the catalyst for changes in the family dynamic. Though in the present, Bart and Lisa are supportive of Homer and the potential for another Simpson child, this moment seems overshadowed by the changes in Homer's life the episode explores: Homer must take the job at the nuclear plant after a string of bad jobs, leaving Marge to make money, promising to return only when he "was a man."

It is stories of human nature like these that prompted the creative staff to take *The Simpsons* in a new direction. As it grew in popularity, the focus of the show moved away from Bart and more to other characters, specifically Homer. Referred to as the beginning of the Golden Age, which lasted from 1992 to 1997 by various accounts, the writing took a more deliberate turn away from Bart's pranks to exploring the realistic side of the other characters. For voice actor Hank Azaria, these episodes exhibit the same knowledge of family as templates for talking about the American family. He states, "There are episodes, I think particularly the Lisa episodes, where they really involve the journey of a little girl and what would realistically happen: those are beautiful, realistic little stories" (Ortved, 2009, p. 89). Yet, beyond being simply "stories," the episodes allow for a greater evaluation of family life in the Simpson household. Thus, as with any evaluation of character, it makes sense to see Bart as a product of his upbringing.

The Simpsons features many characters that have a family dynamic that is less than optimal: Bully Nelson lives with his mother, a train wreck of a parent, waiting for the day his "papa" will come home; another bully, Jimbo Jones references his mother's boyfriends, usually as a one-liner delivered to further the development of a storyline; lastly, Kearney, the indiscriminately aged fourth grader, often references his own son. However, bullies alone are not models of dysfunctional families. Helen and Reverend Lovejoy have a troublesome daughter. Ned has been forced to raise Rod and Todd alone since Maude Flanders's death in season eleven. In a similar fashion, dysfunction enables the reality of childhood fears to be compared to familial tensions. Bart's fears of isolation and abandonment are equivalent to Homer's fears of not being able to provide for his family. Where Homer is impulsive, Bart is introspective. This is best seen in the episode "Yokel Chords" (Price & Dietter, 2007). After a prank at school goes wrong, Bart is sent to a psychiatrist. While the main focus of the episode is Lisa acting as a tutor to Cletus's eight children (a deliciously witty parody of *The Sound of Music*), the sub-plot focuses on Bart's advancing recognition of his self pity and anger. After the money Springfield Elementary paid runs out, Marge brings Bart back to Dr. Swanson for a final visit. Marge tells Bart the following:

> Marge: Bart, honey, this is all we can afford for now. If it doesn't work, maybe when you're an adult you can pay some lady to make you happy for an hour.
> Bart: You know, I'm pretty sure I will. (Price & Dietter, 2007)

On the surface, the message is that Bart may indeed be paying women for a little therapy. However, the breakthrough in the episode comes after Bart realizes the sacrifices his parents make for him and his sisters:

> Bart: And I wasn't planned, so when I came, my parents had to get married. And they were too young, and not ready for a kid to screw up their lives. Maybe…I act out because if my parents are mad at me they can't fight with each other. (Price & Dietter, 2007)[8]

Here, we may look to Jean-Paul Sartre's realization of self. Sartre theorizes that we exist as a characterization of social construction; in other words, as we develop a formal identity, we rely on self-deception in order to mask that outward characterization. This aspect, that Sartre defines as bad faith, is precisely the example set forth by Bart's outward society. As Bart becomes aware of his actions, he becomes increasingly aware of his position in the world, further clarifying Sartre's philosophy: "Without the world there is no selfness, no person; without selfness, without the person, there is no world" (Sartre, 1992, p. 157). Like his parents, Bart creates his world in his own way so that he may fit into it in a manner to his liking. This is comparable to Homer's numerous jobs and reinventions of self. The parallel is that while Bart seeks to become someone else, he expects his father to become what he needs to be—a supportive father.

In a similar approach, Homer has breakthroughs in his relationship with his family. After twenty years on television, Homer has a profound realization about parenting after he meddles in the lives of Bart and Lisa, trying to make Bart successful academically and Lisa popular. In the 2009 episode "Father Knows Worst" (LaZebnik & Nastuk), Homer behaves as a helicopter parent, shadowing the lives of Bart and Lisa. Watching Lisa from the hallways of Springfield Elementary, Lisa catches his eye and sends Homer a text message—"I H8 this"— referring to her elaborate new clothing and feigning attitude, which she has learned from a handy book Homer has given her: *Chicks with Cliques*. Catching

Lisa's eye, she comes inside for an end-of-episode moment of clarity, summarizing what we the audience have learned. The episode gives us the following comic vignette between father and daughter:

> Homer: The best thing I can do as a parent is simply check out.
> Lisa: No—there is a middle ground.
> Homer: Lisa, a light bulb is either on or it's off.
> Lisa: Not if you use a dimmer switch.
> Homer: That's what the dimmer switch companies want you to think. (LaZebnik & Nastuk, 2009)

However, Homer is right. Even with a dimmer switch, there is a spark. No matter how dim the light may be, only when the light is off is there complete darkness.

The Simpson family will continue to act inappropriately in times of stress. Homer will still continue to strangle Bart, Marge will still read *Fretful Mother* magazine, and Bart and Lisa will continue to fight one moment and be closer than ever the next. And, what *The Simpsons* continually affirms is that the bond between the family is constituted by parallels—love and compassion over fear and stress. And, while Groening may worry about Bart, the same worry is evident in Homer's family week after week. But, they have nothing to worry about: despite two divorces, Bart will be Chief Justice of the Supreme Court...if only he can change his ways.

Notes

1. In "Blame it on Lisa," Lisa sponsors Ronaldo, a Brazilian orphan. On the plane to Brazil, where the Simpson are heading to rescue Ronaldo from his captors, Bart learns Spanish by a cassette tape. When Marge informs him that they speak Portuguese, Homer tells Bart to "forget every word boy...it's useless." Against Marge's protests, Bart hits himself in the head with an air phone, triumphantly announcing "All gone."
2. In Hegel's words, "Substance is in this way *Spirit*, the self-conscious unity of the self and essence; each has for the other the significance of alienation. Spirit is the *consciousness* of an objective real world freely existing on its own account; but this consciousness is confronted by the unity of the self and essence, *actual* consciousness by *pure* consciousness. On the one side, actual self-consciousness, through its externalization, passes over into the actual world, and the latter back into actual self-consciousness. On the other side, this same actuality—both person and objectivity—is superseded; they are purely universal" (Hegel, p. 295).
3. See Brian L. Ott's "'I'm Bart Simpson, Who the Hell Are You?': A Study in Postmodern Identity (Re)Construction."
4. In "Brawl in the Family" (Cohen & Nastuk, 2002), social worker Gabriel tells Marge that she "medicates her family with food."
5. In fact, this is recalled by Bart, where upon seeing his permanent record labeled "underachiever (and proud of it)," he remarks, "How old is this thing, anyway?"

6. In "Lisa the Greek" (Kogen et al., 1992), Lisa sees spending Sundays watching football with Homer as a bonding moment; Homer sees it as a way to make money from his daughter's genius with probability and numbers.
7. In this future, Homer and Marge are separated, and the episode ends with their reconciliation.
8. Bart is taken to acts of recognition and confessions of fault. Similar moments are seen in "The Parent Rap" (Meyer et al., 2001) and "Simpsons Roasting on an Open Fire" (Pond & Silverman, 1989).

References

Bendetson, B. (Writer), & Moore, S. D. (Director). (March 31, 2002). "Blame it on Lisa" [Television series episode]. In Groening, M., and Brooks, J. L. (Producers), *The Simpsons*. Los Angeles, CA: 20th Century Fox.

Cohen, J. (Writer), & Nastuk, M. (Director). (January 6, 2002). "Brawl in the Family" [Television series episode]. In Groening, M., and Brooks, J. L. (Producers), *The Simpsons*. Los Angeles, CA: 20th Century Fox.

Crittenden, J. (Writer), & Scott, S. O. (Director). (January 22, 1995). "And Maggie Makes Three" [Television series episode]. In Groening, M., and Brooks, J. L. (Producers), *The Simpsons*. Los Angeles, CA: 20th Century Fox.

Daniels, G. (Writer), & Reardon, J. (Director). (March 19, 1995). "Lisa's Wedding" [Television series episode]. In Groening, M., and Brooks, J. L. (Producers), *The Simpsons*. Los Angeles, CA: 20th Century Fox.

Greaney, D. (Writer), & Marcantel, M. (Director). (March 19, 2000). "Bart to the Future" [Television series episode]. In Groening, M., and Brooks, J. L. (Producers), *The Simpsons*. Los Angeles, CA: 20th Century Fox.

Halwani, R. (2001). "Homer and Aristotle." *The Simpson's and Philosophy: The D'oh of Homer*. William Irwin, Mark T. Conard, and Aeon J. Skoble, eds. Peru, IL: Open Court, p. 7-24.

Hegel, G. W. F. (1977). *Hegel's Phenomenology of Spirit*. (A. V. Miller, Trans.). Oxford, UK: Oxford.

Jean, A. (Writer), & Polcino, D. (Director). (October 19, 1997). "Lisa's Sax" [Television series episode]. In Groening, M., and Brooks, J. L. (Producers), *The Simpsons*. Los Angeles, CA: 20th Century Fox.

Jean, A., Reiss, M., Simon, S. (Writers), & Silverman, D. (Director). (January 31, 1991). "The Way We Was" [Television series episode]. In Groening, M., and Brooks, J. L. (Producers), *The Simpsons*. Los Angeles, CA: 20th Century Fox.

Kelley, B. (Writer), & Clements, C. (Director). (January 9, 2011). "Moms I'd Like to Forget" [Television series episode]. In Groening, M., and Brooks, J. L. (Producers), *The Simpsons*. Los Angeles, CA: 20th Century Fox.

Kogen, J., Wolodarsky, W. (Writers), &Moore, R. (Director). (January 23, 1992). "Lisa the Greek" [Television series episode]. In Groening, M., and Brooks, J. L. (Producers), *The Simpsons*. Los Angeles, CA: 20th Century Fox.

LaZebnik, R. (Writer), & Nastuk, M. (Director). (April 26, 2009). "Father Knows Worst" [Television series episode]. In Groening, M., and Brooks, J. L. (Producers), *The Simpsons*. Los Angeles, CA: 20th Century Fox.

Martin, J. (Writer), & Kirkland, M. (Director). (December 3, 1992). "Lisa's First Word" [Television series episode]. In Groening, M., and Brooks, J. L. (Producers), *The Simpsons*. Los Angeles, CA: 20th Century Fox.

Martin, J. (Writer), & Lynch, J. (Director). (December 26, 1991). "I Married Marge" [Television series episode]. In Groening, M., and Brooks, J. L. (Producers), *The Simpsons*. Los Angeles, CA: 20th Century Fox.

Meyer, G., Scully, M. (Writers), & Kirkland, M. (Director). (November 11, 2001). "The Parent Rap" [Television series episode]. In Groening, M., and Brooks, J. L. (Producers), *The Simpsons*. Los Angeles, CA: 20th Century Fox.

Ortved, J. *The Simpsons: An Uncensored, Unauthorized History*. New York: Faber and Faber, 2009.

Ott, L. (2003). "'I'm Bart Simpson, Who the Hell Are You?' A Study in Postmodern Identity (Re)Construction." *The Journal of Popular Culture*, 37(1): 56-82.

Pond, M. (Writer), & Silverman, D. (Director). (December 17, 1989). "Simpsons Roasting on an Open Fire" [Television series episode]. In Groening, M., and Brooks, J. L. (Producers), *The Simpsons*. Los Angeles, CA: 20th Century Fox.

Price, M. (Writer), & Dietter, S. (Director). (March 4, 2007). "Yokel Chords" [Television series episode]. In Groening, M., and Brooks, J. L. (Producers), *The Simpsons*. Los Angeles, CA: 20th Century Fox.

Sartre, J. P. (1992). *Being and Nothingness*. (Hazel E. Barnes, Trans.). New York: Washington Square Press.

Selman, M. (Writer), & Anderson, M. B. (Director). (April 17, 2005). "Future Drama" [Television series episode]. In Groening, M., and Brooks, J. L. (Producers), *The Simpsons*. Los Angeles, CA: 20th Century Fox.

Sheff, D. (2007). "The Playboy Interview: Matt Groening." *Playboy,* 54 (6): P. 57-60.

Chapter Seven

From *Desperate Housewives*–Past and Present–to *The Real Housewives of New Jersey* to Simply *House*: Views on Family and Gender in Popular Culture

Amy R. Neeman and David Newman

From *The Simpsons* to reality TV, popular television shows have found their place as educational tools in the classroom. Examples can be found in English as a Second Language (Low, 2009; Potgieter & Scheckle, 2006), undergraduate anthropology classes (Conklin, 2003) and even in medical school (O'Reilly, 2009). In his discussion of teaching with media, Trier (2006) references Luke (1997) in making a connection between students of this generation and the use of popular culture in the classroom.

The experience the two authors of this chapter have had with integrating popular television shows into the college classroom has also been a positive one in terms of teaching students to make connections between popular and classical works and relating the shows to concepts of family and gender as well as cross-cultural issues. This chapter will provide several examples of how this strategy worked for the authors in their respective English and Sociology classes.

From the English Classroom

In the 2010 season's opening episode of *Desperate Housewives,* there is a scene with Bree, a conservative, perfectionist housewife. Her latest husband has left her—the one who lost the use of his legs while fighting her lover as a small plane crashed into them. She is distraught when she notices a corner of the wallpaper in her living room peeling off. The wallpaper is yellow with a plant-like pattern. The paper resists her attempts to fix it, and as she becomes frustrated with it, she begins to rip the wallpaper off the wall. She strips the room.

There is a parallel here with Charlotte Perkins Gilman's *Yellow Wallpaper,* originally published in 1892. In this classic story, the main character is forced by her husband to take a "rest cure" for her depression. At the end of the story, she goes insane and rips off the yellow wallpaper, freeing herself from the control of her husband and male doctors. Truly, the character of Charlotte in Gilman's story was the first "desperate housewife."

The color yellow is often associated with illnesses like yellow fever and jaundice. Interestingly, in *Desperate Housewives,* Bree's room is repainted by her newest love interest in yellow. A new character, Beth Young, is introduced. After revealing some potential psychological issues and the fact that she married the accused killer she had corresponded with in jail, she appears later in bright yellow clothes. As problems arise for the female characters in this nighttime soap, the camera focuses on yellow flowers and the women are often shown in yellow, even in the next few episodes.

This connection between the classical and the popular, along with topics of gender and the family, is something we try to bring to our students and get them to reflect on. In the English classroom, this may mean studying a literary work alongside the film version to analyze how family roles are portrayed and interpreted, then turning to television to examine how popular characters fulfill similar roles.

NCIS provides a good example of unrelated characters who seem to take on family roles. Jethro Gibbs leads a team of Naval Criminal Investigative Services agents, including the younger Tony, McGee, Ziva, and Abby. James Coon, in "A Metaphorical Analysis of NCIS" (2010) highlighted the familial elements in the show. He saw Gibbs as the father figure, Tony as the older son ("frat boy"), McGee as the younger brother, and Abby as the favorite daughter. Commercials for NCIS likewise reinforce the workplace family relationships, albeit quirky, among these characters.

In "Family on Television" Spigel (n.d.) discusses the "family workplace," which she defines as "relationships … often ambiguously collegial and familial" (www.museum.tv). Bringing this up with students in an English Composition class affords an opportunity to discuss additional shows that have characters who are not related, but behave like family. Take, for example, the television series *House*, in which the main character, a caustic Dr. Gregory House (played by Hugh Laurie), heads a team of doctors who diagnose patients' illnesses. Dr. James Wilson is an oncologist at the same hospital. Wilson acts like a brother to House, even letting House move in with him and returning the pranks House subjects him to. *Monk* is another series that comes up in class discussion. The main character, a former police detective turned consultant, has obsessive compulsive disorder and other phobias which play a major role in his life and is "taken care of" first by the sisterly Sharona and then the more motherly Natalie.

Students contribute to the discussion using shows they know. The show *Friends,* which focuses on the interactions of six close friends in New York City, has come up most often when students are asked to think of characters who behave like family. International students especially always seem familiar with this long-running sitcom, its characters, and the relationships between them and are able to discuss the show at length.

After discussing in class the familial roles characters take on, students think about television shows or films where characters are not related, but where the characters seem to function as if there were family members. They pay particular attention to cultural aspects, describing how the characteristics of the 'family' members reflect the culture of the show's country of origin.

In response to this prompt, one student wrote about how in the film *Toy Story 3,* Buzz Lightyear and Woody act as family members, with Woody as the father figure. The student explained that because Woody is there for everyone and puts everyone else first, he fulfills the traditional role of the American father. This prompted a discussion in class of perceived qualities of fathers in the United States and in other countries.

There are several advantages to such discussions and writing prompts. These types of assignments get students excited; they become animated as they talk about shows they are familiar with. They require students to be creative and original. In an English Composition class, there is also the bonus that plagiarism is rare with this type of work.

For this assignment, students not only got to discuss family, but were forced to define family roles. Students from other cultures afforded the class opportunities to look at cultural contrasts in family roles and behavior. For example, one student from Cyprus wrote about a show hosted by a female psychologist and a twenty-year-old student who offer callers advice for their problems. In his essay, he compares the relationship between the two hosts to that of a mother and son. He describes what he sees as the qualities of a Greek mother, and then the student shows how the psychologist interacts with the student host in this way.

This line of exploration into cultural differences can be quite fruitful. In 2010, Nigro (session chair), Toth, Arner, Papke and Koloski presented a panel at a meeting of the Popular Culture Association in which Kate Chopin's work was discussed in relation to the culture and society of the time. Inspired by this panel, this year when discussing *The Story of an Hour* in literature class, international students were asked to discuss the story from the perspective of their cultures. In the story, written in the 1800s, the main character learns her husband has died, but her grief is quickly replaced by a feeling of freedom. When the husband turns up alive at the end of the story, she realizes the loss of her freedom and dies.

Students work on the following assignment to go with the short story: "Think about the short story 'The Story of an Hour.' Did the story challenge your cultural perspectives? Why or why not?"

In response, one student from China discussed how in ancient times the role of women was mainly limited to marriage and childbearing and how women held little or no power. She went on to support her claim of female powerlessness by discussing arranged marriages and how girls would have their feet bound at a young age. Another student from Korea explained that the story did not challenge his cultural perspectives. He discussed women's roles under Confucianism and talked about how sons were favored over daughters. Both papers also conveyed a sense of anger and frustration over the treatment of women.

These responses convey the writers' emotions in a way many traditional assignments do not. Many students, especially some international students who were not educated in systems where discussions are encouraged and individual opinions sought out, are initially reticent to reveal emotions or opinions or even to speak up in class. Yet, once they write, they seem more willing to speak up and share their views in class. In this way, assignments such as this provide jumping off points for further discussion.

Another assignment asks students to compare gender roles between the United States and other cultures. A discussion of the character of Cuddy on *House,* supported by video clips, could provide a starting off point. The character is a capable, highly placed hospital administrator who often appears in low necklines and in tight clothes. Students would need to consider how a character like this would be viewed in other cultures, especially non-Western ones.

In summary, using popular culture in the English classroom invites students to work from what is familiar to them (films and popular TV) and asks them to think critically in order to make connections and analyze characters and their roles. It also opens a window to exploring cultural perspectives in the classroom while engaging students and enabling them to share their voices. It infuses the class with a certain energy as students discuss gender and family roles, relating concepts from television and literature to their own personal experiences and cultural expectations.

From the Sociology Classroom

Popular culture also has pedagogical value in the sociology classroom. Popular TV, in particular, can be a valuable tool in helping students process the sociological imagination and its concomitant questions: what is the structure of society, where does the society stand in history, and what varieties of men and women prevail in it (Mills, 1959, p. 5-7), and apply these to important topics like family and gender.

In 2010-2011, Introductory Sociology students looked at one episode from four American shows: *Modern Family* and *Brothers & Sisters*—both from ABC—*Parenthood* from NBC, and *The Real Housewives of New Jersey* [the most popular of the Housewives series] from Bravo. The names all tell us that these shows are about family, and the official 2010-2011 season websites for the first three provide a family tree as a way to help us place the characters and their relations to one another (e.g., www.nbc.com/parenthood/exclusives/family-tree).

The first show assigned to the Introductory Sociology class was *Modern Family* (season 2, episode 5, "Unplugged"; episode 19, "The Musical Man"; and episode 20, "Someone to Watch over Lily"). This show revolves around the Pritchett family:

- Father Jay and his second wife, Gloria, an immigrant from Columbia, and her preteen son, Manny, from her first marriage.
- Jay's son, Mitchell, and his partner, Cameron, and their adopted baby daughter from Vietnam, Lily.
- Jay's daughter, Claire, and her husband, Phil, and their three "typical" kids, teen daughters Haley and Alex, and preteen son, Luke.

One of the first things that came up in discussion about family was the gay couple. Mitchell and his particularly flamboyant husband, Cameron, are doggedly insecure about how best to raise Lily. For example, when they discover that all of Lily's playmates have been enrolled in preschool programs, they panic that their failure to do the same for Lily has doomed her to be the only underachieving Asian in America. We then see them try to find the best preschool for her, and bumble their way through interview after interview. Many in the class saw them as buffoons. Initially, this was attributed to their homosexuality—a gay couple, minstrelizing through the story line, is not a challenge to the dominant heteronormativity that pervades American society (season 2, episode 5, "Unplugged").

But as our discussion expanded to the other characters, we realized that all of the principal adult characters were playing the buffoon. When Jay's brother comes for a long overdue visit, Jay prepares for it by posting a picture of his "ass" on his phone link to his brother, so that when his brother calls him, he will see what he really thinks of him, and Jay rigs a chair next to a bottle of whiskey that will break when the brother sits on it. Needless to say, the brother never checks his phone, and Jay sits on the chair. Gloria rants that Jay does not know anything about his brother; for example, Jay does not know that his brother has a granddaughter or even the name of the town where his brother lives. She says that in Colombia everyone knows his brother—everyone respects his brother— she even knows everything about all twenty-nine of her cousins. Jay sarcastically responds that this must be why Colombia is the land of peace (season 2, episode 19, "The Musical Man").

When Mitchell and Cameron drop in unexpectedly at Claire and Phil's one morning, to check out whether they would be good guardians for Lily if Mitchell and Cameron should die prematurely, they witness the following transaction: Haley, the older teenage daughter is screaming at Claire, that she will win the award for the worst mother ever, who, as she is picking up a broken dish from the floor, yells back that she will make sure to thank Haley in her speech. Middle daughter, Alex, comes rushing in to the kitchen, complaining that she was trapped in the garage for twenty minutes and no one responded to her screams, to which Claire harps back, "You were in the garage for twenty minutes, and you still couldn't find the rat traps I sent you for?" The frying pan catches on fire, and Claire calls out to Phil to put it out, who exclaims, "Come on now, every morning?" Cameron asks if they have come at a bad time, to which Claire responds, "Yes. Come back in seven years, five months, when the kids will be gone" (season 2, episode 20, "Someone to Watch over Lily").

Modern Family is a comedy, so everyone makes a mess of things. The class attested that Americans enjoy seeing these characters trip their way through "life" [the show], in part because by laughing at the television characters' mistakes, we can feel better about our own. But what we noticed as a class, as we moved from the sitcom to television dramas, *Parenthood* and *Brothers & Sisters*, and then to the reality show, *The Real Housewives of New Jersey*, was that everyone is making mistakes, bungling things up, second guessing themselves, and playing it by ear. Everyone is acting—and this includes the "real housewives" who are not supposed to be acting—as if regardless of their intentions, they are flubbing the rules.

Parenthood is a drama which portrays three generations of the Braverman family. Unlike *Modern Family*, the tone of the show is serious, and the issues the characters face are always challenging. In *Parenthood* [season 2,"Slipping Away"], we see Adam, the oldest of the Braverman siblings, shocked to hear from his wife, Kristina, that their sixteen-year-old daughter, Haddie, is having sex with her nineteen-year-old alcoholic boyfriend. Both were upset that they were unsuccessful in dissuading her from dating him, and now she is having sex with him. Adam is unsure how to react, and we get the sense that he really seems at a loss. This leads him to pull back from Haddie—to put some distance between himself and his daughter. This, in turn, saddens the daughter who feels rejected and then regrets that she shared the truth with her mother, who is frustrated, yet understanding of both her husband and daughter. We see Adam's sister Sarah, a single mother with two teen children, Amber and Drew, forced to return to live with her parents, Zeek and Camille, because of financial worries. Typical of Sarah, we see her with the best of intentions give a clumsy speech to her kids as she drops them off to their new high school. The kids are embarrassed at her words, and Sarah gives up and awkwardly stops short. Later, we see Sarah drinking shots with a boyfriend, only to be discovered by Drew, to which she responds, "I am so dead." We see Crosby, Adam and Sarah's younger brother, trying to reconcile with Jasmine, his previously estranged girlfriend and the mother of his son, Jabbar. Crosby has slept with Gaby, the behavioral aide to Max, Adam and Kristina's son with Asperger syndrome. Crosby confesses this indiscretion to Jasmine, who then wants nothing further to do with him. Crosby's inept attempt to win her back is unsuccessful.

Brothers & Sisters is another television drama that means to let viewers see the ups and downs of an American family—in this case, the Walker family. In *Brothers & Sisters*, we see two sixty-plus-year-old siblings, Nora and Saul, unable to move forward with new relations. Brody, an old flame from Nora's life forty years ago before her marriage "built on lies," reappears in her life, reminding her that she had had a choice back then and made the wrong one. Will she make the right one now? She is uncertain. Saul has kept his homosexuality closeted from his overbearing mother for his whole adult life, though in fact he admits he really only managed to hide his loneliness from her. Now he is faced with a man who wants to take him to live in Palm Springs where they will build a house together. Like Nora, he is faced with uncertainty, which at times seems overwhelming. At her mother's funeral, Nora says that she can accept what her mother was, but she cannot accept what she wasn't. At this point, Nora flees the service in tears. Justin, her youngest son, does not want his family to throw him a party for his thirtieth birthday, because he is divorced and alone and therefore has no reason to celebrate. He exclaims, that "not everyone gets the life they want" (season 5, episode 5, "Olivia's Choice; Never Say Never").

In *The Real Housewives of New Jersey* [season 2, episode 9, "Posche Spite"], Jacqueline and her husband, Chris, who are part of the Laurita-Manzo extended family, are unsure how and unable to direct Ashley, Jacqueline's teenage daughter from her first marriage, as she grows up and appears to be making one bad choice after the next. Jacqueline is under pressure from Chris to do something. They hold back gifting her a car for her birthday, and eventually kick her out of the house, which throws her into the arms and house of the boyfriend they were trying to keep her from. Ashley tries to make amends to her mother, by attacking and pulling out the hair extensions of the Laurita-Manzo family's arch enemy, Danielle, who then plots to get even by pressing charges against the girl, who posts a threat on her Facebook account. Danielle is herself not free from making bad choices. Actually she is making them all the time, like hiring an ex-con friend to act as her bodyguard to protect her from the Laurita-Manzos. She wants to show her daughters that you cannot let anyone walk all over you. Her daughters do seem to have more sense. In one scene, Danielle is intent on driving her daughters to Jacqueline's house on the night of a party to which they were not invited, but the girls persuade her not to do so.

In the sitcom, the two dramas, and the reality show, we see people trying to do their best, which is not the same as doing "the best." Almost everyone, regardless of the genre, struggles at this. On the 2010-2011 official website for *Parenthood*, Lauren Graham, who plays the Sarah character, says, "No one has a perfect family" (http://www.nbc.com/parenthood). All of these shows bear this out.

After the class reviewed what they had seen in these four shows, they discussed the question "What is going on?" Students noticed a number of themes.

- *Divorce is commonplace.* You find people who have been divorced on all four shows: Jay and Gloria on *Modern Family;* Sarah on *Parenthood;* Justin, Sarah and Tommy on *Brothers & Sisters;* and Jacqueline, Dina, and Danielle on *The Real Housewives of New Jersey.* And most of those who have divorced have remarried or are planning to remarry. The saddest characters are identified as those without a spouse.

- *The nuclear family is present in all the shows, and most of the women work.* Two of the three Braverman women, three of the five New Jersey House-wives, and three of the four Walker women. Neither of the Pritchett women works. Those who do not work are "stay-at-home moms," and one mom, Adam's wife Kristina, is looking forward to returning to work. One of the Braverman men, a brother-in-law, is a stay-at-home dad.
- *There are committed gay couples.* Two of the four shows feature committed couples: *Modern Family,* Cameron and Mitchell, and *Brothers & Sisters,* Scotty and Kevin. In both of these, one of the men is a stay-at-home dad.
- *Cohabitation occurs.* In *Brothers & Sisters,* Sarah, who is divorced, lives with her fiancé, Luc. In *Parenthood,* Crosby was living with his girlfriend, the mother of his son, before his infidelity.
- *Some adult children with children are returnees.* Sarah from *Parenthood* has moved back in with her parents after her divorce, because of financial problems.
- *The relations among couples are relatively egalitarian.* This holds regardless of which partner is working, whether straight or gay, married or cohabiting. This even applies to Jay and Gloria in *Modern Family,* who are separated by a twenty-year age difference. The spousal partnership is the norm for the "fictional television shows," although the stay-at-home partner does take on more domestic responsibilities—regardless of whether the couple is straight or gay, or the individual male or female. In contrast, marriages in *The Real Housewives of New Jersey* appear to fit a more traditional patriarchal model of family, where the wife, even when she is working, often has less authority, power and possession (to borrow from Holden, 2008,) compared to her husband or men in general. And finally,
- *Adult family members often seem uncertain about what they are doing.* However, in spite of this uncertainty, they manage to get things done, even when they are not happy with the results.

As a class, students used the sociological imagination to adequately answer Mills's three questions. The sociological imagination is at the crux of sociology—it is the ability to look past the self to see how the lives of individuals are inexorably linked to one another and to the society in which they reside. Mills's questions are a tool to draw students away from their inclination to view things solely as a personal or, using Mills's language, biographical matter rather than a social one. Students shared that these shows portray *their* lives—the only difference being that the moments are magnified (to borrow from Hochschild) or exaggerated for entertainment's sake on television—even on the reality show, *The Real Housewives of New Jersey.* Divorce, gay marriage, working mothers and stay-at-home fathers, cohabitation, and uncertainties are nothing unheard of to this generation of students.

As they were doing this exercise over the span of a couple classes, they also read Kathleen Gerson's "How a New Generation Is Reshaping Family, Work and Gender in America" (Gerson, 2011) and Carrie Lane's "Man Enough to Let My Wife Support Me: How Changing Models of Career and Gender Are Reshaping the Experience of Unemployment" (Lane, 2009). The class revisited their discussions about the shows. Students came back to class saying that Gerson got it right: There are no longer clear paths to follow to build and maintain stable relations with others. There is no clear model of family—no clear model of how to keep a marriage going or how to raise children. There are no clear templates for manhood or womanhood, but somehow things work out, and as Gerson writes,

> [this generation] is more focused on how their parents met the challenges of providing economic and emotional support than on what form their families took...Families are not a stable set of relationships frozen in time, but a dynamic process that changes – and no outcome is guaranteed. (p. 353)

Lane says that success is now defined in terms of flexibility and not security for a generation which has witnessed their parents facing numerous job changes and layoffs, and having to embrace a new ideal of "co-breadwinning" and partnership between spouses. The class concluded with a pretty strong consensus that people today are all free agents in this neoliberal world, and the best we can do is to try to do the best we can—meeting challenges as they come toward us, knowing we are on our own, but recognizing that we are better when we try to meet these with the help of others—like family—and, yes, like the families we see in these four shows.

Popular culture's appeal as a pedagogical device is its popularity, its accessibility, its shared vocabulary, its use of commonplace tropes that function as portals to academic investigation, and most importantly, its ability to engage the student in the classroom. The use of popular culture in the college classroom, whether the discipline be English or sociology (or something else), can make the teaching of serious academic subjects more effective.

References

Chopin, K. (2007). The story of an hour. In R. DiYanni (Ed.), *Literature: Reading fiction, poetry and drama* (pp. 38-41). New York: McGraw Hill.

Conklin, M. (2003, December 6). Anthropology teachers grounding students in reality: The study of human behavior is hot, and professors find value in analysis of TV shows like 'The Real World.' *Los Angeles Times,* p. E 26.

Coon, J. (2010, April). "A metaphorical analysis of NCIS." Paper presented at the PCA-ACA Annual Conference. St. Louis, MO.

Gerson, K. (2011). *The unfinished revolution. Coming of age in a new era of gender, work, and family.* New York: Oxford University Press.

Gilman, C. P. (2004). The yellow wallpaper. In R. DiYanni (Ed.), *Literature: Reading fiction, poetry and drama* (pp. 542-552). New York: McGraw Hill.

Hochschild, A. R. (1994). The commercial spirit of intimate life and the abduction of feminism: Signs from women's advice books. *Theory, Culture & Society* 11,1-24.

Holden, T. J. M. (2008). The overcooked and underdone: Masculinities in Japanese food programming. In C. Counihan and P. Van Esterik (eds.). (2008). *Food and Culture: A Reader,* 2nd Edition (pp. 202-220). New York: Routledge.

Lane, C. (2009). Man enough to let my wife support me: How changing models of career and gender are reshaping the experience of unemployment. *American Ethnologist* 36 (4): 681-692.

Low, C. (2009). Carnival laughter as an antidote for students' fear and anxiety. *Essential Teacher,* 6(3-4): 27-29.

Mills, C. W. (1959). *The sociological imagination.* New York: Oxford University Press.

Neeman, A. & Newman, D. (2011, April) *From* Desperate Housewives—*past and present—to* Beverly Hills Housewives *to simply* House*: Views on family and gender in popular culture.* Paper presented at the Joint Conference of the PCA-ACA & SW/Texas PCA/ACA, San Antonio, TX.

Nigro K. (session chair). (2010, April). *Kate Chopin resurrected! The story of the Kate Chopin revival.* Panel presented at PCA/ACA Conference, St. Louis, MO.

O' Reilley, K. (2009, January). TV doctors' flaws become bioethics teaching moments. *American Medical News.* Retrieved from http://www.amaassn.org/amednews /2009/01/26/prl20126.htm.

Parenthood family tree. *NBC: Parenthood.* (2011). Retrieved from http://www. nbc.com/parenthood/exclusives/family-tree/.

Potgieter, S., & Scheckle, E. (2006). Using reality tv in the EFL/ESL classroom. *TESOL Video News,* 17(2). Retrieved from http://tesol.org//NewsletterSite/ view.asp?nid=3268.

Spigel, L. Family on television. (n.d.). *Museum of Broadcast Communication.* Retrieved from http://www.museum.tv/eotvsection.php?entrycode= familyontel.

Trier, J. (2006, Feb.). Teaching with media and popular culture. *Journal of Adolescent & Adult Literacy,* 49(5): 434-438.

Part II: Improving Instruction, the Pop of Pedagogy

After reading the theoretical, debatable chapters of Part I, many readers may be left asking, "So now what?" While discussion starters and background information are of value, classroom practitioners are often more desirable of works that provide a blueprint, a plan, anything concrete they can take back and use immediately in their practice. For these educators, Part II will prove valuable, providing specific pedagogical and andragogical tips for instructors in high school, community college, and university classrooms. Indeed, at least one of the editors reacted to Culver's brilliant work extending Tolkien's world with a linguistic analysis with the admiring jealousy of a former teacher of English who never came up with a unit nearly as creative.

This is not to say there is no theoretical basis to the works, as anyone who reads Ellefritz's brilliant and substantive postmodern deconstruction of contemporary political cartoons can attest. However, Part II is more focused on offering concrete suggestions; for example, Reese's work on incorporating technology is valid for instructors both in traditional brick-and-mortar classrooms as well as those who teach primarily online. Those engaging in the training of teachers will appreciate Sourdot's approach to preparing preservice educators in issues of diversity.

The theme of diversity is further taken up by Waweru and Ntarangwi, who both challenge typical approaches to teaching "world" history, calling long-held beliefs into question, and then provide concrete suggestions for improvement by attaching a concrete lesson plan that blends reggae and African history. Rounding out Part II is Parke's work explaining both the value of and techniques behind having students analyze current television shows relevant to their lives in her composition classroom. While grounded in a composition and literature course, the techniques demonstrated by Parke are applicable to a wide variety of postsecondary classrooms.

Chapter Eight

Editorial Cartoons as Education: Political Cartoons as Pathways to the Pedagogy of Popular Culture

Richard Ellefritz

Social reality is socially constructed, or at least sociologists have been claiming as much for the last several decades (Berger & Luckman, 1966).[1] People construct social reality in their everyday interactions in which they exchange symbols in efforts of communication, sometimes modifying them into altered and new configurations. Except in the rare cases of extreme isolation and other maladies that inhibit this basic condition of humanity, people regularly engage in social interactions within social institutions, organizations, and groups, all the while interacting by and through symbols within an always already ongoing social universe. The mass media is an example of one such social institution, comprised of various organizations that produce cultural texts with which people symbolically interact in their daily routines. The globally networked, corporate owned, and state sanctioned mass media apparatus is one example of where culture comes from—others include the family, education, and religion, and from there much of public discourse is produced and shaped by gatekeepers, agenda setters, and a host of other functionaries who profit from producing cultural content to be consumed by masses of people. Newspapers and the Internet in a growing respect, two mainstays of the mass media, house a cultural artifact common to many peoples' experiences (at least in the West), namely that of the editorial cartoon. This chapter addresses this artifact as a popular cultural text from two main perspectives. First, editorial cartoons are addressed from the perspective of social constructionism, but, moreover, as an aspect of popular culture cussed in more detail below, the concept or theory of hegemony is the second perspective that guides this chapter.

Since its introduction into the field of cultural studies in the 1970s, hegemony theory suggests that culture is not simply the product of a culture industry pumping out cookie-cutter molds of easily digestible refuse passively consumed by the mass public. Rather, under this purview culture is viewed as something contested by the public and elites in an ongoing negotiation over the meaning of social reality. Hegemony is a conceptual and theoretical product of Italian social theorist Antonio Gramsci who directed his analysis at class struggles, but the concept has been adopted into the cultural turn in the sense of cultural hegemony, in which the struggle is over meaning and practice in the broader social universe. Moreover, "Gramsci's (1971) enduring contribution was to focus our attention beyond explicit beliefs and ideology to see how the routine, taken-for-granted structures of everyday thinking contribute to a structure of dominance. Gramsci urged us to expand our notion of ideology to include the world of common sense" (Gamson et al., 1992, p. 381). We are not in this chapter addressing particular ideologies, values, or beliefs, but rather we should be thinking about how editorial cartoons, as one example of popular cultural texts, exist as part of the hegemonic social universe in which we all live, love, work and play, and as such we should focus our attention on how they can help reveal socially constructed phenomena in our everyday lives. With this in mind, we can better serve our students' progress toward a more critical awareness of their own private worlds in which they analyze, evaluate, and interpret phenomena, but just as well, and maybe more importantly, we can help them to better comprehend the broader social world in which we all share something that might be called a common social reality.

In this chapter, I spell out some of the fundamental features, aspects, and processes of the concept of the social construction of reality, and I relate those things to how sociologists approach sociological education. I use the term "sociological educator" throughout this chapter specifically in reference to educators who teach from the sociological perspective, but I constructed that term so that by the end of this chapter the reader, teaching from whatever her or his field happens to be, can in some respect be considered a sociological educator. Sociological education entails grasping and transmitting to students the fundamental notion that all things social are products of society and social interactions. Grasping and internalizing this perspective can be like holding a bright light in a once dimly lit room. What was once camouflaged by the normality of everyday life should come to be seen as a product of socially, historically, and culturally relative ways of knowing and doing. What was once viewed as naturally existing, when illuminated with the sociological perspective, takes on a new aura and can be seen more for what it is than for what our society has lead us to believe. In terms of the purposes of the current volume, Mertz (1976) has given an excellent outline of how the social construction of reality can help us understand popular culture, and, reciprocally, how understanding popular culture can help us more fully see the socially constructed nature of social reality.

Following Mertz (1976), I am guided by two assumptions throughout this chapter:

> First, that popular culture in all its forms—magazines, movies, television, popular songs, etc.—is an integral aspect of society's "symbolic universe;" they help to create the universe as well as maintain it. Popular culture, in this view, functions both as a reflection of values as well as a means of stabilizing those values. My second assumption is that all of us attempt to "make sense of the world." ... The second assumption reinforces my view, that, in order for our students to best "make sense" of the world, we need to adopt broader perspectives of curricula. This view would emphasize that the legitimate area of curriculum is all of culture, "that complex whole which includes knowledge, belief, art, custom, and other capabilities acquired by man [sic] as member of society." Within this framework, popular culture would be as important to study as would so-called elite culture. (p. 13)

I do not spend much time defining what popular culture or editorial cartoons are, for those definitions can, respectively, be found throughout this volume and in other resources in the bibliography of this chapter. Nor do I spend any more time than this investigating their link: Editorial cartoonists often use popular cultural icons and references in their products in order to draw upon the cultural capital of their readers so that the intended message is more accurately interpreted by as broad of an audience as possible (Conners, 2007). This aside, I am more interested in this chapter in how editorial cartoons and their cartoonists function within the field of popular culture rather than in any specific image or reference in a set of particular cartoons. The entry for editorial cartoons in the *Handbook of American Popular Culture* (Pogel & Somers, Jr., 1989) suggests that these texts are part of popular culture because of how they are produced (in mass, usually weekly), by whom they are produced (usually by middle- and lower middle-class artists not classically trained), why they are produced (in jest of contemporary social, political, economic, and cultural circumstances, sometimes using graphic humor and depictions), and by whom they are consumed (nearly everybody at some point or another). Thus, they remain as popular cultural texts by, of, and for the masses.

The Ungentlemanly Art (Hess & Kaplan, 1968), the title of a history of American political cartoons that examines why the production of political cartoons is a low, non-elite, or popular cultural practice, suggests another feature of political cartoons that plays itself out in their imagery, namely that editorial cartoonists are almost entirely white men from the middle classes (Lordan, 2006). These aspects of editorial cartoons make for excellent educational opportunities for sociological educators to teach our students about a range of socially constructed phenomena tied to race, class, gender, the political economy, medicine, religion, and other social institutions. Likewise, this particular part of popular culture provides many opportunities to discuss with students the practices of the production and consumption of cultural artifacts, texts that often employ explicit or implicit ideological messages about the meaning of the social universe and its content.

The pedagogical suggestions I give in this chapter are not designed for a particular curriculum or lesson plan. Rather, they are embedded throughout and in its lengthy endnotes in a way designed to meet the broadest possible needs from the broadest audience I can imagine, but, ultimately, in a way designed to imbue, engender, and embolden the readers' (and their students') sociological imaginations. The literature and research on editorial cartoons is extensive, and a recent meta-analysis of educators' uses of this medium suggests that there is a wide variety of ways they can be used in the classroom (Bickford, 2011). Most educators who use editorial cartoons in the classroom use them to assess or build interpretive skills in students, but none suggested in that review use an approach similar to the one taken below, one in which editorial cartoons become gateways to understanding abstract concepts that are often difficult for college students to comprehend and apply to the real (social) world. Engaging students' critical thinking capacities in the classroom, and getting them to see that they are socially embedded observers with value-laden interpretations based upon their location in the social structure—to illuminate their *habitus*—is no easy task. However, by approaching students with a few harmless looking cartoon images and text bubbles, we can eventually show them some of their taken-for-granted assumptions they employ while evaluating and interpreting information in the symbolic, social, and/or cultural universe.

Social Constructionism and Critical Sociological Thinking

Sociologists have long postulated that social reality, whether in the form of social institutions, interactions, knowledge, or human consciousness, is socially constructed, or a product of society and social interactions (Berger & Luckmann, 1966). Through this perspective, social reality is constituted by objective structures (e.g., the interactions, organizations, and institutions within which people engage themselves, which includes human made material and symbolic objects of cultural significance) and subjective phenomena caught up in the symbolic universe of language, communication, and interpretations, which are themselves, at least partly, the internalization of those objective social structures. Internalization, along with its dialectic relationship with the always already ongoing processes of externalization and objectivation (or, reification as it is sometimes known), results, partly, in the acquisition of individually, culturally, and historically idiosyncratic taken-for-granted assumptions, beliefs, norms, and values derived from the symbolic interactions engaged in within an always-already ongoing socio-cultural-historical framework. As a result, the meaning of any object, event, or process has the potential for both a stable, predictable pattern of shared understandings as well as a creative, flexible, and otherwise dynamic possibility to be newly interpreted and modified.

Social constructionism, the main theoretical framework used in this chapter, "as an approach to the social sciences, draws its influences from a number of disciplines, including philosophy, sociology and linguistics, making it multidisciplinary in nature" (Burr, 2003, p. 2). In defining social constructionism, Burr (2003) notes that various writers or theorists who use the approach (aka social constructionists) share underlying, basic assumptions about the nature of social reality. Social constructionists "take a critical stance toward our taken-for-granted ways of understanding the world, including ourselves" (p. 2-3). In light of this, sociological educators have called for a more explicit incorporation of critical sociological pedagogy in the sociological classroom (Braa & Callero, 2006; Fobes & Kaufman, 2008). Critical sociological pedagogy necessarily includes teaching students about the socially constructed nature of their social worlds; Burr gives the example that "just because we think of some music as 'classical' and some as 'pop' does not mean we should assume that there is anything *in the nature of the music itself* that means it has to be divided up in that particular way" [emphasis added] (p. 3). The categories and concepts used to delineate such boundaries as "classical" and "pop" are products of historically and culturally specific contexts, "and are dependent upon the particular social and economic arrangements prevailing in that culture at that time" (p. 4). Lastly, individuals, nested within their socio-historical-cultural contextualized social realities, negotiate the meaning of social phenomena during symbolic interactions, which results in shared, agreed upon, or otherwise contested definitions of social reality.

Internalized and reified social reality abounds and permeates the experience of individuals so thoroughly that we can and often do take our social experiences for granted, like, as is often said of the matter, a fish would of water. *Taken-for-grantedness* is a quality that develops when individuals internalize the cultural assumptions, norms, and values used to symbolically interact within social situational contexts (i.e., social institutions) in our respective societies (e.g., within or between the social institutional contexts of one's family, friends, coworkers, role models, mass media, educational system, religion, government, etc.). Social reality, or any number of social phenomena subsets that occur in social institutional settings, becomes taken-for-granted when the socially, culturally, and/or historically specific ways of thinking and acting that an individual learns from other members of her or his society come to be viewed as natural, self-evident, and/or immutable; that is, they become *commonsense*.

Commonsense explanations of the world are problematic for sociological thinking (Berger, 1963) and sociological educators (LeMoyne & Davis, 2011) because they form semi-permeable barriers to educating students about their taken-for-granted assumptions of the social world. Whereas Berger (1963) was pessimistic in the ability of sociological educators to debunk undergraduates' commonsense notions of reality, because for him "the taken-for-granted structures are far too solidly entrenched in consciousness to be that easily shaken by, say, a couple of sophomore classes" (Berger, 1963, p. 174), contemporary educators argue otherwise: "As the importance of a college education continues to be emphasized as a means to specific job skills, we have a greater opportunity to expose students, at both the community college and university levels, who might have traditionally been excluded, to the sociological imagination and the preponderance of the sociological evidence" (LeMoyne & Davis, 2011, p. 104). Students' commonsense interpretations and explanations of social phenomena can hinder a deeper understanding of how social structures such as race, class, and gender impact the opportunities and constraints of numerous individuals. Editorial cartoons that present a given person, place, event, or idea in any given way can serve as a common focal point for educators and students to grapple with (re)presentations of social reality according to one point of view, and a series of these texts can serve to show a range or spectrum of ways that cartoonists, like other social actors, attempt to socially construct reality in ways that play off commonsense interpretations.

The postulation of a socially constructed social reality has increasingly become an acceptable and demonstrably effective teaching strategy, quality, and goal of sociological educators (Spector, 1976; Pestello, 1987; Anderson & Holt, 1990; Brouilette & Turner, 1992; Orbach, 1999; Rodgers, 2003; Townsley, 2007; Berkowitz, Manohar, & Tinkler, 2010). Top sociological educators want students to leave their classrooms and courses asking questions "about factors that are not immediately apparent" (Persell, Pfeiffe, & Syed, 2008, p. 114) regarding social reality. The goal is to get students to go beyond asking and answering more "obvious" questions about the social universe, questions and answers that only scratch the surface of this multi-layered, multi-faceted, and multi-dimensional social reality. This edification process involves notifying and imparting the notion to students that understanding social reality from this sociological perspective (*there are* other perspectives within sociology) entails "the recognition that social concepts and phenomena that are often viewed as 'natural' or taken for granted (including race, gender, sense of time, or human nature) are actually reflective of social forces and structures and consequently vary over time and across societies" [sic] (p. 117). Of the many top goals leaders in the field of sociology have for students after taking a college-level, introductory sociology course, one is to inspire or facilitate complex and critical thinking, which is necessary to understand the social construction of social reality, and, conversely, internalizing the concept of social constructionism is crucial to developing a critical sociological thinking.

The aim of critical sociological pedagogy is that if, during the one or two sociology courses the average college student takes, sociological educators can show students that there are *at least some* aspects of their social world that they mistakenly assume are natural ways of human existence then those students might take those lessons on with them and apply them to new situations, hopefully for the rest of their lives and in ways that those lessons are similarly transmitted to others. As a central tenet of sociological thinking is that there is no time off from the social, the discipline-specific form of critical thinking Grauerholz and Bouma-Holtrop (2003) conceptualized as "critical sociological think-ing" should be useful long after college students have finished their course work in sociology classes. Critical sociological thinking refers "to the ability to evalu-ate, reason, and question ideas and information while demonstrating awareness of broader social and cultural contexts" (p. 492-3), and "requires sociological knowledge and awareness" (p. 493). As a concept, the social construction of reality is a core component of sociological knowledge, and, when passed on, it can give students the ability to be aware of the mutable nature of a social world becoming increasingly more complex.

Of the intrinsically critical nature of sociological thinking, Buechler (2008) argues that it "is simply the best angle of vision that we have to capture life's complexity, interpret its history, anticipate its future, and guide reasoned action" (p. 319). He goes on to argue that "[s]ociology *requires* a skeptical and restless quality of mind. It continually questions the self-proclaimed reasons for any social arrangement. To be a sociologist is to assume that things are not what they appear to be, that hidden interests are at work, and that claims cannot be taken at face value" [emphasis added] (p. 319). When applied to popular culture, the sociological perspective can help whoever holds it to become more critical, more skeptical, and less assuming about the many leisurely, pleasurable, and informative pastimes with which people regularly engage themselves. As edito-rial cartoons are concise, informative, and entertaining bits of popular culture that attempt to help or motivate readers to affirm or reaffirm a given interpreta-tion of the social world, and as they have been a staple of U.S. history consumed regularly by many types of people for many reasons, this medium should serve as a useful device to help students uncover the nature of social constructionism in a way that is engaging and educational.

From editorial cartoons throughout U.S. (and world) history, iconic images have emerged that have become the mainstay of the images people have for *po-litical personalities*, e.g., Theodore "Teddy" Roosevelt lent his nickname to the construction of the now well-known cuddly kids' toy when he was pictured along with a bear cub in a cartoon by Clifford Berryman in a 1902 *Washington Post* edition after the cartoonist learned of a bear hunting expedition in which the then president refused to kill a bear cub tied to a tree by his hunting party; *political parties*, e.g., the first Republican elephant was a construction by Thom-as Nast, a famous cartoonist responsible for many image constructions, includ-ing the popularizing of the modern Western conception of Santa Claus, which was further popularized by Norman Rockwell and Coca-Cola; and *political pro-cesses*, e.g., political redistricting took on a new image when "[Elkanah] Tils-dale's map turned the redistricting of Essex County, Massachusetts, into a men-acing, dragon-like image," (Lordan, 2006, p. 105). Just by using these examples, students could be shown that there are reasons for the existence of names and images that they might already be familiar with, but taken to a general level of popular culture as a whole, students could be encouraged to find the reasons for the existence of other names, slogans, or images with which they are familiar— for example, students could be asked to find the possible origins of the popular slogan "Vote or Die" with the expectation that they would be able to eventually trace it back to 'America's first political cartoon' authored by Benjamin Franklin, "Join, or Die."[2]

I do not mean to say iconic images have "emerged" through editorial cartoons in a preordained or natural way, in fact, that is exactly one lesson that students would be well off to learn from the pedagogy of political cartoons: Editorial cartoons are often created exigently, as responses to existent or foreseen social circumstances. Political cartoons are sometimes a push back against instances of injustice and folly as recognized by cartoonists, and their publication can have serious contemporary effects on public opinion and lasting implications for popular imagination (Morrison, 1969; Lamb, 2004). In kind, these cartoons' authors are products of their socio-cultural-historical environments, and as such are caught up in the affairs of their societies—just as are you, I, and our students, but they project their thoughts and aspirations out to their vast audiences via their preferred medium, one substantially different than a classroom setting. Pointing out the various textual incantations these imagineers have instituted throughout history is one way to begin to discuss with students the socially constructed nature of social reality.

One lesson that can come out of all of this is that students should be aware that they enter into a negotiation process when reading, decoding, evaluating, and/or interpreting editorial cartoons, as they do with any other (popular) cultural text. If students assume that there is one ultimate meaning that can come from their reading of a cartoon, then under this critical pedagogical program oriented toward elucidating the social construction of reality sociological educators could entice students to uncover the motivations of the cartoonist, students' own taken-for-granted background assumptions, and how the text might be interpreted under alternative ideologies (e.g., capitalism vs. socialism, progressivism vs. conservatism, etc.). The very fact that political cartoonists editorialize social phenomena means that what is communicated is by its nature contestable. If students assume that what is presented is uncontestable, then engaging them in that debate should prove fruitful on grounds that they take for granted their ability to contest and critically analyze information presented to them. If students assume that what is presented *is* contestable, but that their own interpretation is the best or most suitable, then engaging their ability (or inability) to take multiple perspectives should prove fruitful on grounds that have yet to show their sociological educator that they are aware of the socio-historical-cultural contingencies upon which they draw their conclusions. In any case, seating students at the negotiating table, and in some cases chairing the meeting between socially embedded actors and texts, should very well facilitate critical sociological thinking that can be applied to new situations throughout students' lives.

Hegemonic Struggles to Socially Construct Reality

To say that social reality is negotiated, that it is the product of negotiations between symbolically interacting people nested within socio-cultural-historical contextualized situations, deprives social reality of its content: *What*, exactly, is negotiated? Editorial cartoons provide an excellent avenue to explore this question with students because editorial cartoonists engage themselves in the negotiations of the meaning of political, economic, cultural, and other socially significant phenomena, all the while asking their audiences to accept their terms (but in no way must their readers).[3] Antonio Gramsci's concepts of "hegemony" and "organic intellectuals"[4] serve as useful conceptual tools here to both identify the nature of editorial cartoons, political cartoonists, and the social reality they interpret and (re)produce. While an in depth discussion of that is a matter more appropriate for an entire article, chapter, or book of its own right, and because over the years there have been numerous expositions from various fields of study about Gramsci's contributions to our understanding of the socio-cultural-historical, and, more specific to Gramsci, the politico-economic universe (e.g., see Salamini, 1974; Urbinati, 1998; Fischman & McLaren, 2005), and due to space constraints, I will be rather brief on my exposition and application of his concepts here. Drawing my references from Storey's (2003) manifesto on popular culture, incidentally a book in which the author states that how he thinks "about the relations between culture and power is informed by the work of Italian Marxist Antonio Gramsci" (p. 48), I propose only one way in which to theorize the function of editorial cartoons and their cartoonists in contemporary society (partly because this is not the purpose of this chapter, as well as for reasons spelled out in the fourth endnote for this chapter).

Before getting to the application of hegemony theory to editorial cartoons, it is worth noting a few points of interest regarding the editorial page in general:

> The editorial page is the intellectual focal point of any newspaper. Editorials serve to provoke, debate, set agendas, crusade for change, persuade, and often challenge. While they express the opinion of media owners, editorial writers serve as keepers of the public conscience. The chief duty of its practitioners is to provide the information and guidance toward sound judgments that are essential to the healthy functioning of a democracy. Therefore, the editorial writer is challenged to draw fair conclusions from stated facts, basing them on the weight of the evidence and the publication's concept of the public good. (Hamlet, 2009, p. 477)

And, regarding the specific component of interest to this chapter in relation to the editorial page, Lordan (2006) has this to say: "The editorial cartoon is a key component of an editorial page that, in many ways, serves as an 'intellectual town hall': a place where some of the nation's leaders in government, education, and industry share views about the most important issues of the day" [sic] (p. 107). The main difference between written editorial contributions and editorial cartoons, setting aside for the moment the differences in the texts' formats, is the fact that editorial cartoons are often contributed to newspapers by a relatively small set of homogeneous people whereas editorials are often contributed from a broad set of a relatively heterogeneous people. Not everybody has the artistic talent to condense a complex set of ideas into a small number of images and words, and, furthermore, to do so in a somewhat humorous way. If the editorial page is the bastion of democratic debate, a marketplace of ideas where the nation's leaders and followers negotiate over the value and meaning of current affairs, then the combination of "artistic skill, rhetorical exaggeration, and biting humor [that draws] attention to corruption [and highlights] society's ills" (Makemson, 2009, p. 253) posits editorial cartoonists further than their editorialist counterparts into the role of the intellectual organizers of the masses, a role ripe for the organization and contestation of hegemony.

"Hegemony is 'organized' by those whom Gramsci designates 'organic intellectuals'" (Storey, 2003, p. 50). So, what is hegemony, and who are these organic intellectuals? These concepts are defined differently depending on what source one uses, but, according to Storey (2003), the concept of hegemony refers to *a condition in process in which the consent of subordinate groups and classes is achieved through the moral and intellectual leadership by dominant groups or classes in societies* (here I will continue to use the term "group" instead of "class" to [overly] simplify the matter). *Hegemonic domination* produces a state in which cultural artifacts, including popular cultural texts such as editorial cartoons, take on a natural, uncontested state in which both producer and consumer see them as transparent, taken-for-granted aspects of the cultural landscape. *Hegemonic struggle* is the contestation over meaning and practices, and this struggle is the battle for hegemonic domination. The concept of hegemony, again, refers to a process, and this process is an ongoing struggle, a negotiation between those in the dominant and subordinate groups over resources, both material and non-material. Hegemony involves hegemonic and counterhegemonic struggles, and both are organized by a given group's organic intellectuals—for example, members of the subordinate or dominant group who perform an intellectual function of articulating messages (what we might think of in one instance as claimsmakers). Organic intellectuals have the task of organizing the respective groups (or classes) from which they originate or on which they focus by establishing and contesting the meaning of any given claim that competes for hegemonic domination. Hegemony should be distinguished from domination because of the fact that hegemony involves an always ongoing attempt by the dominant (for example, those groups with more resources or better access to resources) and subordinate groups to define and redefine the meaning of social phenomena.

As opposed to cultural theories that propose popular culture is a structural, top-down feature of society produced for the double purposes of profit and to pacify the masses through their passive consumption of it, or conversely that popular culture is entirely a bottom-up production of authentic, local texts created to resist oppressive social systems, hegemony theory proposes that a compromise equilibrium is produced whereby the commodities produced by culture industries are made into popular culture by the masses through their uses of those commodities. Through this process hegemonic domination is achieved by one group gaining the willing consent and compliance of one or more subordinate groups to adhere to the dominant group's moral, political, economic, and/or other definitional constraints of social reality. Hegemonic domination is not easily (if ever) completely established, though, for it must be continuously constructed, fortified, restructured, and in some cases conceded, partially or in whole, in the light of hegemonic struggle. We should not assume that subordinate groups are passive, for to do so would devalue the very proposition set forward in this chapter: Students of sociological education can learn to see the operation of hegemony and the social construction of reality, and once a glimmer of that light is cast upon the shadows, distortions, and illusions so prevalent in popular cultural texts, they can begin to ask and answer less obvious questions of the nature of the social world they inhabit.

Editorial cartoons house essential characteristics of many pop culture texts, namely condensed communications through images and the written word. These cartoons' authors intentionally construct their image to impress in the minds of their audiences certain interpretations, impressions, perceptions, or meanings of social reality.

> A key question for cultural studies is: "Why do particular meanings get regularly constructed around, say, particular cultural practices and thereby achieve the status of 'common sense,' acquire a certain taken-for-granted quality?" Although this is a recognition that the culture industries are a major site of ideological production, constructing powerful images, descriptions, definitions, frames of reference for understanding the world, Gramscian cultural studies rejects the view that "the people" who consume these productions are "cultural dupes," victims of "an up-dated form of the opium of the people." [sic] (Storey, 2003, p. 52)

A common cultural practice in the United States, and around the world, is the production and consumption of the newspaper. It is so common that its existence is most likely in the realm of the taken-for-granted by most people (imagine what would happen in the conversations if newspapers one day just stopped being produced). What is of interest in terms of hegemony theory is that this medium can be used by organic intellectuals in the editorial section to construct and contest the operations of society. Editorial cartoonists can articulate messages that support or criticize the status quo, and any particular organic intellectual in this enterprise can orient themselves along any number of combinations of ideological lines (political, economic, cultural, etc.). A task for students, then, could be to pick apart the manifest and latent messages and meanings a given cartoonist presents their audiences in order to decode the ideological content of the text. In terms of hegemony theory, though, texts should be analyzed together, across a number of portrayals of a given person, event, or issue in order to analyze the hegemonic struggle and social construction of the given aspect of social reality in question. Students should be able to identify not only the assumptions of the cartoonist, but they should more importantly be able to eventually identify the operation of their own background assumptions that guide their analysis.

In order for a (counter) hegemonic articulation to be performed, both the editorial cartoonist (claimsmakers and organic intellectual) and her or his readers must share in the meaning of the symbols within the cartoons. "Editorial cartoons in newspapers depend on the fact that readers will understand such symbols; a figure in a Klansman's robe and hood denotes racism, a smokestack belching smoke symbolizes pollution, and so on" (Greenberg, 2008, p. 146). In packaging their claims with condensing symbols, editorial cartoonists as claimsmakers rely upon a shared cultural or social stock of knowledge to communicate complex ideas to their readers. "The social stock of knowledge differentiates reality by degrees of familiarity. It provides complex and detailed information concerning those sectors of everyday life with which [people] must frequently deal" (Berger & Luckmann, 1966, p. 43). The shared stock of knowledge between author and audience, between claimsmakers and their readers, and among organic intellectuals and their acolytes and detractors is often taken-for-granted precisely because the shared stock of knowledge is constituted by those symbols that are part of the commonsense understanding of social reality (it *is* a rather circular argument, but, then again, so is the process of the social construction of reality). As put by one researcher of the topic, "[W]hile cartoons are normally understood by readers to be satirical depictions of real events, they nevertheless draw from an available stock of public knowledge and reproduce a common-sense view of the world" (Greenberg, 2008, p. 194).

If there were no shared stock of knowledge between claimsmakers and readers then there could be no, or at least very little, communication of the deeper meanings, but the efficiency of communication depends on the coding of the messages and the ability to effectively decode the messages. The entire intended package of a claimsmaker is not always [fully] accepted by [all] readers; different readers might accept one part of a claim while rejecting others, or some might reject it entirely, and this can happen when readers agree or disagree with how acceptable or accurate a particular symbol that is used to portray a concept, person, event, process, or issue is considered to be. While people with similar taken-for-granted assumptions, values, and norms might be able to interact through the shared recognition of common symbols in that they can all read, for instance, English, or recognize similar popular icons, the definitions of the deeper meaning of condensed symbols requires that a shared definition of the situation exists. Definitions of a situation depicted in cartoons can differ based upon cartoonists' and readers' differences in the (e)valuation of a particular aspect of a given topic, it can arise from differential socialization processes they individually experience, by occupying different social structural positions (e.g., age, education, ideology, political party, race, sex, social class, etc.), as well as living in different social contexts of a broader socio-cultural-historical milieu. By and large, though, the content of any particular editorial cartoon, or cultural artifact for that matter, should be assumed to have multiple meanings that become ap-

parent once individuals together begin to negotiate the meaning(s), and this tran-
spires between any given political cartoonist and her or his audience upon the
consumption of these, or any other, cultural texts.

In terms of hegemony theory, interesting lines of questioning for students
would be stretched between the processes of production and consumption of
editorial cartoons (and any other popular cultural text). Students should be aware
that editorial cartoons do not appear from nowhere: Cartoonists are agenda setters just as much as the editorial staffs at the newspapers in which they wish to
publish their work. Students might be asked if a given cartoonist and/or newspaper presents consistent ideological messages in their editorial cartoons. Students
might be asked to compare cartoons about a given topic, such as abortion or
freedom of expression, and in doing so they might be challenged to express the
parameters of debate and/or to identify why hostilities might form over contestation of the meaning of a cartoon or series of cartoons. Students themselves
should be pressed to always at the same time be aware of the assumptions that
guide their interpretations and assessments. This is made somewhat easy in sociology textbooks because theoretical frameworks such as structural-
functionalism, symbolic interactionism, and conflict theories (Marxism and feminism) are used in this way. However, for sociological educators who do not
have a background in sociology to this degree, it should be enough to pass on or
inspire critical sociological thinking in students by notifying or imparting to
them the notion that the social construction of reality, especially in the context
of the corporate owned and state sanctioned mass media, takes shape through
hegemonic and counter hegemonic struggles to define or set the definitional
constraints on the meaning of any given social phenomena.

Deep Politics of Editorial Cartoons

As an application of this discussion of editorial cartoons, social constructionism, and hegemony, I would like to first highlight a blog entitled, "Cartoon
Plagiarism Case Offers a Metaphor for the Abortion Debate" (Baradell, 2005).
The blog contains two editorial cartoons that are *almost* identical, hence the plagiarism. Bob Englehart's cartoon, "When Does Life Begin," which was first
published in 1981 in *The Hartford Courant*, was all but entirely reproduced
twenty-four years later by Dave Simpson of the *Tulsa World*. Both cartoons,
which can also be found on the Association of American Editorial Cartoonists'
(2005) website, are nearly identical. They depict from left to right three white
males answering the question of when life begins: First, a Catholic priest, nearly
indistinguishable in both cartoons, states that it begins "at the moment of conception;" pictured in the middle is a judge, depicted as a white male, donning a
black judge's robe, holding a gavel by both hands (but otherwise somewhat dis-
similar looking from one carton to the next), answering the question with, "At
birth;" and last in line is a somewhat younger looking white male. The younger

looking male on the right of the cartoons was drawn much differently by Simpson than it was by Englehart, whose depiction of the standard male youth of the early 1980s was a skinny-faced, pizza eating, white, male teenager wearing a letter jacket over an Argyle sweater. Compared to this, Simpson's depiction is of a fat-faced, white, male teenager wearing a backwards baseball cap with some type of large necklace (commonly referred to as "bling") hanging over a patterned t-shirt. The teens in both pictures say that life begins "when you get your driver's license." In terms of the above discussion on the social construction of reality and the process of hegemony as played out through editorial cartoons, what are we to make of this, both for ourselves and in terms of a lesson for our students?

Baradell's (2005) metaphor for the abortion debate, which he drew from this particular case of plagiarism, is interesting for our purposes in answering this question. Evidentially, Baradell thinks that "we haven't made much progress in the abortion debate over the last quarter century." If I were teaching from this example,[5] I might ask my students if they agree or disagree with Baradell's metaphor. Abortion is often covered in introductory sociology textbooks, and I have found that students bring with them to the classroom background knowledge about the topic that they have picked up from their interactions with family and friends, within educational and religious settings, and from various mass media sources. What is of interest in terms of the discussion here is whether they believe or not that the issues surrounding abortion are immutable, that is to say, if they take the abortion debate for granted. Research has shown that the abortion debate did not arise from nowhere, that it did not form out of a void onto a predestined or preordained path toward the current state of it being framed in terms of pro-life Republicans and pro-choice Democrats (Carmines, Gerrity, & Wagner, 2010). While at first glance one might readily accept the message that the Catholic Church has always been an unwavering pro-life voice in the debate; that judges have always been pro-choice activists, and that youths have always been enthusiastically uninformed and apathetic, further investigation into the matter shows otherwise (see Reagan, 1997; Dellapenna, 2006). The abortion debate is much more complex than depicted in these cartoons, and the fact that a claimsmaker from the Internet has chosen to use this example to make the claim that the debate has changed little over the years makes the case that there are in fact people who choose to ask and answer the most obvious, surface-level questions about social phenomena.

In terms of hegemony, it should be noted that an underlying or implicit articulation in both Englehart's and Simpson's versions was that of the central importance in the abortion debate of the voice of white men. Had Simpson updated the youth to an African American female, he might not have been sanctioned for plagiarism (although he might have been sanctioned for other reasons) because of his re-articulation of this frame within the abortion debate; but, he did not do this. He, along with most other editorial cartoonists, is a white man, and his, as with most characters in editorial cartoons, are white men. This can be a taken-for-granted aspect of editorial cartoons that is part of the underlying current in the struggle over cultural hegemony. Multicultural feminist voices are often left unheard in mass media (Brooks & Hebert, 2006), and so the predominance and/or normality of white and masculine voices in popular cultural texts should lead some students to overlook these aspects, taking them for granted in a way that indicates what type of hegemony is at play. The questions I would want my students to ask themselves after a class period with this example at center stage would be along the lines of, yes, whether the abortion debate has changed or to what degree it has changed since its inception, but I would want them asking themselves about whose voices are represented (if any, realistically) and *why* it is the opinion of some (such as Barradell) that these particular cartoons represent the core, or at least a pillar, of the abortion debate. Students should be left asking themselves not only about what is (re)presented in the cartoons, but also about what is not (re)presented.

In a similar vein, Mikhaela Reid's (2011) four panel comic strip, "Every Sperm Is Sacred," which "reflects Reid's anxiety about the crusade to not only overturn *Roe v. Wade* but to limit the availability of contraception" [sic] (Wallis, 2007, p. 135), was rejected by her editors because "'they felt the image [in the fourth panel] of women basically being tied up and raped by the Sperminator machine was too reminiscent of a recent murder of a young woman in New York City who went to a bar and was found later tied up and murdered'" [sic] (Wallis, 2007, p. 135, quoting Reid). Whichever cognitive or social devices that were at work to bring the editors' focus on the fourth panel is an empirical question better answered through interviewing those editors. What is theoretically plausible and useful from the discussion so far is that while the cartoonist symbolically condensed her message in the fourth panel in a way she felt fitting to make known to her readers her anxiety over reproductive issues related to abortion, the editors' stock of knowledge—whether in terms of the panel being offensive to their own personal sensibilities, or by sparking fears in them of losing their jobs or revenue if/when their customers became offended—contained an inclination to interpret the cartoon as not suitable for publication. As sociological educators, we must ask what the role of race, class, and gender had in these (non)productions, and those are often part of the taken-for-granted aspects of the social world that are often overlooked and/or disregarded by college students (Kleinman & Copp, 2009).

Reid's attempt at symbolically condensing her claim of the social problem of these reproductive issues itself was negotiated in a way that lead to the socially constructed reality of *not* having her message made known to her intended audience. This is a clear example of hegemonic and counterhegemonic struggles. Reid articulated her symbolic message to (re)define the reality of abortion, but the organization in which she worked stopped her chances of materializing that message by implementing their authority over the control of the means of cultural production. The act of editorializing reproductive issues within the cartoon contained an inherent bias for one interpretation over another, but before readers could interpret the [framing of the] issue for themselves, the cartoonist's editors implemented their roles through censoring the entire package from readers. In this case, the killing of the cartoon is itself an act of editing, one that constructs social reality through the omission of a claimsmaker's message that was a direct attempt at framing a social problem in a manner so as to convince readers of a certain way to interpret a social phenomenon, in this case abortion. Here we can see that the dialectic relationship between objective and subjective aspects of social reality was involved in socially constructing reality and hegemonic struggles.

In an example of editorializing social reality through *commission*, the twelve Danish cartoons published in the *Jyllandsposten* that satirized the Prophet Muhammad drew much domestic and international debate over the seemingly clashing issues of the freedom of expression, the freedom of the press, and the freedom of religion. Muller and Ozcan (2007) found that, generally, "the majority of the Muhammad cartoons depict the Prophet in an unpleasant, threatening way. In most of the cartoons, Muhammad is depicted with aggressive looks, a dark and wild beard, and thick eyebrows" (p. 289). The meaning of the cartoons is open to interpretation by individual readers, and those interpretations are likely to be shaped by one's socio-historical-cultural context in which they live and socialize. Also shaped by socio-cultural-historical contexts, the production and reception by the Danish authors and audience was likely the product of Western hostility to Muslims and Islam that predated the terrorist attacks in the United States on 09/11/2001, which are typically blamed on nineteen Muslim, terrorist hijackers. However, the social context of the cartoons' production was likely influenced by the heightened association in Westerners from the 9/11 terrorist attacks of the supposed equivalency of Muslims and Islam with terrorists and terrorism. The reception by the Muslim community and those in the Arab world was likely contextualized by the religious taboo of visually depicting or representing the Prophet Muhammad, but is also likely contextualized by the perceived and real encroachment of Western culture, markets, and military on their societies. When teaching about such a topic with cartoons that made such an impact on various levels of societies throughout the world, it is important to note that things are not always what they seem.

Claimsmakers were at work all the way through the process of production, consumption, and reception of the case of the Danish-Prophet Muhammad cartoons. As one researcher put the matter:

> *Jyllandsposten* and the Danish government attempted to define this issue in terms of freedom of speech, posing the Muslim reactions as being the crucial problem, while several governments in Muslim countries, multiple Muslim organizations, and a variety of other actors promoted an intolerance frame, pointing to anti-Muslim sentiments in Denmark as being the fundamental problem. (Shehata, 2007, p. 139)

With the framework of a subjectivist view of social problems as a product of the claimsmaking process, the question is left open as to what exactly the problem was and how it arose. For example, Yilmaz (2011), reviewing the case some five years after the initial publications, concludes that the publishers intended to set an anti-Islamic agenda due to their adherence to the hegemony of populist, radical, rightwing politics. In other reports it has been noted that some newspaper publishers refused to print the cartoons and some governmental actors reprimanded newspapers that published the caricatures (Dafrizal & Ahmad, 2011).

According to one observation of the Danish/Muhammad cartoon incident:

> The images that linger are those of embassies on fire and angry crowds burning Danish flags. To the casual observer it may seem as if these manifestations emerged spontaneously and spread through some sort of contagion process. But closer examination reveals a different story: mobilization was driven by elites and by mass media, with civil-society manifestations, such as riots and demonstrations, being only the most visible expression. In fact, the number of people on the streets around the world was relatively small, and, more importantly, most street protests were chronologically preceded by mobilization attempts and diffusion activities by national governments, international institutions, and national and transnational media. (Olesen, 2007, p. 37)

For some, the problem was the depiction of Muhammad and a general anti-Islam zeitgeist in the West, for others the problem was the restriction on the freedom of expression and of the press based upon the opposition to those freedoms by a perceived hostile ethnic group. In our post-9/11 era, political elites around the world are differentially motivated to address religious claims involving Islam; as an event in which Muslims protest freedoms that U.S. citizens value and take for granted, this could have been an opportunity for Western elites to further an anti-Islamic agenda. The Danish cartoonists did not, though, simply have a one-to-one, direct impact on readers in the Western, Muslim, and Arab worlds; the diffusion of the claims involved politically, socially, and culturally motivated attempts to both criticize the original production and intent of the cartoons by some (pro-Islamic/multicultural) elites, as well as to defend the cartoonists' rights to produce such images by other (anti-Islamic/nationalistic) elites (Asmal, 2008).

As another researcher observed, though, dividing the issue between competing elite mobilization efforts is a misguided frame of the event for the central issue does not necessarily resolve the controversy between the priority over the freedom of speech and press versus that of religion, but rather it ostensibly comes down to a fundamental misrecognition of cultural assumptions, norms, and values. Hussain (2007) pointed out, for instance, that a BBC report, which both reflects and shapes how [some of] its audience thinks about the issues, that decreed "depictions of Muhammad or Allah are banned in Islam" (p. 115), was inherently flawed because it not only portrays Islam as a monolithic religion, but the use in the same sentence of Muhammad and Allah, who *are* depicted by Muslim artists from time to time, is ambiguous. The denotation of Allah refers to the monotheistic God of the Abrahamic religions, but placed in this context, it could be interpreted by ignorant Westerners (not that we all are) as an entirely different, totally unconnected deity than that worshipped by Christians who interpret the world through the lens of *their* Western, Christian-dominated hegemony. Moreover, placed in that context, it is unclear whether the intent of the BBC was to make the distinction that neither the Prophet Muhammad nor Allah could be depicted, or if it meant that the Prophet Muhammad is the same as Allah, which in either case is incorrect. At essence, the Danish cartoonists fabricated an image of the Prophet Muhammad which was socially constructed through their readers' receptions of the cartoons; however, the social construction of *the case* of the cartoons involved many social, cultural, and historical factors that can and did lead to factional interpretations. This likely lead to misinterpretations by individual readers based on their idiosyncratic socializations within their respective socio-historical-cultural contexts. While the cartoons themselves make for an interesting case for social constructionism, the hegemonic and counterhegemonic struggles by Westerners and the Muslim and Arab worlds are also, maybe more, interesting for the sociological classroom.

In these two illustrations, of abortion and the Danish cartoons, I have attempted to show that cartoonists, their editors, and audiences/readers, and not to mention editorial cartoons themselves, are all (along with a multitude of other social institutions, actors, and contexts) involved in the social construction of reality and the process of struggles for hegemony. Cartoonists attempt to package a claim about a feature of social reality, often times symbolically condensing a social problem into a hyperbolic generalization of a complex phenomena into a few images and lines of text. They attempt to construct social reality for their readers, and while doing so make (counter)hegemonic claims about the nature of social phenomena, which are always-already socially constructed through similar processes. Before cartoonists can interact with their audiences/readers, editors decide whether or not a cartoon or series of cartoons is permissible in their respective publications, sometimes "killing a cartoon" before it is published. While the factors that contribute to the publishing of some cartoons and the censoring of others is an interesting topic itself, how and why cartoonists construct and readers interpret and evaluate the message of a cartoon is an important aspect of how editorial cartoons (and other modalities of claims) factor into the social construction of social reality. If students can be shown that things like individual editorial cartoons do not just appear from nowhere, but are in fact a product of motivated claimsmakers supported by an equally motivated culture industry and consumer base, then they might begin to question other aspects of popular culture and the larger universe of social reality.

Political or Editorial Cartoons?

As the denotation is somewhat indistinguishable, editorial cartoons are often called political cartoons, and vice versa. Although I have at times used them interchangeably, in this chapter I have more often used the term "editorial" as opposed to "political" in reference to our cultural texts of interest because the connotation of "editorial" implies a broader universe of discourse. "Political" is not necessarily a restrictive term, for it can readily refer to a broad world of struggles over power and resources from the interpersonal up to international levels, both on material and non-material planes, and talented cartoonists can and have tied together any number of combinations of these features into their works. In part, though, I avoid the term "political" because I do not want to suggest that educators focus on, for instance, struggles between Democrats and Republicans over any of the myriad issues that arise between these groups, nor do I wish to suggest that when using this aspect of popular culture for educational purposes, educators should focus on political issues *per se*.

As pointed out in an article in *The Chronicle of Higher Education*, defining all subject matter as political issues would be akin to asking the question, "But *everything* is political, isn't it?" [emphasis added] (Fish, 2002). In answering this, Fish states that:

> The question is insistent, it always comes back, in part because there is more than a little truth to the assertion it presupposes. Everything is political in the sense that any action we take or decision we make or conclusion we reach rests on assumptions, norms, and values not everyone would affirm. That is, everything we do is rooted in a contestable point of origin; and since the realm of the contestable is the realm of politics, everything is political.
>
> But this sense in which everything is political is so general (no action escapes it) that there isn't very much that can be done with it; it doesn't tell you anything about the entities (all entities) to which it applies. If everything is political, to say of something that it is political is not to distinguish it from anything else; and if you want to know what a particular thing is or how it works, you will have to go back to the ordinary distinctions that will still serve to mark one thing off from another even if, on a very abstract level, they are both political. ("Is Everything Political?")

Many editorial cartoons focus topically and thematically on political ideas, figures, events, and/or processes, but not all do so; some focus exclusively or inclusively on cultural, economic, environmental, historical, (inter)personal, and/or social issues or topics.

Teaching students about the socially constructed nature of social reality is not a task left to a day's worth of teaching, nor to a semester, but it can take years to fully grasp the essence of the concept. I approach such a program with multiple lessons in which I implement multiple media formats to introduce students to the matrix of socially constructed social phenomena, and editorial cartoons are only one way I use to show my students this feature of social reality. Like with some other popular cultural texts (such as YouTube videos or movie clips), editorial cartoons can provide comic relief while generating discussion on controversial topics (Dougherty, 2003), and in line with this and the fact that editorial cartoons have historically been a mainstay of newspapers, they should be treated as serious pedagogical sources to inspire critical sociological thinking.

When discussing the socially constructed nature of social reality and processes such as hegemony with students, especially younger students who are still under the ideological wings of their families, friends, religions, education, media, and other ideological (state and corporate) apparatuses, and for the type of pedagogy illustrated in this chapter in general, it is important to always keep in mind that we as educators approach the topics we do with certain biases that not all students appreciate or view as legitimate.

Using "political" instead of "editorial" in reference to cartoons commonly found on editorial pages might suggest to students that *all* subject matter represented is of a political nature, and, while some—myself included—might argue that all features of social reality contain struggles over power and resources, this description is somewhat limiting. I have found that students use the term "political" more often than "editorial" in reference to these cartoons, and so that might be one or the first thing to go over with them in this style of teaching. At this point in my career I wonder if a perception of political bias by at least some students is unavoidable. Students identify a wide range of behaviors by their teachers as politically biased (Tollini, 2009), and the discrepancy between what we as educators define as politically biased and what they as our students define as politically biased can sometimes be at odds in subtle and surprisingly unobvious ways (Tollini, 2010). The mere presentation of editorial cartoons could potentially be defined as biased, but I personally try to avoid this by showing what might be considered to be "both sides" of a given issue. But, what students consider being "both sides" and what sociological educators consider to be "both sides" might not be the same thing at all.

Keeping in mind that hegemony theory does not assume that cultural consumers are passive dupes, but that they take part in an active process of (re)defining what a given cultural text means, it is important to show students that there *are* aspects of popular culture, the zone of social reality where they will likely continue to spend so much time thinking and doing, that are shaped or shaded by their taken-for-granted assumptions about the way society works and what any given symbol, object, practice, event, or issue ultimately means. Getting students to the point where they see familiar cultural texts as "strange texts" (Jacobs & Brooks, 1999) is as difficult as getting them to see how their position in social structure affects their consciousness. This is a large part of the process of inspiring students' sociological imaginations (Mills, 1959), and this is the goal of most sociological educators (Dandaneau, 2009). It would be a loss if a student or a number of them were turned off from the sociological perspective by a lesson or professor who chooses to highlight only, let us say, the positive aspects of the Democratic party and negative aspects of Republicans (or vice versa). It would be a further loss for this pedagogical program to only focus on political cartoons regarding party politics because there are volumes of editorial cartoons depicting just about any topic imaginable in one way or another. When teaching students that social reality is by its nature socially constructed a simple lesson based on the preference of "editorial" over "political" might just be one way to begin a day's, week's, or month's lesson plan.

Conclusion

Showing students that their commonsense notions of social reality are not always germane to understanding deeper meanings of familiar texts can be a difficult and tricky task. Using editorial cartoons to do so is one way of achieving that goal. Avoiding the idea that editorial cartoons only present opinions and interpretations of political parties, processes, or personalities is an important aspect of using this medium to teach about the broad realm of our socially constructed social reality. There exists a plethora of editorial cartoons for educators to sift through, so many so that it sometimes becomes difficult to edit out some funny and relevant cartoons to save for time and pacing in the classroom. The breadth and depth of issues illustrated by editorial cartoonists makes this a ripe avenue for educators to explore in the search for engaging and relevant material. My students have indicated that they are more than willing to accept their use as legitimate, but they are also aware that using this medium can easily lead to a politically biased situation.

When using political cartoons to cover value-laden topics such as abortion, religion, and other sociologically important topics for a course or lesson, we should keep in mind that *our* own taken-for-granted assumptions guided by our years of experience in higher education can and will color our classroom performances and for some students in an unfavorable light. That is why it is important when constructing and presenting our (counter)hegemonic claims to try to cover various sides to the issues we address in the ways described in this chapter. The college classroom is an opportune time to begin introducing students to the various issues present in contemporary society, but we should keep in mind that, and especially for students who are early in their vocations, college students might not have the necessary conceptual tools and social stocks of knowledge to interpret any given editorial cartoon presented in its intended meaning by the cartoonist or educator. While early studies on the matter have shown that adults in the general public do not often interpret editorial cartoons with their intended meanings (Carl, 1968), another early study has shown that young learners also produce interpretations inconsistent with cartoons' intended messages (Bedient & Moore, 1985). But, this situation can easily be (re)defined as an opportunity.

Editorial cartoons have been used with success in several college-level educational settings (e.g., see Kleeman, 2006; Ewing et al., 2008; Hammett & Mather, 2011), but none that I am aware of have applied their use to teaching social constructionism and hegemony theory to college students. These two theoretical frameworks would make for an interesting analysis of the functions of editorial cartoons and cartoonists in society, but elucidating how sociological educators can use this media format to illustrate to students the existence of their taken-for-granted assumptions has been the goal of this chapter. Future work could delve into a deeper analysis of editorial cartoons by picking up where others have started and left off (e.g., see Morris, 1993), but the goal here has been to provide a method for sociological educators to use mass media formats in popular culture that illustrate the process of the social construction of reality and hegemony in such a way that the sociological imagination will be sparked in students' consciousness, lighting their paths in the journey of their lives. Once lit, hopefully the fires of critical sociological thinking will burn bright enough to illuminate the unseen dimensions of all those other aspects of popular culture they take for granted. Hopefully, successful sociological educators working from this program can inspire their students to become further luminaries for all those students who have not yet experienced the sociological classroom.

Endnotes

1. A guiding assumption in this chapter is that the reader will allow the author to privilege sociological knowledge and the sociological perspective. As the author's educational background, sociology provides the backbone, foundation, or framework for this chapter, but much consideration has been made to inform readers not familiar with this field about the central content and why it is important to teach students of all fields. Another assumption is that this chapter will be read in the context of educational practices that take place in the United States. The content should be applicable universally, but most examples involve the United States in some way. Lastly, I would like to thank the editors of this volume, Denni Blum and Edward Janak, for the opportunity to write this chapter. Were it not for Dr. Blum's course on popular culture and pedagogy, and her subsequent encouragement to continue to work with my term paper from that course, this chapter and other associated works would never have blossomed. Dr. Janak's dedication to this volume, accommodating editing of this chapter, and general encouragement were indispensable to this book's and chapter's productions.

2. For references, see Fresh's (2004) article, "Diddy Launches Citizen Change Vote Initiative," and Belyeu's (2012) article regarding the "Join, or Die" cartoon. If or when researching this for a class project, students would likely come across the Wikipedia article on Citizen Change (n.d.), in which its author states the following about the campaign: "The stated aim was to get young people to vote. The campaign's message, promoted on t-shirts and other things, is '**Vote or Die!**'" [emphasis in original]. Regarding the relationship between Combs's "Vote or Die" slogan and pop culture, the article's author states the following: "Many American television shows (most notably *South Park* and *The Daily Show with Jon Stewart*) have parodied this campaign as laughably hyperbolic, unnecessarily violent, and its ironic presentation of a false choice" [sic]. Whether or not the two slogans are actually related is a matter for further research, but this should nonetheless make for an

interesting research project for students; it involves the social construction of slogans that are themselves designed to socially construct reality, albeit in a more materially political way.

3. Here, I will leave up to the reader her or his preferences for the topic or theme they would want to address through the medium of editorial cartoons for I have very few ways of predicting the preferences of my readers. Furthermore, I have attempted to write this chapter thus far in a way that leaves open the topical possibilities of using editorial cartoons so that readers do not get the impression that the avenue for using editorial cartoons in the classroom is narrow. In fact, I would argue that the plethora of political cartoons available will provide more than enough cartoons for many educators' needs. Choosing a constructed or contested terrain to illustrate through political cartoons will come down to the preferences of the reader, and so please know that the editorial cartoons I selected to discuss in this chapter in no way establish the permissible parameters of available content.

4. There has been no comprehensive or empirical study to date on the matter, but here I take just one approach to identifying the intellectual function of editorial cartoonists. Because this is not the appropriate venue, and moreover because I do not have the data, I cannot elaborate in a systematic way on how editorial cartoonists function as intellectuals, but the sociology of intellectuals can help in the matter. Kurzman and Owens (2002) identified four periods in the development of the sociology of intellectuals, but the traditions that began at the founding of the field continued through the mid- to late-twentieth century and into the twenty-first century. "Three approaches developed at this time, each distinguished by its consideration of intellectuals as a class: one, pioneered by Antonio Gramsci, viewed intellectuals as bound to their class of origin; a second, associated with Karl Mannheim, treated intellectuals as potentially class-less; a third, popularized by Julien Benda, proposed that intellectuals form a class in themselves" (p. 64). Without the proper data and analysis, it would be difficult to say which tradition is most or least appropriate to use in identifying the intellectual functions editorial cartoonists play in society, and so it should be noted that while I use Gramsci's concept of "organic intellectuals," I do not wish to propose that this is the only or best way to approach them as a category in society. Taking off from Gramsci, for instance, Eyerman (1994) conceptualizes "movement intellectuals" as leaders of social movements in a broader sense than how "organic intellectuals" lead social classes. If social classes are interested in divesting themselves of socioeconomic bonds, social movements are interested in divesting themselves of socio-historical-cultural bonds. Because editorial cartoonists' subject matter is not only (or often) on "class issues," I suspect that "movement intellectuals" might be a more appropriate term for editorial cartoonists, but the fields of cultural studies and education are no doubt more familiar with the Gramscian concept compared to its Eyermanian counterpart. As a note to how they relate, though, "[w]hat movement intellectuals do, then," much like what editorial cartoonists might do for society, "is to articulate (and project) the knowledge

interests of social movements at the same time as they are criticizing society or the social issues, thus projecting their own needs and criticisms on to a reconstructed social force" (Eyerman, 1994, p. 198). This is a matter to pick up in future research.

5. In an effort to remain fair and balanced in the eyes of my students, I have taught with several different editorial cartoons that take up the topic of abortion, ranging from pro-life to pro-choice and beyond. There are many reasons for and ways of discussing abortion in the sociology classroom, and, respectively, one is to illustrate the issue of claimsmaking and framing in the social problems process by way of showing how different claimsmakers package their claims. By showing students cartoons on a single subject, such as abortion, in a multi-perspective manner, I attempt to facilitate a discussion that helps students develop an awareness of the various frames that claimsmakers produce in their struggles to define what abortion means. I try to balance out the discussion by showing both the pro-choice and pro-life sides, and I attempt to connect abortion to other issues, such as slavery, human rights, and to Constitutional rights of expression and bearing arms. In this way, there are a number of possibilities for educators to help a wide variety of students to evaluate their own commonsense understanding of what is represented in popular cultural texts.

References

Anderson, L., & M. Holt. (1990). Teaching writing in sociology: A social constructionist approach. *Teaching Sociology*, 18(2), 179-184.

Asmal, F. (2008). Islamophobia and the media: The portrayal of Islam since 9/11 and an analysis of the Danish cartoon controversy in South Africa (Master's thesis). Retrieved August 7, 2012, from http://hdl.handle.net/10019.1/3326.

Association of American Editorial Cartoonists. (2005, August 15). Plagiarism rears its ugly head in two cases. *News*. Retrieved January 29, 2012 from http:// editorialcartoonists.com/news/article.cfm/483/.

Baradell, S. (2005, November 11). Cartoon plagiarism case offers a metaphor for the abortion debate. [Web log comment] Retrieved January 29, 2012, from http://www.ideagrove.com/blog/2005/11/cartoon-plagiarism-case-offers-a   metaphor-for-the-abortion-debate.html.

Bedient, D., & D.M. Moore. (1985). Student interpretations of political cartoons. *Journal of Visual Verbal Learning*, Fall, 29-35.

Belyeu, M. (2012). Primary source: Join, or die snake. *Teacher Resources*. Retrieved August 6, 2012, from http://www.history.org/history/teaching/enewsletter/vol ume5/november06/primsource.cfm.

Berger, P.L. (1963). *Invitation to sociology: A humanistic perspective*. Garden City, NY: Doubleday & Company, Inc.

Berger, P.L., & T. Luckmann. (1966). *The social construction of reality: A treatise in the sociology of knowledge*. New York: Anchor Books.

Berkowitz, D., N.N. Manohar, & J.E. Tinkler. (2010). Walk like a man, talk like a woman: Teaching the social construction of gender. *Teaching Sociology*, 38(2), 132-143.

Bickford, J.H., III. (2011). Students' original political cartoons as teaching and learning tools. *Social Studies Research and Practice*, 6(2), 47-59.

Braa, D., & P. Callero. (2006). Critical pedagogy and classroom praxis. *Teaching Sociology*, 34, 357-369.

Brooks, D.E., & L.P. Hebert. (2006). Gender, race, and media representations. In B.J. Dow & J.T. Wood (Eds.), *The Sage handbook of gender and communication* (297-317). Thousand Oaks, CA: Sage.

Brouilette, J.R., & R.E. Turner. (1992). Creating the sociological imagination on the first day of class: The social construction of deviance. *Teaching Sociology*, 20(4), 276-279.

Buechler, S.M. (2008). *Critical sociology*. New York: Paradigm Publishers.

Burr, V. (2003). *Social constructionism*. New York: Routledge.

Carl, L.M. (1968). Editorial cartoons fail to reach many readers. *Journalism & Mass Communication*, 45(3), 533-535.

Carmines, E.G., J.C. Gerrity, & M.W. Wagner. (2010). How abortion became a partisan issue: Media coverage of the interest group-political party connection. *Politics & Policy*, 38(6), 1135-1158.

Citizen Change. (n.d.). In *Wikipedia*. Retrieved August 6, 2012, from http://en.wikipedia .org/wiki/Citizen_Change.

Conners, J.L. (2007). Popular culture in political cartoons: Analyzing cartoonist approaches. *PS: Political Science & Politics*, 40, 261-265.

Dafrizal, F.I., & F. Ahmad. (2011). Framing of controversial caricatures of Prophet Muhammad: A study of two Malaysian mainstream newspapers. *Malaysian Journal of Communication*, 27(2), 77-95.

Dandaneau, S.P. (2009). Sisyphus had it easy: Reflections of two decades of teaching the sociological imagination. *Teaching Sociology*, 37(1), 8-19.

Dellapenna, J.W. (2006). *Dispelling the myths of abortion history*. Durham, NC: Carolina Academic Press.

Dougherty, B.K. (2003). Comic relief: Using political cartoons in the classroom. *International Studies Perspectives*, 3(3), 259-270.

Ewing, E.T., H.L. Gumbert, D. Hicks, J.L. Lehr, A. Nelson, & R.P. Stephens. (2008). Using cartoons to teach the suffrage campaign in European history. *Journal of Women's History*, 20(3), 144-165.

Eyerman, R. (1994). *Between culture and politics: Intellectuals in modern society*. Cambridge, MA: Polity Press.

Fischman, G.E., & P. McLaren. (2005). Rethinking critical pedagogy and the Gramscian and Freirean legacies: From organic to committed intellectuals or critical pedagogy, commitment, and praxis. *Cultural Studies ←→Critical Methodologies*, 5(4), 425-447.

Fish, S. (2002). Is everything political? *The Chronicle of Higher Education*. Retrieved December 13, 2011, from http://chronicle.com/article/Is-Everything-Political- /45993.

Fobes, C. & P. Kaufman. (2008). Critical pedagogy in the sociology classroom: Challenges and concerns. *Teaching Sociology*, 36, 26-33.

Fresh, R. (20 July 2004). Diddy launches citizen change vote initiative. *Allhiphop.com*. Retrieved October 29, 2012, from http://allhiphop.com/2004/07/20/diddy-launches- %C2%91citizen-change%C2%92-vote-initiative.

Gamson, W.A., D. Croteau, W. Hoynes, & Theodore Sasson. (1992). Media images and the social construction of reality. *Annual Review of Sociology*, 18, 373-393.

Grauerholz, L., & Bouma-Holtrop, S. (2003). Exploring critical sociological thinking. *Teaching Sociology* 31, 485-496.

Greenberg, J. (2008). Framing and temporality in political cartoons: A critical analysis of visual news discourse. *Canadian Review of Sociology*, 39(2), 181-198.

Hamlet, J.D. (2009). Editorials. In *Encyclopedia of journalism* (Vol. 2, pp. 472-477). Thousand Oaks, CA: Sage Publications.

Hammett, D., & C. Mather. (2011). Beyond decoding: Political Cartoons in the classroom. *Journal of Geography in Higher Education*, 35(1), 103-119.

Hess, S., & M. Kaplan. (1968). *The Ungentlemanly Art: A History of American Political Cartoons*. New York: The Macmillan Company.

Hussain, A.J. (2007). The media's role in a clash of misconceptions: The case of the Danish Muhammad cartoons. *The Harvard International Journal of Press/Politics*, 12, 112-130.

Jacobs, W., & D. Brooks. (1999). Using strange texts to teach race, ethnicity, and the media. *The Velvet Light Trap*, 44, 31-38.

Kleeman, G. (2006). Not just for fun: Using cartoons to investigate geographical issues. New Zealand Geographer, 62, 144-151.

Kleinman, S., & Copp, M. (July 2009). Denying social harm: Students' resistance to lessons about inequality. *Teaching Sociology*, 37(3). 283-293.

Kurzman, C. & L. Owens. (2002). The sociology of intellectuals. *Annual Review of Sociology*, 28, 63-90.

Lamb, C. (2004). *Drawn to extremes: The use and abuse of editorial cartoons in the United States*. New York: Columbia University Press.

LeMoyne, T., & J.M. Davis. (2011). Debunking common sense and the taken for granted: A pedagogical strategy for teaching social problems. *Teaching Sociology*, 39(1), 103-110.

Lordan, E.J. (2006). *Politics, ink: How America's cartoonists skewer politicians, from King George III to George Dubya*. Lanham, MD: Rowman & Littlefield Publishers, Inc.

Makemson, H. (2009). Cartoonists, political. In *Encyclopedia of journalism* (Vol. 2, pp. 253-260). Thousand Oaks, CA: Sage Publications.

Mertz, M.P. (1976). Popular culture and the social construction of reality. *English Education*, 8(1), 12-21.

Mills. C.W. (1959). *The Sociological Imagination*. New York,: Oxford University Press.

Morris, R. (1993). Visual rhetoric in political cartoons: A structuralist approach. *Metaphor and Symbolic Activity*, 8(3), 195-210.

Morrison, M.C. (1969). The role of the political cartoonist in image making. *Central States Speech Journal*, 20(4), 252-260.

Muller, M.G., & E. Ozcan. (2007). The political iconography of Muhammad cartoons: Understanding cultural conflict and political action. *PS: Political Science and Politics*, 40(2), 287-291.

Olesen, T. (2007). Contentious cartoons: Elite and media-driven mobilization. *Mobilization: An International Quarterly*, 12(1), 37-52.

Orbach, B.K. (1999). Demonstrating the social construction of race. *Teaching Sociology*, 27(3), 252-257.

Persell, C.H., K.M. Pfeiffer, & A. Syed. (2008). How sociological leaders teach: Some key principles. *Teaching Sociology*, 36, 108-124.

Pestello, F.P. (1987). The social construction of grades. *Teaching Sociology*, 15(4), 414-417.

Pogel, N., & P. Somers, Jr. (1989). Editorial cartoons. In M.T. Inge (Ed.) *Handbook of American Popular Culture, 2nd ed.* (Vol. 1, pp. 367-415). New York: Greenwood Press.

Reagan, L.J. (1997). *When abortion was a crime: Women, medicine, and law in the United States, 1867-1973.* Los Angeles, CA: University of California Press.

Reid, M. (2011). Every sperm is sacred! *The Boiling Point.* Retrieved December 19, 2011, from http://www.mikhaela.net/cgi-bin/showpic.cgi?picdir=toons&picname =sacredsperm.gif.

Rodgers, D.M. (2003). "The stigmatizers and the stigmatized": Enacting the social construction of difference and discrimination. *Teaching Sociology*, 31(3), 319-324.

Salamini, L. (1974). Gramsci and Marxist sociology of knowledge: An analysis of hegemony-ideology-knowledge. *The Sociological Quarterly*, 15(3), 359-380.

Shehata, A. (2007). Facing the Muhammad cartoons: Official dominance and event-driven news in Swedish and American elite press. *The Harvard International Journal of Press/Politics*, 12, 131-153.

Spector, M. (1976). The social construction of social problems. *Teaching Sociology*, 3(2), 167-184.

Storey, J. (2003). *Inventing popular culture.* Malden, MA: Blackwell Publishing.

Tollini, C. (2009). The behaviors that college students classify as political bias: Preliminary findings and implications. *Teaching Sociology*, 37(4), 379-389.

Tollini, C. (2010). A comparison of faculty members' and students' definitions of political bias in the classroom. *International Journal of Sociology and Anthropology*, 2(5), 77-81.

Townsley, E. (2007). The social construction of social facts: Using the U.S. Census to examine race as a scientific and moral category. *Teaching Sociology*, 35(3), 223-238.

Urbinati, N. (1998). From the periphery of modernity: Antonio Gramsci's theory of subordination and hegemony. *Political Theory*, 26(3), 370-391.

Wallis, D. (ed.). (2007). *Killed cartoons: Casualties from the war on free expression.* New York: W.W. Norton & Company.

Yilmaz, F. (2011). The politics of the Danish cartoon affair: Hegemonic intervention by the extreme right. *Communication Studies*, 62(1), 5-22.

Chapter Nine

Using Technology to Engage Millennials in Learning

Bob Reese

Engagement of the student in the learning process has been seen as necessary even before Socrates devised his Socratic method (Corno & Mandinach, 1983). Kearsley and Schneiderman (1998) further developed this concept with the formalization of their *Engagement Theory* which hypothesizes that students learn best when "meaningfully engaged in learning activities through interaction with others and worthwhile tasks" (p. 20). The National Research Council embraced the necessity of engagement theory in *How People Learn* (Bransford, Brown, & Cocking, 2000). Carini, Kuh, and Klein (2004) provided evidence that student engagement is linked positively to desirable outcomes such as critical thinking and grades. There is little disagreement about the need for engagement to enhance learning in the achievement of student learning objectives. Engagement, however, became a priority in education with the entrance of the Millennial Generation into secondary school and higher education.

The Millennials are generally defined as those persons born between 1982 and 2000. The term Millennials was coined as the first of this young cohort entered high school as the new century began. And they are different—some say much different—than the preceding generations. They have different needs, challenges, and demands. Howe and Strauss (2000, 2003, 2007) have accused them of thinking of themselves as special, with a confidence that is unfounded. Many feel entitled to a good grade or a top job without having to work for it. More positively, they are described as team oriented achievers and as grade driven. Many feel pressured and stressed by consistent over-programming and overwhelming expectations for achievement, and many are terrified of making mistakes or saying anything wrong. These last descriptions appear linked to being overly sheltered by protective parents who unduly work to make sure they suffered few of the insults and injuries associated with traditional growth and development (Howe & Strauss, 2000, 2003, 2007; Mueller, n.d.; Taylor, 2006; Twenge, 2006).

Finally, they are considered the "wired" generation because they have grown up with rapidly advancing technology that quite often overwhelms their elders. Because of this concurrent development there is a perception that this generation is competent with *all* emerging technology. This perception—accurate or not—is reinforced by their seeming preoccupation with their constant and continuous use of their cell phones, which seem more like appendages than communication tools. College and universities have feverishly tried to adapt to the technology needs of this cohort by changing from desks to tables replete with plugs and Wi-Fi to better accommodate laptops, tablets, and smartphones. As part of this phenomenon, millennials consider themselves consummate multi-taskers. For example, they text one friend while they simultaneously engage in conversation with another. Or, they take pictures and post them to their Facebook page without missing a beat as they order their favorite coffee drink and chat with the person behind them. They do not agree—or do not care—that multitasking has been shown to be ineffective (Spink, Ozmutlu, & Ozmutlu, 2002; Ophir, Nass, & Wagner, 2009; Drews, Yazdani, Godfrey, Cooper, & Strayer, 2009). It is the way they conduct their social life. They see no reason to change for the classroom.

Millennials seem addicted to interactive technology and to multi-tasking. They sit in class peering at the screens of their laptops and iPads, instead of their instructors. As instructors speak, they are busy tapping the keyboard. Are they taking notes, searching Google, or are they texting, tweeting, or e-mailing? One cannot know for sure, which leads to classroom engagement challenges. Classroom instructors who try to compete head-on with this reality often face the frustration of Sisyphus. In order to successfully engage learners, instructors must find ways to incorporate technology and complement the multi-tasking mind-set of the millennial generation.

Student Response System (SRS)

One way to address this challenge of engagement is with a student response system (SRS), often referred to as *clickers*. SRSs have been around since 1998 and are common now in many higher education settings. SRSs are relatively inexpensive for both colleges and students.

Most college classrooms are already equipped with computers attached to multi-media projectors to accommodate PowerPoint (PPT) presentations. All that is needed is a SRS base unit, which is plugged into the computer. Base units can cost anywhere from $200 to $700 and usually come with two or more instructor clickers. Depending on the brand, base units are often free with the minimum purchase of clickers by the school bookstore. The clicker device itself costs the student about $25-$30, and can be used in any class requiring SRS.

Students can keep their units for the duration of their college career. Upon graduation, they can sell them back to their bookstores or online.

Once students register their clickers, their username is now associated with their clicking grades. This information may be easily uploaded into educational learning platforms such as Blackboard, which makes them also useful for taking attendance. Instructors build questions into PPTs (many textbooks have pre-developed clicker questions available for download into PPT); and students easily click-in their answers. Results are tabulated instantly and can be viewed after the vote, or even as the voting progresses if so desired.

There are several advantages gained by using SRS. Data show that SRS increase engagement, learning, and attendance. They encourage students to debate with their neighbors when their results are split. There is immediate feedback to the student and to the instructor. All students feel they have a voice, and they can answer without the fear of embarrassment often associated having an incorrect answer. The student's role changes from passive receptacle to active participant (Briggs, 2008; Duncan, 2007; Wood, 2004; Porter & Tousman, 2010). Research consistently shows that students positively evaluate clickers in the classroom (Cusumano & Reese, 2008; Reese, 2011).

Models of SRS Engagement

There are three basic questions most instructors want to know about students: (a) Are they here (attendance)? (b) Are they interested and paying attention (engagement)? (c) Are they learning (comprehension)?

Attendance is noted as soon as the first iClicker question is asked. Therefore, it is not necessary for instructors to create a question specifically for attendance. By not having a question specifically for attendance, students are encouraged to answer substantive questions so as to display attendance, along with comprehension of course materials.

Engagement is an intrinsic benefit of clickers. Students must pay attention because they have only a limited time (15-60 seconds) to click in their answer after the instructor asks a question. This dynamic promotes general curiosity (another form of engagement) to learn correct answers to questions (promotion of comprehension). This brings us to two models for engagement: (a) questions to generate discussion; and (b) testing for comprehension.

Because answering via clickers is anonymous, motivation to engage and to learn is encouraged as students compare their performance with that of other students as the results of the clicker questions are projected on a screen. Survey-style questions that are answered anonymously encourage engagement, comprehension, and discussion. This model is particularly valuable in courses with hot-button issues like gay marriage, racism, prejudice, and other wedge issues. After a survey question on opinions or attitudes students generally find that they are not alone in their viewpoint and are more likely to engage in discussion. (The instructor must ensure that the classroom provides a safe environment for these open face-to-face discussions.)

Tests for comprehension may include questions reviewing material from the last class, from assigned readings, or from in-progress teaching. Points are given for clicking in and for correct answers, which can later be uploaded to Blackboard as class participation points. This stimulates students to read text material prior to class. Comprehension of current information being taught is informed by questions at the end of a module. This allows instructors to see if understanding has occurred. If so, they can move on to new material. If not, a review is advised. Some instructors utilize a pre-test/post-test model thereby priming students for what information will follow and affording repetition of important concepts.

Some challenges are presented with the use of SRS systems. Some colleges use more than one brand and students have to buy more than one clicker. If students are required to buy clickers, judiciousness requires that they be used for more than attendance. Using them requires preparation and planning as questions must be inserted into PPTs prior to class. The learning curve of usage is short and not very steep, but it does require some practice. Using SRSs takes up class time as you wait for students to click in and then examine results.

Voice-Over PowerPoint (VO-PPT)

While SRS systems immediately engage students present in brick-and-mortar facilities, they are not the only type of students needing to be actively engaged in today's universities. A grave concern in education is the engagement of online students (Conrad & Donaldson, 2011) as their numbers expand. Online learning ignores the audio component of learning that makes up such a huge ingredient of on-ground classes (Dunn, Dunn, & Freeley, 1984). Incorporating VO-PPT addresses both of these concerns.

There are several pedagogical advantages to including Voice-Over Power-Point (VO-PPT) in online courses or portions of hybrid courses that are conducted online. They can also be used in on-ground courses as supplements to a topic that the text does not cover in depth. VO-PPT is both flexible and learner-centered. It adds the audio component to online learning, and "hearing" the instructor enables a rapport with the instructor that helps keep the online learner from feeling isolated. VO-PPT also employs a mastery approach to learning in that students can access individual slides, they can review slides repeatedly, and they can do both with or without the audio (Reese, 2008).

Production of VO-PPT is easy and inexpensive—it is built into Microsoft PowerPoint (PPT). The only extra equipment you need is a microphone. I suggest one that is mounted on a headset so that it is always the same distance from your mouth. This keeps sound levels consistent. Also, microphones with a USB plug seem to work best; they eliminate a distracting hum that seems to accompany standard audio plugs.

First, create and save your PPT. Print out a handout so that you will know the order of the slides. (This will keep you from getting ahead of yourself.) Then, under to the Slide Show tab, click Record Narration. Imagine yourself in front of the class and speak in the same tone and pace you would in class. In my Course Introduction VO-PPT I try to be relaxed and friendly: "Hi, I'm Bob Reese and I want to welcome you to Psychology 101, Introduction to Psychology. If you have a problem or a question, don't hesitate to e-mail me at the e-mail address on the slide. By the way, when you do contact me, you may address me as Bob or Dr. Bob. I don't do well with Dr. Reese or Mr. Reese."

There are some cautions. Do *not* read from a script as it will most likely record as a monotone, which is, of course, boring. Another no-no is never read the slide verbatim (unless you are really trying to drive home a point).

On the constructive side, add emotion where appropriate—let your passion for what you are teaching come through. Creating "broadcast quality" recordings is unnecessary. My experience is that if you speak conversationally, the listeners tend to normalize the audio and the "ums" and "ahs" that are part of routine speech are not distracting.

The learning curve is short and has a gentle slope. Instructor preparation takes no more time than planning and delivering a solid lecture. Advantages of VO-PPTs for the instructor include using them multiple times and perhaps, with slight modifications, using them in multiple courses.

One drawback is that the completed VO-PPT must be compressed before downloading into educational platforms such as Blackboard in order not to chew up too much viewer RAM. In the past this required expensive software such as Articulate or Camtasia. Now, this obstacle has been removed with the access to free—and easy to use—programs like iSpring.

Overall, the positives for use of iClickers and VO-PPTs easily outweigh the negatives. Because students are engaged—they enjoy them. They have inspired my creativity and enhanced my pedagogy!

Measuring Student Engagement

Evaluation of the efficacy for both iClickers and VO-PPT was accomplished by end-of-term surveys completed by students. Survey questions were formulated in standard evaluative research fashion with the questions presented in both a positive and negative fashion to eliminate response error bias and enhance reliability (JCSEE, 1994; Fitzpatrick, Sanders, & Worthen, 2004). Answers to negative questions were reversed coded for evaluation purposes. Surveys were delivered online using a Blackboard Survey consisting of a 5-point Likert scale [1—strongly disagree; two—disagree; three—neither agree nor disagree; 4—agree; and 5—strongly agree].

The brand of SRS utilized for this study is *iClicker*. For the iClicker portion of the survey there were a total of three categories of survey questions posed in a positive and negative manner: (a) helpful to learning the material vs. not helpful to learning the material; (b) iClickers encouraged participation in class discussion vs. did not encourage participation; and (c) a recommendation of continued use in future classes.

For the VO-PPT portion of the survey there were a total of three categories of survey questions posed in a positive and negative manner: (a) helpful to learning the material vs. not helpful to learning the material; (b) viewing the VO-PPTs was interesting and engaging vs. boring and a waste of time; and (c) a question regarding the use of the technology itself—that is, it was easy to use versus difficult to use. A positive or negative evaluation was determined by the percentage of the positive versus negative student responses.

On-ground and hybrid courses contained questions from both surveys. Students were rewarded with a nominal amount of bonus points for completing the survey. The bonus points were not enough to significantly impact their grade. For example, 10 bonus points were awarded in classes where approximately 1,800 points were earnable via academic assignments.

The iClicker evaluation was measured in eight undergraduate class sections of psychology classes all taught by the researcher/author. Four of these were traditional on-ground classes, and four were hybrid classes that met once a week in the classroom for 1.5 hours and 1.5 hours online (asynchronously). Classes occurred over a total of seven standard fifteen-week semesters. There were a total of 158 students enrolled, of which 122 responded to the survey for an overall response rate of seventy-eight percent.

The results of the iClicker evaluation showed an eighty percent positive evaluation for iClicker use in the classroom. Eighty-five percent found the iClickers to be helpful to their learning versus five percent who found them not helpful. Sixty-nine percent felt that iClickers encouraged their participation versus fifteen percent who said it did not. And ninety percent recommended continued use versus only two-tenths of one percent who thought they should be eliminated (see Table 1).

The VO-PPT evaluation was measured in fifteen undergraduate classes of psychology classes all taught by the researcher/author. Classes occurred over a total of six standard fifteen-week semesters and two ten-week summer semesters. Six of the fifteen classes were totally online courses; three were traditional on-ground classes; and three were hybrid classes that met once a week in the classroom for 1.5 hours and online for 1.5 hours (asynchronously). There were a total of 297 students enrolled, of which 231 responded to the survey for an overall response rate of seventy-eight percent.

The results of the VO-PPT evaluation showed a seventy-three percent positive evaluation for VO-PPT use in the class. Seventy-five percent found the VO-PPTs to be helpful to their learning versus eight percent who found them not helpful. Sixty-five percent felt that VO-PPTs encouraged their participation versus eleven percent who said they did not. Eighty-one percent recommended continued use versus nine percent who thought they should be eliminated (see Table 2).

Discussion

The inclusion of iClickers and VO-PPTs encourage engagement by students. Ongoing research consistently shows that iClicker and VO-PPTs are efficacious in assisting learning and enhancing student participation. In an open essay question included at the end of the survey for overall course improvement suggestions, some students commented on iClickers and VO-PPTs. Some of their comments are included in the Appendix.

References

Bransford, J. D., Brown, A. L., & Cocking, R.R. (Eds.). (2000). *How people learn: Brain, mind, experience, and school.* Washington, DC: National Academy Press.

Briggs, L.L. (2008). Using classroom clickers to engage every student. Retrieved from http://campustechnology.com/printarticle.aspx?id=67903.

Carini, R.M., Kuh, G.D., & Klein, S.P. (2004). Student engagement and student learning: Testing the linkages. *Research in Higher Education, 47*(1), 1-32.

Conrad, R.M., & Donaldson, A. (2011). *Engaging the online learner.* New York: Jossey-Bass.

Corno, L., & Mandinach, E.B. (1983, Summer). The role of cognitive engagement in classroom learning and motivation. *Educational Psychologist, 18*(2), 88-108. Retrieved from: http://psycnet.apa.org/?fa=main doiLanding&uid=1984-16166-001.

Cusumano, J., & Reese, B (2008, October) *Using iClickers to teach psychology: Two different models.* Symposium conducted at the 7th annual meeting of Southeastern Teaching of Psychology Conference (SETOP) Getting Connected: Best Practices in Technology-Enhanced Teaching & Learning in Psychology. Atlanta, GA.

Drews, F.A., Yazdani, H., Godfrey, C.N., Cooper, J.M., & Strayer, D.L. (2009). Text messaging during simulated driving. *Human Factors: The Journal of the Human Factors and Ergonomics Society 2009, 51:* 762. Retrieved from http://hfs.sagepub.com /content/51/5/762.

Duncan, D. (2007). Clickers: A new teaching aid with exceptional promise. *Astronomy Education Review, 5,* 70-88.

Dunn, R., Dunn, K., & Freeley, M.E. (1984). Practical applications of the research: Responding to students' learning styles-step one. *Illinois State Research and Development Journal, 21*(1), 1-21.

Fitzpatrick, J.L., Sanders, J.R., & Worthen, B.R. (2004). *Program evaluation: Alternative approaches and practical guidlines* (3rd ed.). Boston: Allyn & Bacon/Pearson.

Howe, N., & Strauss, W. (2000). *Millennials rising: The next great generation.* New York: Random House.

Howe, N., & Strauss, W. (2003). *Millennials go to college: Strategies for a new generation on campus.* American Association of Collegiate Registrars & Lifecourse Associates: Great Falls, VA.

Howe, N., & Strauss, W. (2007). *Millennials go to college: Strategies for a new generation on campus* (2nd Ed). Lifecourse Associates: Great Falls, VA.

JCSEE. (1994), *The program evaluation standards: How to assess evaluations of educational programs* (2nd ed.). Joint Committee on Standards for Educational Evaluation. Thousand Oaks, CA: Sage.

Kearsley, G., & Schneiderman, B. (1998, September-October). Engagement Theory: A framework for technology-based teaching and learning. *Educational Technology,* 38 (5), 20-23. Retrieved from: http://eric.ed.gov/ERICWebPortal/search/detailmini.jsp? nfpb=true&_&ERICExtSearch_SearchValue_0=EJ573955&ERICExtSearch_Search Type_0=no&accno=EJ573955.

Mueller, W. (n.d.). Meet the millennials. *Living with Teenagers.* Retrieved from http://www.cpyu.org/Page_p.aspx?id=77190.

Ophir, E., Nass, C., & Wagner, A.D. (2009, September 15). Cognitive control in media multitaskers. *PNAS: Proceedings of the National Academy of Sciences of the United States of America,* 106(37), 15583-15587. Retrieved from http://www.pnas.org/ content/106/37/15583.abstract?sid=ba6a9801-963f-479d-bb2c-79aab65882ca.

Porter, A.G. & Tousman, S. (2010). Evaluating the effect of interactive audience response system on the perceived learning experience of nursing students. *Journal of Nursing Education,* 49(9), 523-527.

Reese, B., (2008, October). *Engaging Audio Learning with Voice-Over PowerPoint.* Poster presented at the 7th annual meeting of Southeastern Teaching of Psychology (SETOP) Conference, Getting Connected: Best Practices in Technology-Enhanced Teaching & Learning in Psychology. Atlanta, GA.

Reese, B. (2011, January). *Engaging audio learning with Voice-Over PowerPoint.* Poster presented at 3rd Annual Conference on Higher Education Pedagogy, Virginia Tech Center for Instructional Development & Educational Research (CIDER), Blacksburg, VA.

Spink, A., Ozmutlu, H. C., & Ozmutlu, S. (2002). Multitasking information seeking and searching processes, *Journal of the American Society for Information Science and Technology,* 53(8), 639-652. Retrieved from http://onlinelibrary.wiley.com/doi/ 10.1002/asi.10124/full.

Taylor, M. (2006). Generation NeXt comes to college: 2006 updates and emerging issues. *A Collection of Papers on Self-Study and Institutional Improvement,* 2, p. 48-55.

Twenge, J.M. (2006). *Generation Me: Why today's young Americans are more confident, assertive, entitled, and miserable than ever before.* New York: Free Press.

Wood, W.B. (2004). Clickers: A teaching gimmick that works. *Developmental Cell,* 7, 796-798.

Appendix

Table 1

iClicker EVALUATION: 80% Positive Evaluation
• 8 Class Sections (All Undergraduate; 4 Traditional on-ground / 4 Hybrid)
• 158 Students; 122 Respondents = 77% overall response rate

• 7 Semesters (15 wk semesters)						
Evaluation Summary, iClickers	**-** **1**	**-** **2**	**-/+** **3**	**+** **4**	**+** **5**	**Total**
Helpful learning vs. Not helpful learning	3	10	24	90	117	244
Encouraged participation vs. Did not encourage participation	9	27	39	78	91	244
Recommended continued use of iClickers in my classes	0	2	9	34	77	122
Total #	12	39	72	202	285	610
Total %	2%	6%	12%	33%	47%	100%
TOTAL %	8% -			80% +		88%

Table 2

VO-PPT EVALUATION: 73% Positive Evaluation						
• 15 Class Sections (All Undergraduate)						
• 297 Students; 231 Respondents = 78% overall response rate						
Evaluation Summary, VO-PPTs	**-** **1**	**-** **2**	**-/+** **3**	**+** **4**	**+** **5**	**Total**
Helpful learning vs. not helpful learning	13	23	77	212	130	455
Interesting & engaging vs. Boring & waste of time	17	34	109	195	104	459
Easy to use vs. Difficult to use	7	34	46	206	167	460
Total #	37	91	232	613	401	1374
Total %	3%	7%	17%	44%	29%	100%
TOTAL %	10% -			78% +		83%

Unsolicited student responses regarding iClicker use in the classroom.

- I liked the i clicker questions; they helped me understand the material.
- The iclicker portion of the class is a great and fun way to get the students thinking.
- The i-clicker questions every class were EXTREMELY helpful with learning the material. It was a nice review and kept you up to date on the certain chapters you were going thru in class (along with the notes). I thought it added a lot to the classroom experience and was a valuable tool.
- I really liked the iClicker. It gave me a chance to "put it all together" and gave me a taste of what test questions would be like. The extra points were helpful too!
- I enjoy the I-Clicker, it helped me to know whether I was grasping the information.
- I thought the iclickers were very useful and that they should continue to use them.
- I loved the I-clicker—helped myself and other students to follow along in class. Questions were studying tools for our tests

Unsolicited student responses regarding Voice-Over PPT use in the classes.

- More VO powerpoints, I learned more from those than I did from reading the book.

- The VO-PPT are very helpful in my actually learning the material—I would like more of them.
- I really found the VO-PPT very helpful and think that I would have [add] more.
- I would like to have more VO-PPT. I learn material better when it is explained to me. With the VO-PPT, Bob explained things perfectly and I was able to understand the material easier.
- VO-PPTs I thought they were pretty useful, ... I liked being able to watch them multiple times.

Chapter Ten

Amending Eurocentric Narratives of African History in the U.S. Classroom: A Popular Culture Approach

Fred N. Waweru and Mwenda Ntarangwi

Introduction

Ask yourself what words come to mind when you hear Africa. My students have helped me create lists of words that come to mind using such an exercise. Within a few minutes, a class frequently generates thirty or forty words that Americans associate with Africa. Native, hut, warrior, shield, tribe, savage, cannibals, jungle, pygmy, pagan, voodoo, and witch doctor are commonly associated with 'traditional' Africa. There are also 'new words,' including coup, poverty, ignorance, drought, famine, tragedy, and tribalism. (Keim, 2009, p. 4)

While these constructions and perceptions of Africa by American students are derived from a single institution where Curtis Keim teaches, they are shared by many and have endured over a long period of time. In a 1993 essay on how so-called educational films mythologize Africa, for instance, Sheila Walker quotes similar words of students given to Maynard in 1974 including: savages, lion, jungle, primitive, and spear (Walker & Rasmimanana, 1993, p. 3). Why are these images and constructions of Africa so powerful despite remarkable advances in the academic field of African Studies since the discipline was established in the 1950s? Probably one area to look into for answers to this question is the noted disconnect between African history scholarship and the actual teaching of Africa in the world history classroom (Reynolds, 2004; Goucher, 2004; Hunt, 2004). Of particular concern is the teaching modus operandi that frames contemporary/post-colonial African history through the lens of Eurocentric narratives, which lays emphasis on the colonial dichotomy of elite versus subaltern.

In this perspective, there is a belief that the Western world—which is an extension of Europe and United States—is the distinguished power center of civilization and consequently perceived as the yardstick against which every other place in the world must be measured. The tenet to this approach also assumes that all, or at least most, of the well-known events that take place in developing countries are consequential results produced by the actions of the Western world (Gran, 1996). African history is then taught through two key themes—slavery and colonialism—that force teachers and learners to only understand Africa through a Western prism. Inevitably, this practice leads to a narrative approach where any non-Western history is projected from a passive perspective.

The Eurocentric narrative of Africa's historiography that emphasizes the binaries of colonizer/colonized, Western/non-Western, primitive/modern, and underdeveloped/developed has consistently developed a very lopsided view of African history in the American classroom.[1] Human agency in African history is not only found in the deeds of great men or great states "but (also) in the struggles of ordinary people against the forces of nature and the cruelty of men" (Liffe, 1987, p.1). The docile representation of African history has many implications in the twenty-first century where global networks and connections are the contemporary world order. In academia, learning world history serves as a critical element in students' formation of their cognitive map of world histories as well as their own since all history is interconnected. Misrepresenting Africa through the teaching of its history also causes some students to assume a deterministic approach towards economic and instability issues currently facing Africa. As Reynolds (2004) shows, if certain components of world history are consistently omitted or misrepresented, then what sort of understanding of the world, past and present, will the learners establish as they create a cognitive map of world history? Today's global interconnectedness through economic, cultural, and political spheres calls for a nuanced understanding of world history and as a result the understanding of African history is no exception.

The purpose of this chapter is to propose a balanced approach to the teaching of African history that invites learners to go beyond the external dualism of colonizer/colonized in the effort to understand the complexities mutually experienced by both the colonizer and the colonized in African history. We show that one can teach African history using some of these enduring themes but provide learners with different ways of looking at and understanding past events by centering the narrative on Africans' experiences and expressions rather than European interpretations and projections of such history. The general arguments made in the chapter are that the othering of Africa, the presentation of Europe and the West as the prism through which non-Western cultures and histories are to be understood, and the continued perception of Africa as one monolithic political, geographic, and cultural space, have all contributed to the distorted perceptions of Africa exemplified in the words cited above by students in the American classroom.

This chapter is divided into three parts. In the first part, we discuss the core values of modern African history in the context of world history, and highlight how teaching through Eurocentric narratives consigns African history to oblivion. In the second part, we underscore less covered but influential contributions Africa has made to the rest of the world; and as a result break away from the trend of lumping African history into one big whole evident in many history textbooks (see, for instance, Hunt, 2004; Goucher, 2004; and Vaughan, 1994, among others). We find this common trend to be misleading given Africa's diverse cultures, geographies, politics, and economies that ought to be analyzed and presented individually rather than be addressed as one big empire. Even in cases where some history teachers move beyond the simplified depiction of the continent and cover more topics, the emphasis is placed on such areas as the economic imperatives that led to slavery, Egyptian civilization, Kingdoms such as that in Mali, and the apartheid system in South Africa. In this chapter we want to emphasize the value of not only highlighting such important historical factors but also how a deeper analysis of historical events and individuals can allow for an African history that helps show the deep connections Africa has with the rest of the world even into today's issues. To show the value of such an approach, we choose to provide a slice of African history that clearly demonstrates African agency by focusing on the history of an African "states-man" and Ethiopian leader, Emperor Haile Selassie I. We argue that the complexities that emerge from moving away from general blocks of history into specific histories of individual countries and even leaders are necessary in allowing students to see how complex African history is and encourage teachers to introduce African history through popular culture. Lastly, we propose a lesson plan that incorporates and highlights the specifics of history covered in Part II by using popular culture music to teach African history in a manner that breaks away from the current trend of Eurocentric approach.

Why Learn about Africa?

Apart from being the birthplace of the human race, Africa has a fundamental relevance in world history. The value of learning African history is cogently argued by a 1990 Rockefeller Foundation report titled *A Greater Voice for Africa in the Schools* based on the findings from a panel formed to discuss changes in teaching about Africa in the United States. The report chaired by Evelyn Jones Rich, indicated that:

> Myths and misapprehensions, distortions, sheer neglect, and covert racism . . . continue to prevail in our schools. ... These issues particularly plague the study of Africa, a continent of diverse and dynamic peoples, many of whose descendants have been major forces in the growth and definition of our own democracy and in the African diasporas throughout the world. The study of Africa and Africans has special meaning and importance as we go about the task of learning not only how to live as global citizens but also how to define ourselves—all of

us, black, white, Asian, Native American and others—as citizens of our own democracy. (Rich, 1990, p. 4-5)

In spite of long historical ties between Africa and the United States, post-colonial African history remains oblivious to many learners in the United States. This ignorance is caused by three interrelated factors. One, too many education textbooks reference Africa in one or two chapters, where Africa tends to be represented as a passive continent with less significance in world history. This limited coverage leads to the second factor, where textbooks represent African history based on popular stereotypes that offer fragmented and often inaccurate representations, instead of providing an understanding of how life is experienced by the 'majority' of Africans (Cooper, 1994; Reynolds, 2004). The limited coverage of African history in history textbooks, and the parochial representation of African history in formal education leads to a third and perhaps the most pressing factor—teachers' competency to teach African history. As we have established so far, the narrative characteristics of African history in U.S. education contexts tends to portray the opposition of civilized colonizer and primitive colonized, among many others. Unfortunately, many teachers of world history are caught up in this narrative with many of them having had a limited exposure to African history during the course of their formal education and teacher training (Hunt, 2004). This lack of exposure causes most teachers to automatically follow the grassroots norm of teaching African history through Eurocentric approach. As Rich goes farther to assert, "When Africa is included in the curriculum, in many cases what is taught reinforces stereotypes. Teachers approach Africa with Western values and a history of American and Western racism..." (Rich, et al., 1990, p. 11). Indeed, all the three interrelated factors are rooted in the Eurocentric approach, which presumes the Western culture as superior.

Africa in the Context of World History

Africa's past is truly a global tale full of rich, diverse, and dynamic characteristics. Archaeological evidence shows that Africa is the birthplace of the human species and home to many present and past great civilizations.[2] Nonetheless, in the realm of the Western world's history and beyond, Africa is connected to the dark ages of slave trade that resulted in the depletion of ancestry to many African descendants in Europe, North America, and South America. This degrading characterization and depiction of Africa's history is not unusual given many assumptions about its place in the world for many writers who worked in the eighteenth and nineteenth centuries. Writers such as Georg Hegel, giving lectures between 1830 and 1831, saw no value in looking at African history, stating that "[a]t this point we leave Africa, not to mention it again. For it is no historical part of the World; it has no movement or development to exhibit. Historical movements in it—that is in its northern part—belong to the Asiatic or European World."[3] Such a view was not isolated but shared among many scholars and writers who already brought to their study of Africa certain assumptions about its people and geography.[4] Indeed, as distinguished African historian Ali Mazrui (1993) notes, "the same events which one historian regards as an illustration of Africa under external influence could be viewed by another historian as an example of Africa's impact upon the outside world" (p. 21). Acclaimed African writer Chinua Achebe illustrates this impact in his highly acclaimed novel *Things Fall Apart*, when he discusses that Europe did not bring "civilizations" to "savages," but rather, Africa had a history that was sometime "superior to that of the imperialist" (Bernth, 1991, p. 38; Goucher, 2004). We similarly illustrate below that, through its struggle for freedom, Africa was also an active continent that had defining impacts around the world. This function of Africa, in the context of world history, has however been overshadowed in education by the highly exaggerated, generalized, and stereotyped "notions of Africa"[5] that focus on external dimensions, and the modern problems facing Africa (Hunt, 2004; Reynolds, 2004).

We provide world history teachers a specific piece of African history that can help both novice and expert historians connect African history to world history without conforming to the homogenized Eurocentric terrain that gives distorted images of Africa. In this endeavor, our aim is not to substitute addressing the devastations of colonialism in Africa, but rather an attempt to generate an informed dialogue in the classroom that represents Africans not just as the colonized, but also as people who, through the struggle for independence, influenced themselves as well as changed the course of world history. While this illustration is but a single story, it does provide an entry point into a more complex African historical reality than is often presented in many classrooms in the United States. We later provide a resource for teachers of world history who would like to teach this piece of African history through the pedagogic approach of pop-culture music.

The narrative of "great men of geniuses" is a category central in history (Hook, 1992/1945, p. 4). Nevertheless, the most critical aspect underrepresented in the Eurocentric narrative of modern African history is the significance of outstanding and influential figures. With perhaps the exception of the rise to fame of Nelson Mandela in the mid-1990s, the Eurocentric narrative of modern African history downplays the exploits of great individuals who empowered Africans during their struggle for liberation. Its omission in the world history has critical implications to the perception of Africans. In particular, its absence illustrates the subaltern's lack of leadership, and benevolent characteristics. More importantly, it feeds the existing fatalistic conceptualization of issues facing the African continent. Regaining independence from colonial rule has not necessarily led to utopia in Africa. In fact, there are troubling events that continue to cause friction in the development efforts of Africa. Nonetheless, there are some positive and influential modern histories of Africa that, if brought to light, could change the pessimistic perceptions of Africa held by many students.

Among these influential histories of Africa is the ruling history of Ethiopia in the twentieth century, which is of significance to Africa for three main reasons. First, Ethiopia was one of the only two African countries that were never colonized (the other was Liberia). Second, Ethiopia is the only country in Africa that avoided colonization through military means. Third, the history of Ethiopia is connected to that of the first African emperor–Haile Selassie I–whose enduring legacy became inextricable in Africa and the post-industrialist world. It is the influence of his historic legacy in the context of Africa that we endeavor to bring to light and show teachers history how such an approach allows students an opportunity to get a more nuanced understanding of African history.

Born in 1892 as Tafari Makonnen in Ethiopia (known then as Abyssinia), the heir of emperor Haile Selassie I's dynasty can be traced back to the thirteenth century, and from there on to King Solomon and Queen of Sheba (Haggai 2002, p. 192). Tafari's father, Makonnen, was a former general who had commanded the 1896 Battle of Adwa, which led Ethiopia to defeat an invading Italian army, making Ethiopia the only African state to retain its independence by military action (Page, 2003, p. 247-248). In 1916 Tafari was elevated to the rank of 'Ras' (Duke) before becoming an emperor in 1930 after the death of his father (Page, 2003, p. 247-248). It was then as an emperor that he took the name Haile Selassie I., which means Might of the Trinity (Imperial Ethiopia, n.d). He also bears other names such as Rastafari, King of Kings, and Lion of Judah.

The legacy of Haile Selassie dates back to 1923 when he abolished slavery in Ethiopia and built a school for the slaves in the capital city of Addis Ababa. The abolishment of slavery was the first diplomatic move by Selassie, which in turn secured Ethiopia's admission to the League of Nations (LON, or what is currently the United Nations) in 1926. A decade after Ethiopia's admission to LON, its sovereignty came under attack again in 1935 by the Italian army in the plain watch of the LON. Even though it was clear that the then Italian leader Benito Mussolini's army was the aggressor, it was not until Germany and Italy became Europe's greatest enemy at the beginning of WWII that the LON came to Ethiopia's aid in 1939 (Allain, 2006). The reluctance of the LON to assist its signatory Ethiopia, although dismaying, became a turning point for Selassie and also a defining moment for his contribution to Africa; and hence to world history.

Although he had not lived under colonial rule, Selassie was cognizant of the struggles for freedom that his fellow African countries were experiencing. In addition, owing to his keen interest of global affairs, he was aware of oppressiveness that people of color were facing in the Western world. For instance, starting in 1954 he travelled to United States on state visit six times—more visits than "most of any reigning foreign head of state up until that time" (Vestal 2011, p. ix). The awareness of suffering by African descendants gave Selassie the motive to root for a Pan-African—literary meaning all Africans—movement that attempted to unite all African "traits," whether in the African continent or in the Diaspora, in an effort to create an economic and political independence (Campbell, 2006). This bold vision for Africa by an African led to the 1963 formation of the Organization of African Unity (OAU)—currently known as African Union (AU) and has fifty-three member states with its headquarters in Addis Ababa, Ethiopia.

The formation of OAU made Selassie an international voice for Africa, particularly towards the Western hemisphere where majority of partakers were still colonizing many of the Africa nations. As a central mouthpiece of Africa, Selassie benevolently bullied global immorality that was integral then in the LON. When the LON was established in 1919 after WWI, the mandates of its covenant stated the goals of the League were to "prevent war through collective security, disarmament, and settling international disputes through negotiation and arbitration" (Basic Facts about the United Nations, 2000). While these mandates sounded assuring and admirable goals to achieve, the events of the time suggest that they were nothing but Western ideologies, because most of the League's signatories were still occupying Africa. Selassie challenged the LON's lack of integrity to its mandates by increasingly protesting against imperialism in Africa. With the full support of OAU, Selassie menaced the Western world's global imperialism through the famous speech that he uttered to the United Nations General Assembly in New York City on October 4, 1963. In this excerpt of the speech, Selassie protested that:

> Until the philosophy which holds one race superior and another inferior is finally and permanently discredited and abandoned: That until there are no longer first-class and second class citizens of any nation; That until the color of a man's skin is of no more significance than the color of his eyes; That until the basic human rights are equally guaranteed to all without regard to race; That until that day, the dream of lasting peace and world citizenship and the rule of international morality will remain but a fleeting illusion, to be pursued but never attained; And until the ignoble and unhappy regimes that hold our brothers in Angola, in Mozambique and in South Africa in subhuman bondage have been toppled and destroyed; Until bigotry and prejudice and malicious and inhuman self-interest have been replaced by understanding and tolerance and good-will; Until all Africans stand and speak as free beings, equal in the eyes of all men, as they are in the eyes of Heaven; Until that day, the African continent will not know peace. We Africans will fight, if necessary, and we know that we shall win, as we are confident in the victory of good over evil. (United Nations, 2000)

As this historic utterance indicates, Selassie was not only presenting the full weight of Africa's determination to liberate itself, but he was also generally calling to the end of racial oppression around the world. The speech also seems to infer the fact that bloody revolutions were inevitable in a world blighted by oppression. The concern for bloody global revolutions made Selassie to become a world ambassador for peace and tolerance through his diplomatic circuit that was recognized as far as the Caribbean. In Jamaica, he was cherished as the "Black peoples" liberator, and his strong stand against colonialism inspired po-

litical movements in Jamaica that later came to topple the political order instituted by the British occupiers. He also inspired spiritual identity for many African
descendants around the world through the Rastafarian movement. While this
messianic movement originated in Jamaica through the influence of other Pan-
Africanists, such as Marcus Garvey, it hailed Haile Selassie's unrelenting
worldwide advocacy for African descendants and adopted a tenet that the emperor was the "Black Messiah" who appeared in flesh to redeem all 'Blacks'
exiled in the world of White oppressors (Barret, 1997, 1). Even though Black
Jamaicans are the overwhelming followers of Rastafarianism, the movement has
diverse members around the world such as Chinese, East Indians, Afro-Chinese,
Afro-Indians, mulattoes, Afro-Jews, and even Whites (Barret, 1997, p.3). This
diversity of the movement is significant in understanding the numerous ways
that Haile Selassie influenced people beyond Africa.

The powerful utterance by Selassie to the LON was significant to Africa's
history and remains relevant in the twenty-first century. In particular, it played
an enormous role in changing global history, by redefining the ethics of racism
around the world and strengthening international morality. However, his contributions to the world history remain obscured in the Eurocentric narrative, as has
been most of African history. It is at this juncture that we call for balanced narratives of African history in the world history classrooms to include Africa's
contribution to the social harmony that the world enjoys today. Given that many
U.S. students may have some encounter with or knowledge of reggae or Rastafarianism, it would make sense if they were also made aware of its historical
roots and the role played by individuals such as Haile Selassie in shaping contemporary global popular culture. Indeed, as globalization continues to bring
disparate locations and peoples closer, it is crucial to model positive attitudes in
young learners in an effort to continue supporting this tolerance. Through planting positive attitudes of other countries in the world, students have the potential
to become more tolerant and hopefully rally for justice and equality for all. How
might this be achieved? While there are various ways to teach African history,
we propose a pop culture medium to teaching this slice of African history
through music.

Pedagogical Approach of Pop Culture

Teachers must move away from the usual dichotomous approach to teaching
African history that mainly tends to highlight economic and political history of
oppression and exploitation. While not denying these historical realities and
their continued effects on the continent to date, a popular culture approach allows for African agency to define the continent's history. This agency says that
Africans did respond variably to slavery, colonization, and imperialism and
highlights the different outcomes of such responses. One of these responses, as
mentioned above, is the desire for a unified Africa that was pursued by Haile

Selassie and other African leaders that culminated in the formation of the Organization of African Unity. We now see that this approach also connects Africa to the Diaspora as Bob Marley takes up Selassie's speech to the LON and turns it into a song titled "War." In the song, Marley sings "Until the philosophy which holds/One race superior and another inferior/is finally and permanently discredited and abandoned/I say war" (www.elyrics.net).

Popular culture allows for African history to become alive and to show the ways in which Africans are not only active in shaping their lives but also connected to others located far away but who share a similar heritage and aspirations. Teaching African history through popular culture also allows students to see the value of using material culture as windows into people's past. Moreover, using Bob Marley as well as Haile Selassie together in a history lesson allows for clear connections to be made between Africa and the African Diaspora, which in itself departs from a tendency to teach Africa as a separate entity from the world.

Perhaps more importantly, since the usual representation of Africa's relationship to world history has been through two major themes of colonialism and slavery, which tend to emphasize power relations, educators miss out on seizing the opportunity to address issues of chauvinistic attitudes by teaching students how to live as global citizens. Here we provide an example of how to introduce similar issues but through popular culture, which not only allows students to see music as a window into African history, but also connect the continent to the rest of the world (Caribbean, Americas, Israel, Europe, etc.).

Historically, music has been an art form that reflects societies' cultures. In recent history, popular music has become a synthesizing platform for both entertainment and a source of power for the oppressed to voice their political and social messages. Hence, these are the dominant characteristics of reggae music, which originated from the Trench Town ghetto of Jamaica in the 1960s. From its inception, reggae music became a manifesto for liberty as the lyrics mainly expressed the dire conditions experienced by the poor, who were mainly Blacks, living under the rule of European occupation in Jamaica. Reggae music expanded its reach and became the genre widely associated with Pan-Africanism as well as liberation for all oppressed peoples. Its strong lyrical incantation has been espoused around the world because they tend to propagate political resistance, peace, anti-colonialism, Pan-Africanism, anti-racism, social injustice, and poverty struggles among other issues that dominate the global order. One particular vocalist of Haile Selassie's legacy and who is widely recognized by many is legendary Reggae musician Bob Marley[6] who in 1976 produced the song "War" whose lyrics are interpolated from Selassie's speech to the LON. We choose this song not only because is it well produced and entertaining, but also because the lyrics have the potential to encourage students to think critically in regard to the strong resolve of Africa during the struggle for freedom. Teachers of African history can use this lesson as a good window to introduce students to other facets of African history as well due to the easy accessibility of popular music and its ability to connect with diverse student groups in ways that texts may not.

Lesson Plan

The Legacy of Haile Selassie and Africa's Place in World History

Audience and Discipline
This lesson is intended for advanced high school and introductory college courses. It is best suited as a three-hour unit in a world history course or African history course.

Commentary
This lesson is centered in the discussion of Africa in relation to world history. It is not a substitute for addressing the devastations of colonialism in Africa, but rather an attempt to incite a dialogue in the classroom that portrays Africans not just as the colonized, but also as people who, through the struggle for independence, influenced themselves as well as the entire world history.

Lesson Summary
In this lesson unit, students will uncover the inextricable legacy of Emperor Haile Selassie in relation to the Pan-African and independence movement that contributed to the liberation of African descendants in Africa and in the Diaspora.

Facilitating Discussion
• Understand the students' perception of Africa by having them generate a list of the things they know about the African continent and write them on a board.
• From the list, analyze the stated and the unstated assumptions of Africa in relation to world history.
• Help students deconstruct some of their assumptions by providing more nuanced information about the continent. For instance, if students mention civil war and drought as their images of Africa, help them actually identify the number of countries out of the fifty-three that are involved in civil war and show the danger of using a few cases to represent a vast continent.

- Facilitate a dialogue with the students on how those assumptions develop and how they may impact their own relations to Africa and Africa's place in and relations to global affairs.
- Ask students to identify positive things about Africa and then go through steps similar to those above in helping them understand how such images come about and how they would shape their own relations with Africa as well as Africa's relations to the world.
- Encourage students to reflect on those positive things as they engage in the learning of this lesson and if possible find stories that students can identify with which articulate such positive things about Africa.

Instructional Materials
- Media player
- A copy of Haile Selassie I speech
-              A map of Africa
- The 1976 *War* by Bob Marley

Learning Objectives
- To highlight African history from a balanced approach that recognizes Africa as an active player in world history.
- To familiarize students with the legacy of Haile Selassie and the pan-African movement that led to the formation of Organization of African Unity (currently known as African Union).
- To aid students understand the world, past and present, as they create a cognitive map of world history.
- To prompt a critical worldview in order to promote tolerance as communities around the globe increasingly become connected.

Lesson Content
- How Ethiopia evaded colonization by fighting two wars with Italian invaders (the 1896 Battle of Adwa, and the 1936-1939 war against Benito Mussolini's army).
- The rise to the throne and influence of Haile Selassie in the African struggle for independence.
- The impetus that led to the establishment of the Organization for African Unity.
- The influences of Haile Selassie in promoting tolerance and social liberties around the world.
- The linkage of Haile Selassie to Pan-Africanism and the Rastafarian movement.

Lesson Procedures

Pre-Lesson Students' Preparation

- Ask the students prior to the lesson to conduct a brief research about Bob Marley, Rastafarianism, or Haile Selassie and bring an artifact of their choice to the classroom. For instance, students could bring to class some examples of songs by Bob Marley that they like or have listened to and explain why they like them. The teacher can then assist the students make some connections between the relevant artifacts with Africa, the Reggae movement, Bob Marley, Ethiopia and Rastafarianism.
- Students might also bring a hat, scarf, or bumper sticker of Rastafarianism and have the teacher help them make sense of the dominant colors on the artifacts and what they symbolize of Africa and its Diaspora.

Instructional Procedures
- This lesson would be best offered as a lecture that incorporates students discussion.
- Provide biographic literature of Haile Selassie.
- Provide students with a copy of the October 4th, 1963 speech that Haile Selassie gave to the League of Nations (currently United Nations) available at http://www.whattheproblemis.com/documents/aw/aw_Haile_Selassie_1963_UN_Speech.pdf.
- After the students have read the speech, play the 1976 Bob Marley song "War", whose lyrics are interpolated from the speech and can be found here: http://www.youtube.com/watch?v=2PF3AoKakAw.
- Form discussion groups and let students apply critical thinking as they discuss the context and content of the speech and report their analysis to the class.
- Provide short remarks on other African eminent figures that contributed to the liberation of Africa, such as Kwame Nkrumah, Patrice Lumumba, Nelson Mandela, and Amilca Cabral.
- Wrap up with questions and comments from students.

Students' Learning Outcomes

- Learners will be able to explain how Ethiopia evaded colonization through the two battles with Italian invaders.
- Learners will be able to state how Ethiopia became the first African country to be a signatory of the United Nations.

- Students will be able to explain the conditions in Africa that led to the formation of the Organization of African Unity (OAU).
- Learners will have the ability to state the rationale that established Pan-Africanism and hence the impetus for the Rastafarian movement.
- Learners will have the ability to analyze various ways that Africa has changed the course of modern history—particularly, the use of decolonization to institute the current global morality that is free of adverse imperialism.
- Learners will recognize the role popular culture plays in providing a window into history.

Conclusion

As the world increasingly becomes more and more interconnected and people from different social, economic, and political backgrounds interact and work together, a nuanced understanding of where they are coming from and their historical connections to today's word are critical. Part of our global changes have been brought by increased technological advancements and the exchange of information and even ideas, but the more information seems to be available to us, the less time (it seems) people are willing to invest in getting a deeper understanding of self and others. Clearly Reggae is a worldwide musical phenomenon, and Bob Marley is a household name in many parts of the world. And yet few high school and college students have probably made any connections between African history and Reggae. As teachers, we have a great opportunity to introduce students to the intricate history of Africa and other areas of the world, and one way to engage them is to bring to our teaching fresh perspectives and approaches that not only complicate otherwise assumed simple historical matters regarding Africa but also provide them a tool they can relate to in approaching such a perspective. By using Reggae and the life of Haile Selassie I, we have deliberately moved history teachers from the well-travelled path and introduced them to an exciting and hopefully more engaging way of teaching African history. In doing so we hope that African history will be treated with the complexity it deserves while allowing students to dive into it through a familiar window of popular culture.

Endnotes

1. See discussions of this kind of teaching in, among others, E. Perry Hicks and Barry K. Beyer, (1970), "Images of Africa," *Journal of Negro Education*, Vol. 39 (2):158-166; Barbara Wass Van Ausdall, (1988), "Images of Africa for American Students," *The English Journal*, Vol. 77 (5): 37-39; Barbara B. Brown, (1994), "Africa: Myth and Reality," *Social Education*, pp. 374-375; and Sheila S. Walker and Jennifer Rasmim-

anana, (1993), "Tarzan in the Classroom: How 'Educational' Films Mythologize Africa and Miseducate Americans," *The Journal of Negro Education*, Vol. 62 (1): 3-23.
2. John Reader's *A Biography of the Continent: Africa* gives a detailed biography of the African continent over time. This biography chronicles Africa beginning from the continent's formation, emerging of humanity, the early African civilizations and empires, migrations, foreign influences, settlers, and postcolonial Africa.
3. See Georg Hegel, *The Philosophy of History*, p. 99.
4. See the 1975 essay by Chinua Achebe, "An Image of Africa: Racism in Conrad's *Heart of Darkness.*" Also see Achebe's interview in *Things Fall Apart.*
5. See the discussion about the common representation of Africa based on selected "notions" of Africa in Jonathan Reynolds, "So Many Africas, So Little Time: Doing Justice to Africa in the World History."
6. Bob Marley also dedicated other songs to the esteem of African identity such as "Zimbabwe" which he performed in 1980 as a guest of honor during Zimbabwe's independence ceremony, and "Exodus," which he recorded in 1977.

References

Achebe, C. (Winter, 1977). An image of Africa. *The Massachusetts Review*, 18(4), 782-794.
Achebe, C. (2009). *Things Fall Apart.* [Irele Francis, ed]. New York: W.W. Norton & Company, Inc.
Allain, J. (2006). Slavery and the League of Nations: Ethiopia as a civilized nation. *Journal of the History of International Law*, 8, 213-244.
Bernth, L. (1991). *Approaches to Teaching Achebe's 'Things Fall Apart.'* New York: The Modern Languages of America Associations.
Brown, B.B. (1994). Africa: Myth and reality. *Social Education*, 54 (6), 374-375.
Campbell, C. (2006). Sculpting a Pan-African Culture in the art of Negritude: A model of African artist. *Journal of Pan-African Studies*. 1(6).
Cooper, F. (1994, December). Conflict and connection: Rethinking colonial African history. AHR Forum. *American Historical Review*.
Goucher, C. (2004). Connecting African History to the Major Themes of World History. *World History Connected*, 2(1).
Gran, P. (1996). *Beyond Eurocentrism: A New View of Modern World History.* Syracuse, NY: Syracuse University Press.
Haggai, E. (2002). *The Cross and the River: Ethiopia, Egypt, and the Nile.* Boulder, CO: Lynne Rienner Publishers.
Hegel, G. (1956). *The Philosophy of History.* New York: Dover Publications.
Hicks, E.P., and Beyer, B.K. (1970). Images of Africa. *Journal of Negro Education*, 39 (2), 158-166.
Hook, S. (1992). *The Hero in History: A Study in Limitation and Possibility.* New Brunswick, NJ: Transaction Publishers.
Hunt, D. (2004). Teaching about the Africa in the context of World History. *World History Connected*, 2(1).

Imperial Ethiopia. (n.d). Reflections on Haile Selassie. Retrieved from http://www.imperialethiopia.org/selassie.htm.

Keim, C. (2009). *Mistaking Africa: Curiosities and Inventions of the American Mind*, 2nd ed. Westview Press.

Leonard, B. (1997). *The Rastafarians*. Boston, MA: Beacon Press.

Liffe, J. (1987). *The African Poor: A History: Vol. 58. African Studies*. Cambridge, NY: Cambridge University Press.

Mazrui, A. (1993). *Africa since 1935. Vol. VIII UNESCO General History of Africa*. Heinemann, CA. UNESCO.

Marley, R. War. *Elyrics.net*. Retrieved 8/8/12 from http://www.elyrics.net/read/b/bob-marley-lyrics/war-lyrics.html.

Page, M. (2003). *Colonialism: An International Social, Cultural, and Political Encyclopedia*. Santa Barbara, CA: ABC-CLIO, INC.

Reader, J. (1997). *A Biography of the Continent*. New York: First Vintage Books.

Reynolds, J. (2004). So many Africas, So Little Time: Doing justice to Africa in the world history. *World History Connected, 2*(1).

Rich, E., et al. (1990). *A Greater Voice for Africa in the Schools: A Report Prepared for the Rockefeller Foundation*. New York: The Foundation.

United Nations. Basic Facts about the United Nations, 2000. Retrieved from http://www.un.org/aboutun/history.htm.

Van Ausdall, B.W. (1988). Images of Africa for American students. *The English Journal, 77* (5), 37-39.

Vaughan, M. (1994). Colonial Discourse Theory and African History, or has postmodernism passed us by? *Social Dynamics*. 20(1), 1-23.

Vestal, T. (2011). *The Lion of Judah in the New World: Emperor Haile Selassie of Ethiopia and the Shaping of American Attitudes toward Africa*. Santa Barbara, CA: ABC-CLIO, LLC.

Walker, S. & Rasmimanana, J. (1993). Tarzan in the classroom: How 'Educational' Films Mythologize Africa and Miseducate Americans. *Journal of Negro Education, 62*(1), 3-23.

Chapter Eleven

Popular Culture and Teacher Education in the Twenty-First Century: The Pedagogical Possibilities of *Aliens in America*

Ludovic A. Sourdot

In the past thirty years, America's classrooms have become increasingly more diverse. In April 2010 the Census Bureau reported that in that time frame (1980-2007), the percentage of speakers of non-English languages grew by 140 percent while the nation's overall population grew by 34 percent. Other significant data indicates that more than 55.4 million individuals (or 20 percent of the population five and older in the United States) reported speaking a language other than English at home (United States Census Bureau, 2010). It is estimated that there are more than three-hundred languages other than English spoken in homes across our country. At the same time, the teaching population in the United States has remained homogeneous. According to data released by the National Center for Education Information, the public school teaching force is still dominated by white females: 84 percent of all teachers are white female, up from 69 percent in 1986. However, a new trend has emerged in the past decade: the development of alternative certification programs has helped the raise the number of male Hispanics and Blacks into the teaching profession (National Center for Education Information). It appears that alternative certification programs are able to attract individuals looking for a second career or people who did not originally major in education.

Despite recent progress in the diversification of the public school teaching population in the United States, much more needs to be done to prepare pre-service teachers to serve the needs of all students in the United States. Looking back at my own training, I often felt that I was not adequately prepared to meet the needs of English Language learners or students whose background was different than mine. In my past experiences teaching in public schools and now at the college level (preparing a new generation of educators) I have found that using popular culture was helpful in presenting and debating questions about diversity with teacher candidates. I first speculated about the possibilities *Aliens in America* (Guarascio & Port, 2007) present for education with my colleague Steve Carpenter a few years ago (Carpenter & Sourdot, 2011). I have used the television sitcom *Aliens in America*[1] for several years and I have found it to be a very useful tool in preparing pre-service educators to apply culturally responsive teaching strategies and in turn empower students to embrace diversity and the democratic principles of our nation. In this chapter, I describe the ways in which I have since used *Aliens in America* with teacher candidates and how such programming can be used as an effective teaching tool to prepare future teachers to meet the challenges of the twenty-first century classroom.

Alien Identity

I first became interested in *Aliens in America* because it describes the struggles of a foreign exchange student coming to America to pursue his education. In the show, Raja Musharraf struggles to adapt to a new environment, culture, and customs. While Raja's character is fictional, the difficulties he experiences in the show are very close to what I personally encountered when I came to the United States in the mid-1990s. Upon watching several episodes of the series, I realized that the "Alien" in America portrayed on the screen was a true reflection of myself fifteen years ago. My personal background, life history, and education have clearly influenced my decision to investigate *Aliens in America*. My upbringing in France, my life experience, and my education on two continents have had a profound impact on my beliefs and values. My experiences growing up in France, the education I received in the United States while attending university help my worldview but also traveling as a young man visiting foreign countries such as, Australia, the United Kingdom and several other countries in Western Europe.

As stated above, my investigation of *Aliens in America* is not an autobiography, but since the inspiration for this study is deeply rooted in my own personal experiences, I feel that using the first person in this study is appropriate. Over the past several years several scholars have argued that using first person accounts are appropriate in qualitative research. Denzin (1989) described a personal experience story as a narrative study of an individual's personal experience usually found in one or more episodes, private institutions, or communal folklore. In this chapter I share a few personal experiences as described by Denzin (1989) that provide insight into my own perspective. The examples I share also provide the reader insights into my own identity. Slattery gives the following definition for autobiography:

[Autobiography] can be understood as a partial narrative or a comprehensive life history of the self, psychoanalytic investigations of the self, analysis of identity constructions, investigations of past, present, and future dimensions of the self by an individual, a written text describing one's life journey and future goals, or possibly even distortions, delusions, and embellishments about one's life history. (P. Slattery, personal communication, March 7, 2009)

Slattery (2009) and Denzin (1989) tell us that a researcher's voice is not only acceptable within qualitative research, but that it may also help make significant connections between one's experiences within a cultural or social context. In this study I will therefore use the first person. I feel that Leggo (2008) summarized best my beliefs on inserting autobiographical elements to academic writing:

Because so much of my teaching, writing and researching emerge from the intersections of the personal and the professional, I contend that autobiographical writing is always both personal and professional, and that we need to write autobiographically in order to connect with others. (Leggo 2008, p. 90)

In this chapter, I not only aim to connect with others, but to share my work about *Aliens in America,* a television sitcom with tremendous possibilities for education. Over the past few decades, the television medium has evolved and has become a legitimate area of study by scholars; a brief overview of this evolution informs on the possibilities television presents for education.

Television

Indeed, the development of the cable and satellite industry in the past twenty-five years has allowed audiences in the United States and around the world to enjoy a wider variety of television programming. In turn, this evolution has sparked the interest of scholars around the globe to investigate television programming, specifically television genres, audience and its effects on TV viewers. For instance, the field of television studies has emerged and gained prominence in the past twenty years; Buckingham (2003), Bignell (2004) and McQueen (1998) specifically looked at the way television has evolved over time and all provided ways to analyze and explore television texts. Buckingham (2003) defines the influence of the media in our lives: "The media, it is often argued, have now taken the place of the family, the church and the school as the major socializing influence in contemporary society" (Buckingham, 2003, p. 5). Buckingham's work informs on the ways the media, including television programming, should be analyzed and carefully studied to prepare a new generation of informed students. Bignell (2004) explains that the field of television studies has emerged in part because of the development of popular television around the world; he believes that popular programming is a legitimate site of inquiry specifically because of its large audience:

> The academic subject of television studies has taken popular television seriously; because it is the television most people watch the most. This is despite the common criticism in the press, and sometimes in the television industry itself, that popular television is unimportant, 'just' commercial, and lacking in artistic values. (p. 3)

In recent years, television networks have capitalized on the popularity of social networking sites such as Facebook, MySpace, and Twitter to enhance and prolong the viewing experience of television audiences. In 1998, McQueen also emphasized the fact that television programming was a worthy subject of inquiry: "How can we afford *not* to study something that has become so central to modern society?"(McQueen, 1998, p. 4). Buckingham (2003), Bignell (2004) and McQueen (1998) all agree that the media, including popular television, are important to study and analyze since they occupy such a big part in the lives of Americans. Scholars in the field of education share the view of Buckingham (2003), Bignell (2004), and McQueen (1998) on the need to study popular culture and especially television and its application to educational contexts. Back in the 1980s, Giroux and McLaren (1989) saw popular culture as a site of interest for educators as "popular culture represents not only a contradictory terrain of struggle, but also a significant pedagogical site that raises important questions about the elements that organize the basis of student subjectivity and experience" (Giroux & McLaren, 1989, p. 238). Over the years several scholars (Jhally & Lewis, 1992; Freedman, 2000; Trier 2005) have investigated the content of television shows, their research primarily focused on race and stereotypes in television shows.

New Shows and the Need for More Research

In the past few years the television landscape has evolved tremendously in the United States. Premium cable channels such as Home Box Office (HBO) and Showtime have produced television shows that have been innovative and at times controversial in nature (*Sex and the City, Big Love, Californication, Breaking Bad, Dexter*). Cable channels such as Comedy Central and MTV have also offered more controversial programming with shows such as *South Park* and more recently *Skins*.[2] The increased dominance of reality TV in recent years appears to have also influenced TV executives into promoting shows that are more provocative than in years past (*Nip/Tuck, Gossip Girl*). In *South Park* and *Reno 911!*, as is also the case with several other shows, humor is very often achieved while poking fun at a character's religion, gender, ethnicity, physical appearance, and sexual orientation. Therefore, there is a need for more research on the television medium and its implications for education. I chose to focus my attention on the television show *Aliens in America* broadcast on the CW network between October 2007 and May 2008. I selected this particular show because I felt it offered an interesting combination of factors worthy of inquiry.

Why Investigate *Aliens in America*?

Aliens in America, primarily dealing with the interactions of a young Pakistani Muslim in a predominantly white state (Wisconsin) in the post 9/11 era, was especially interesting to me. The plotline that consists of transplanting outsiders to a new environment is not revolutionary; this concept has been used in many occasions on television, most notably with the *Beverly Hillbillies* (1962-1971), *Beverly Hills 90210* (1990-2000), and *The O.C* (2003-2007). In the *Beverly Hillbillies* a hillbilly family leaves a southern state to move to California, the show chronicled the clash of cultures between the hillbillies and the sophisticated Californians. In *Beverly Hills 90210*, the Walsh family moved from Minnesota to Beverly Hills where Brenda and Brandon had to adapt to a new lifestyle. In *The O.C.* (2003-2007) a wealthy family adopts a troubled teenager; the show centered on the interactions of the adopted son with a group of local teenagers. In January 2007, The Canadian Broadcasting Corporation premiered *Little Mosque on the Prairie*, a sitcom about a small community of Muslims living in Central Canada. The Canadian Broadcasting Corporation became the first major North American media outlet to broadcast a show about Muslims. A few months later, *Aliens in America* premiered on the CW network becoming the first sitcom in the United States to feature a Muslim character in a starring role. I felt that a show focusing on a Muslim character evolving in a predominantly white region of the United States deserved further scrutiny.

Aliens in America is a sitcom set in suburban Wisconsin and centers on the lives of a white family who welcome a foreign exchange student into their home. The Tolchucks anticipate that their teenage son Justin will become more popular at school by associating with an international student. In the first episode, their plan takes an unexpected turn when the family, expecting to host a blond-haired, blue-eyed Scandinavian high school student, instead meets Raja, a Muslim teenager from Pakistan. The title of the show, *Aliens in America*, is a play on words in that the lead characters Justin, an American student, and Raja, a Pakistani exchange student, are both treated, constructed, and consider themselves as *aliens* at school and at home. They are both aliens in different ways, and this reality renders them quite similar. *Aliens in America* is also interesting because it portrays teenagers interacting with one another in and outside of school. The show also deals with the representations of interactions between Muslims and Americans in the post 9/11 era and presented many areas of interest when working with teacher candidates.

My decision to use *Aliens in America* was also motivated by the work of multicultural educator Walter Stephan (1999) whose research on the subjects of prejudice stereotypes had a tremendous influence on my life and teaching. Based on his examination of research, he concludes that stereotypes are "frequently negative, overgeneralized, and incorrect" (Stephan, 1999, p.16); this definition summarizes very accurately the depiction of Muslims in the news media following the attacks of 9/11. News reports were too often inaccurate and portrayed Islam as a religion of hate. In his research Stephan also points out that "people tend to pay more attention to information confirming stereotypes and remember it better than disconfirming evidence" (p.17). This last finding shows that it would take a significant amount of positive media coverage in order to change the way TV audiences feel about Muslims.

Aliens in America first aired on the CW in October 2007. However, David Guarascio and Moses Port (the creators of the show) started planning for the sitcom in 2005. In an interview with National Public Radio (N.P.R), they explained that they used the geopolitical situation between the United States and the rest of the world as a source of inspiration (Gross & Miller, 2007). Therefore, the show cannot be dissociated from the geopolitical context of the post 9/11 era. However there are several other reasons why *Aliens in America* deserved a closer examination. The first reason has to do with the fact the CW network is the only broadcast network that targets young adults between the ages of eighteen and thirty-four. Several shows broadcast on this network portray teenagers and children, therefore people that are younger than the targeted audience are likely to watch these shows. The CW network emerged after the WB network (owned by Time Warner) and the United Paramount Network (owned by CBS) ceased their broadcasting operations in September 2006 (Seid, 2006). The acronym CW combines the "C" from CBS and the "W" from Time Warner. The decision to combine the two operations came after years of low ratings for the two networks, combined with losses in advertising revenue.

In order to reach their goal of reaching young adults between the ages of eighteen and thirty-four the network has developed a strong presence on the Web to support and promote their programming. For example, the CW has set up several "lounges" or online communities on its web site to allow viewers to interact and share ideas and feelings about the show with other viewers across the country. The CW is also very active on the social networking site Facebook where viewers have access to previews of their favorite show, watch behind-the-scenes footage and interviews of cast members. The CW's target audience combined with its innovative efforts to reach younger viewers on the World Wide Web through blogs and social networking influenced my decision to investigate a show broadcast on the CW network.

The broadcast networks took notice and realized that in order to bring viewers back they would have to be creative. The ABC network, owned by Disney, released two new shows during the 2004-2005 season: *Lost*[3] follows the lives of several individuals who after surviving a plane crash try to adapt to living on a deserted island, while *Grey's Anatomy*[4] follows a group of surgical interns in and out of Seattle Grace hospital. These two shows are significant since they are representative of new marketing strategies launched by the American Broadcasting Corporation (ABC) and other major cable outlets. These networks set up multimedia platforms to promote their shows, spark interest in the public, and make devoted fans out of the viewers. Newspaper and magazine advertisement campaigns are now supplemented by exclusive previews on the network's World Wide Web site. In the past decade, the American broadcasting Company (ABC) has become a leader in web presence to promote shows. The network, owned by The Walt Disney Company, spared no expense in promoting the show; it even created a web site for Oceanic airlines, the fictional airline whose jetliner crashed on the island (Oceanic Air, 2003). ABC also markets T-shirts with lines or quotes from *Grey's Anatomy* on its web site. *Grey's* fans can interact with other fans of the show on bulletin boards, learn about the journey each character went through since first appearing on the show, or even find out more information about a medical condition or injuries described in the latest episode. TV viewers can also catch up on their favorite show online where every episode is streamed the day after the show airs on ABC. They may also elect to download their favorite episodes from iTunes or hulu.com; *Lost* was one of the first television shows offered on iTunes in October 2005 (Apple Inc., 2005).

These marketing strategies are new and were made possible because of an increase in the number of households in the United States with broadband Internet access. *Lost* and *Grey's Anatomy* are not only relevant because of their marketing strategies but also because of the quality of the plots. According to Johnson (2005), the fact is that these types of shows make viewers think:

> Some narratives force you to do work to make sense of them, while others just let you settle into the couch and zone out. Part of that cognitive work comes from following multiple threads, keeping often densely interwoven plotlines distinct in your head as you watch. But another part involves the viewer's "filling in": making sense of information that has been either deliberately withheld or deliberately left obscure. Narratives that require that their viewers fill in crucial elements take that complexity to a more demanding level. To follow the narrative, you aren't just asked to remember. You're asked to analyze. This is the difference between intelligent shows and shows that force you to be intelligent. (Johnson, 2005, pp. 63-64)

It appears that shows such as *Aliens in America* are the result of a reaction of broadcast networks to the success of shows offered on premium cable networks such as HBO and Showtime. The increased dominance of reality TV in recent years has also pushed TV executives to promote and offer shows that are more provocative than in years past. In recent years, in several shows such as NBC's *Outsourced,* MTV's *Jackass,* Fox's *Family Guy,* CBS's *Two Broke Girls,* and TBS's *Sullivan and Son* humor is often achieved while poking fun at a character's religion, gender, ethnicity, physical appearance, or sexual orientation. *Aliens in America* falls under this new wave of more provocative television programming.

Television programming is not static, it evolves and adapts to new technology. Viewers crave interactivity (Johnson, 2005) and enjoy being challenged to think about a complicated plot in *Lost*, to identify with bad guys such as *Breaking Bad*, to fantasize about romance and love with ABC's *Revenge* or the CW's *The Vampire Diaries*, or to simply go back to their high school years and identify with characters and issues encountered by the characters in *Aliens in America*.

Popular Culture, Television, and the Challenges for Educators

The television medium falls under the broader umbrella of popular culture. In 1987 art educator Paul Duncum defined popular culture as "as a mass-produced, mass-distributed, and mass-consumed artifact; typically involving content that is relatively clear and simple; and produced by a small group of professionals for the consumption of others" (Duncum, 1987, p. 6). Cultural scholars Joe Kincheloe and Peter McLaren see popular culture as a domain of struggle:

> Dominant and subordinate cultures deploy differing systems of meaning based on the forms of knowledge produced in their cultural domain. Popular culture with its TV, movies, video games, computers, music, dance and other productions plays an increasingly important role in critical research on power and domination (Kincheloe & McLaren, 2005, p. 310).

In 1994 another scholar of critical pedagogy, Henry Giroux, called for educators "to be informed by [the] emphasis on popular culture as a terrain of significant political and pedagogical importance" (Giroux, 1994). He believed that popular culture is a powerful influence on students; he wrote, "How we understand and come to know ourselves and others cannot be separated from how we are represented and imagine ourselves" (Giroux, 1997, p. 14). Giroux believes that the news media and popular culture are powerful forces that influence the way children see themselves and others. Brady (1997) also wrote about the relationship between education and popular culture:

> School is an important site where the construction of a narrow range of identities not only takes place but can be challenged pedagogically. ...It is around the relationship between popular culture and education that an approach can be theorized that will enable people (teachers, parents, boys, girls, administrators) to intervene in the formation of their own subjectivities and to enable and exercise power in the interest of transforming forms of domination and conditions of oppression into emancipatory practices and democratic possibilities. Educators must become more attentive to the various pedagogical sites (both in and out of narratives of a national past, present and future. (Brady, 1997, p. 224)

Brady (1997) was concerned with the ways in which the relationship between popular culture and education could be beneficial and lead to emancipatory and democratic practices. It appears, that several scholars have agreed and followed Brady (1997) in the study of what she described as "the relationship between popular culture and education" (p. 224). Giroux (2000) revisited the work of cultural studies theorist Stuart Hall and concluded that Hall's work "provides an important theoretical framework for developing an expanded notion of public pedagogy" (Giroux, p. 341). Wright & Sandlin (2009) describe public pedagogy as "a term referring to the educational force of popular media" (Wright & Sandlin, p. 118). They also looked at popular culture's applications to adult education and noted that popular culture presents is a powerful pedagogical tool:

> Individual life experiences, beliefs, morals, ethics, political choices, and personal philosophies—our identities—are filtered through the images, commentary, and artful editing of the forces that operate through popular culture. Popular culture as a facilitator of, and catalyst for, self-directed learning can bring about learning that is far more powerful, lasting, and lifelong than learning in formal educational settings and other traditionally researched areas of teaching and learning. It must also be a site for ever-expanding educational research into that learning. (Wright & Sandlin, 2009, p. 135)

While Wright and Sandlin recognize the power of popular culture for lifelong learning, they also recommend that more research be conducted on the subject. Sandlin, along with Schultz and Burdick, brought together a group of artists, scholars, activists, and public intellectuals to help define the field of public pedagogy. This work informs on the "concepts and practices" of public pedagogy and "provides new ways of understanding educational practice, both within and without schools" (Sandlin, Schultz, & Burdick, 2011). Brady (1997), Giroux (2000), Wright and Sandlin (2009), Sandlin, Schultz and Burdick (2011) all agree that popular culture is a powerful pedagogical tool; they also realize that more research needs to be conducted on this topic. However, popular culture is also worthy of inquiry because of the challenges it poses to educators across the country.

Cortés (2000) is also concerned with the influence of popular culture on children and introduced the idea that children are exposed to several curricula on a daily basis. He identified "the immediate curriculum, the institutional curriculum, and the media curriculum" (Cortés, 2000, p.18). In a television interview with *The Open Mind*, Cortés explained that the media curriculum is "very powerful and can greatly influence children of all ages" (*The Open Mind*, 2000). Multicultural theorist Geneva Gay also felt that television can have a negative effect on our youth and our schools: "The images are too easily accessible and their influence is too powerful for teachers to ignore how ethnic groups and issues are represented in television programming. …Students bring this information and its effects to the classroom with them" (Gay, 2000, p.123). Mahiri (2000-2001) takes a different stand and argues that educators must find ways to adopt some elements of popular culture in their teaching to connect with students:

If schooling is to survive ...I suggest that teachers continue to become more aware of the motives and methods of youth engagement in pop culture in terms of why and how such engagement connects to students' personal identifications, their needs to construct meanings, and their pursuit of pleasures and personal power. Teachers should explore how work in schools can make similar connections to students' lives, but the real challenge is to make these connections to and through changing domains of knowledge, critical societal issues, and cognitive and technical skills that educators can justify their students will actually need to master the universe of the new century. (Mahiri, 2000-2001, p. 385)

Scholars view popular culture and television as a site of struggle that influences students. They agree that it should not be ignored but instead studied and utilized in the curriculum to reach children. Over the years, several scholars have investigated television shows seeking to answer different questions. A quick review of this body of work is necessary to place this study of *Aliens in America* in context.

Research on Television and Teacher Education

Over the years, several scholars have investigated the content of various television shows. Jhally & Lewis (1992) conducted a study about stereotypes in *The Cosby Show*. This study is very interesting since these researchers presented the show to black and white American audiences and collected their reactions to the show. McKinley (1992) investigated how the television show *Beverly Hills 90210* influenced the ways in which young female viewers constructed their identity. Freedman (2000) studied the television show *Dangerous Minds* with pre-service teachers through a cultural studies framework and examined its influences on their perceptions of students of color. Trier (2005) has studied extensively the ways in which students and teachers are represented in films such as *Mr. Holland's Opus, The Breakfast Club,* and *Dangerous Minds.* Watson (2006) provided an interesting analysis of the television show *Ally McBeal* broadcast between 1997 and 2002 in the United States on the Fox television network. These scholars specifically analyzed why this show became so popular and examined issues of sexuality and feminism in the show. Finally, Bindig (2008) explored the television show *Dawson's Creek* through a feminist cultural studies perspective. These studies were very informative and allowed me to understand the type of shows that had been investigated in the past. It also helped me realize that television programming had evolved tremendously in the past decade. These studies also provided me with some valuable background into the way these movies and television shows are being watched and analyzed by viewers. However, Jhally and Lewis's study was published fifteen years ago. Trier's analysis is more recent, but he utilizes movies produced in the 1980s and 1990s. Freedman conducted her study in 2000, but here again she investigated a television show that aired during the 1996-1997 season. McKinley's work was published in 1992; Bindig's book was published in 2008, but her analysis is about a show that had been off the air for five years, as did Watson (2006).

Therefore, there is a need for more research looking at television programming that specifically targets young viewers, since in the past few years the television landscape has evolved so much in America. It is why I selected *Aliens in America,* which belongs to this new category of shows, for this study. The show targets young viewers, specifically while achieving humor poking fun at ethnic, cultural, racial, religious, and other forms of identity.

In the past few years, the development and widespread use of mobile technology has made television programming available to more people virtually anywhere. Individuals wanting to watch TV have more options and more choice than ever; major television-set manufacturers have launched TV equipped to receive 3-D signals. Television viewers are now even able to catch their favorite shows on the go through Hulu.com, Netflix.com, and Apple's iTunes. Television is, therefore, more relevant than ever.

Research Design

In this study, my goal was to examine the content of the television medium through the study of the sitcom *Aliens in America* broadcast on the CW network. I was especially interested in the ways in which teacher candidates would read and perceive the show, and how the show may be used as a tool to prepare future educators to meet the challenges of the twenty-first century classroom. I have used *Aliens in America* with several groups of undergraduate students over the past two academic years. I have shown the television sitcom to teacher candidates enrolled in a learning theory course I teach several times a year. Most students enrolled in this course are undergraduate students majoring in interdisciplinary studies; a few students major in another field (art, dance, history, mathematics, and science majors) and minor in education. In order to become certified to teach in the state of Texas, undergraduate students must hold a bachelor's degree, complete observation hours in public schools, successfully complete a semester-long in the field (student-teaching) and pass two certification tests. The first test aims at assessing their content knowledge, the second one at assessing their mastery of Texas education law, professional responsibilities, and best practices. Each course taken by teacher candidates is therefore tied to the pedagogies and professional responsibilities test (PPR). The learning theory course I teach focuses on the work and practical classroom application of theorists such as Jean Piaget, Lev Vygotsky, Erik Eriksson, Lawrence Kohlberg, Carol Gilligan, Albert Bandura, Urie Brofenbrenner, and Howard Gardner. Once students have gained a good understanding of the work of these influential theorists I invite them to investigate different ways to connect with students, through popular culture. I indicate on the syllabus distributed at the beginning of the semester that popular culture will be discussed; however, students are not aware of the nature of the activity in advance. I intentionally choose not to reveal how popular culture is going to be discussed in class in order to get teacher candidates to think about the pedagogical possibilities of popular television in various educational settings.

For this study a qualitative research approach was used. Merriam (1988) explained that in a qualitative approach the main objective is to understand "the meaning of an experience" (p. 16). She added that "qualitative research assumes that there are multiple realities—that the world is not an objective thing out there but a function of personal interaction and perception. It is a highly subjective phenomenon in need of interpreting rather than measuring" (p. 17). She concluded, "in qualitative research one is interested in process, meaning, and understanding" (p.19). Denzin and Lincoln (2005) explained that the qualitative researcher uses various methods to make sense and interpret phenomena, Creswell (2007) went further and explained that the final report of a qualitative study is an extensive document reflective of the views held by all parties involved: "The final written report involves or presentation includes the voices of participants, the reflexivity of the researcher, and a complex description and interpretation of the problem, and it extends the literature, or signals a call for action" (Creswell, 2007, p. 37).

For these reasons, I felt that a qualitative approach would allow me to accurately describe and interpret the perceptions of teacher candidates to the show. This approach also allowed me to understand the meaning-making process they went through while watching the show. For this study, I used a questioning technique originally developed by art educator Terry Barrett to interpret works of art. I turned to Barrett (2002) because his questioning strategies allow viewers of art (in this case a television sitcom) to describe, analyze and interpret. Barrett's definition of the interpretive process matches what I wanted to achieve with teacher candidates in this study: "To interpret is to respond in thoughts and feelings and actions to what we see and experience, and to make sense of our responses by putting them into words" (Barrett, 2002, p. 291). In order for teacher candidates to interpret the actions depicted on the screen, I distributed a handout to teacher candidates with Barrett's three questions:

1) What do you see?
2) What does it mean?
3) How do you know?

These questions allowed teacher candidates to describe and interpret what they were seeing on the screen. The third question "How do you know?" allowed teacher candidates to back up their claims with specific examples found in the episode of the television sitcom they were watching. Teacher candidates were therefore, encouraged to go beyond the surface and justify their claims with evidence. Teacher candidates were invited to watch the pilot episode of *Aliens in America* while using the three questions to guide their interpretation. Once teacher candidates watched the pilot episode, they were invited to discuss their interpretation of the show with the class. I also gave them an opportunity to

work in small groups and focus specifically on one part of the episode when Raja (the exchange student) is introduced to the class by his teacher. Students were asked to ponder three questions:
1) Do you think the teacher introduced Raja properly?
2) How would you have introduced Raja to his classmates?
3) Please comment on any other themes/situations depicted in the show.

This second activity allowed teacher candidates to go beyond their initial observations about the show. They were also asked to reflect on what was taking place on the screen and provide a solution to a real classroom situation they could face in the future. After the class, I gathered each student's response to allow for a microanalysis of data by using a "detailed line-by-line analysis [used] to generate initial categories (with their perspectives and dimensions) and to suggest relationships among categories" (Strauss & Corbin, 1998, p.57; Sanderson, 2008, p.920).

A Closer Look At *Aliens In America*

As stated earlier in this chapter, *Aliens in America* is about a white suburban family from Wisconsin. The first episode I showed participants in the study was the pilot of *Aliens in America* first broadcast on the CW network on October 1, 2007. In this first installment, viewers are introduced to Justin Tolchuck, a sixteen-year-old high school student who has trouble fitting in with his peers in high school in Medora, Wisconsin. His mother, Franny, desperate to improve his social life, meets with school counselor Mr. Matthews, who convinces her to welcome an exchange student into their home and help Justin's social skills. The Tolchucks travel enthusiastically to the airport a few days later to pick up their exchange student. The Tolchucks, expecting to welcome a Scandinavian student are very surprised when their new guest turns out to be Raja Musharraf, a sixteen-year-old Muslim from Pakistan. Franny Tolchuck spends the rest of the episode plotting to send Raja home while the young Pakistani attempts to survive his first day of school in the United States. In the end Franny Tolchuck learns that Raja is an orphan and, despite her fears of Muslims and foreigners, she decides to let Raja stay in her home.

The show chronicles Raja's experiences as an exchange student in the town of Medora, Wisconsin. The plot of the show is centered on Raja's interactions with the Tolchuck Family. I showed the pilot episode of the show to teacher candidates in order to get a better understanding of the ways in which they perceived the show. The pilot episode (described above) gave teacher candidates a good overview of what *Aliens in America* was about. For example, they had the opportunity to witness the ways in which several racial, ethnic, and religious groups were portrayed in the show. In addition, they were also able to see how the characters interacted with each other in school and in the community. Teacher candidates were able to gain a good understanding of the overall tone and structure of the show, including the ways in which specific groups were portrayed and how humor was achieved.

A close examination of the data collected reveals that participants were concerned with the portrayals of specific characters and institutions. Teacher candidates also made interesting connections between *Aliens in America* and their lived experiences, and focused on the structure of the show, the historical context, the state of the television industry, and its underlying message.

The first and most obvious finding for this study is the level of engagement of teacher candidates in the activity. They were not aware that they would be watching a television show; the syllabus simply stated that the topic to be covered that day was "Popular culture and education." I intentionally decided not to tell students about the activity, since I did not want them to read about *Aliens in America* or view excerpts of the show on Youtube or iTunes. I wanted them to discover and discuss the show with their classmates. I believe that this strategy proved effective since most teacher candidates had never seen a full episode of *Aliens in America* and were therefore able to provide their own opinion about the show. Once they viewed the pilot episode, several students expressed interest in the sitcom, wanting to know more about the show, its creators, and when the show aired. Another interesting finding is the fact that the group of teacher candidates I worked with showed a deep appreciation and knowledge for popular culture.

This knowledge of popular culture was on display when students picked up on references to other television shows. This practice is known as intertextuality. French philosopher and semiotician Julia Kristeva coined the word intertextuality in 1969 in *Word, Dialogue and Novel* (reprinted in Moi, 1986). Allen (2005) gave a useful working definition of intertextuality: "The fundamental concept of intertextuality is that no text, as it might like to appear so, is original and unique-in-itself; rather it is a tissue of inevitable, and to an extent unwitting, references to and quotation from other texts" (Allen, 2005, p.1).

Intertextuality runs rampant throughout the series. For instance, in the pilot episode Raja is walking through the hallway at Medora High School. In the background, comments from random students can be heard, such as, "Apu where is my Slushee." This comment, a racially charged reference to Apu Na-hasapeemapetilon, the Indian convenience store clerk in the popular cartoon television show *The Simpsons,* is directed at Raja, who is from Pakistan. The comment not only assumes no distinction about the contentious relationship between Pakistan and India but also appears to be an attempt by show creators to reference *The Simpsons* and get a laugh out of viewers. In *The Simpsons,* humor is often achieved while making fun of Apu's culture and religious beliefs. During this scene teacher candidates picked up on the reference to *The Simpsons* and understood that this example was simply the reflection of the type of abuse that may take place on high school campuses every day across the country.

During the activity, much time was spent analyzing the portrayal of Claire Tolchuck's boyfriend, Jeffrey. He appears briefly at the end of the pilot episode when all family members are gathered around the dinner table. Jeffrey is an athletic African American; during his first on-screen appearance, he wears a bright red football jersey at the dinner table. Several participants were uneasy about the ways in which Jeffrey was portrayed wearing a football jersey. Most teacher candidates also denounced the stereotypical ways in which Raja and his religious beliefs were portrayed in the pilot episode. They noted that Raja was treated like a terrorist, and that he was not welcomed at school. Other teacher candidates noted that the (white) father constantly asked Raja to do chores at home, "like a servant." The comments made by teacher candidates regarding the portrayals of Raja and Jeffrey sparked a discussion on the depictions of people of color on television. Several participants expressed concerns about the lack of diversity on television shows on broadcast networks.

A majority of teacher candidates were also concerned with some of the sound effects which appeared to cue and influence television viewers to react certain way to the action on the screen. They noted that the creators of the show used audio cues to achieve humor, and also raised interesting points regarding their intentions. Having a screeching sound play in the background when the Tolchucks first meet Raja at the airport clearly appear to suggest that the audience should also feel frightened by individuals who look like the teenage Pakistani Muslim seen on screen. Teacher candidates brought up a point that is crucial to this study: how will younger viewers negotiate this content?

A surprising finding of this study is the fact that teacher candidates appeared to connect with characters depicted in the show. They connected with Raja, a fictional character on the screen, on a personal level, and realized that the situations depicted on the screen were very close to what they had personally experienced themselves while in school. At that particular moment, it appears that teacher candidates recognized that life in schools had not changed that much since they had left high school. In the end, they perceived the show as an accurate reflection of what they could expect to experience in their own classrooms a few months away...this time as teachers.

During a group activity, teacher candidates were also asked to analyze and deconstruct the ways in which Raja was introduced by the teacher and to explain how they would have introduced the young exchange students themselves. I describe the scene below: Raja arrives at Medora High School. Medora is a fictional town used by the show creators. Students stare at Raja and make comments about the *salwar kameez* he is wearing. In this scene, the teacher makes the following announcement as if to take advantage of a teachable moment.

> Today I am going to put aside our lesson because we have a special guest. For one year we will be in the presence of a real-life Pakistani who practices Muslimism. That means we have an opportunity to learn about his culture and he about ours. So let's be in a dialogue. Raja, you are so different from us, how does that feel? (*Aliens in America*, pilot episode).

Raja answers, "I am not sure I understand?" The teacher tells him to "think about it." She turns to the class and asks, "How does everyone else feels about

Raja and his differences?" In response, a student raises her hand, and the teacher invites her to speak. "Well, I guess I feel angry, because his people blew up the buildings in New York," declares the student. The teacher answers "That's good." Raja tries to object and says, "But that is not true." The teacher interrupts, "O.K. Raja, in America you have to wait until you are called on, and I would appreciate a raised hand" (showing Raja how to raise his hand). The teacher then turns to the class again and asks, "Who else is angry at Raja?" Most of the students raise their hands.

This activity allowed teacher candidates to provide their own responses to the "teachable moment" depicted on the screen. In doing so they pictured themselves in the classroom and solved a problem they may encounter in their daily interactions with students. During the activity, all teacher candidates recognized that the teacher did not introduce Raja (the exchange student) properly. They pointed out that the teacher objectified Raja, making him the center of attention, and focusing on the fact he was different than his classmates. Several teacher candidates felt that the teacher's actions set him apart from his peers, making him an outcast instead of making him feel welcomed.

When asked how they would have introduced Raja, teacher candidates showed compassion and described culturally responsive strategies aimed at making Raja feel comfortable in the class. They explained that Raja should have been given an opportunity to introduce himself to his classmates and that the teacher should have focused on the similarities between Raja and his American counterparts. I was encouraged to see that a majority of teacher candidates exhibited empathy for Raja and offered appropriate ways to make him feel welcomed in the classroom. I also felt that teacher candidates were not shy about criticizing the "on screen" teacher, they were more comfortable deciphering and dissecting the teaching strategies (or lack thereof) utilized by the "on screen" teacher instead of having to directly assess their peers.

Throughout the activity teacher candidates were asked to think like teachers, analyze and deconstruct real-life situations. In the discussions that followed the showing of *Aliens in America,* teacher candidates were reminded that America's classrooms are increasingly becoming more diverse (Banks, 2008) and that they will be teaching students with diverse linguistic and cultural backgrounds. Watching *Aliens in America* also reminded them about the necessity to acquire skills and utilize teaching strategies to meet the needs of all students. During this activity it appears that teacher candidates also benefited from seeing a fictional teacher handle specific classroom situations when they reflected on how they would have responded to similar challenges in their own classrooms. Pauly (2006) explained that teacher candidates must be aware that images are powerful modes of communication since they "participate within discourses of meaning and power that have real consequences in children's lives" (Pauly, 2006, p. 118). I also see *Aliens in America* as a great way for teacher candidates to connect with their students and gain a better understanding of the type of television programming their students engage with on a daily basis. Pauly (2006) believes that teacher candidates should know that images are powerful and carry much power: "images, like other languages, carry historically accented, power-bearing meanings, into particular historical, social and political conditions" (Pauly, p. 128). I also believe that if teacher candidates understand the pace, tone, and type of entertainment their students are used to watching they may elect to adjust their pedagogical style to make learning more relevant to students.

Conclusion

My interest in *Aliens in America* stemmed from my own personal experiences as an exchange student in the United States. Upon further investigation, I have found that *Aliens in America* can be an effective tool in preparing teacher candidates to meet the challenges of the twenty-first century classroom. The questioning techniques I used with teacher candidates allowed them to decipher, deconstruct, and analyze the teaching strategies utilized on screen. During the activities, teacher candidates were also given several opportunities to picture themselves in the classroom and reflect upon their own practice. I have also found that using *Aliens in America* enables teacher candidates to formulate their own responses to specific real-life situations they will face in the classroom. Finally, using *Aliens in America* is critical in promoting culturally responsive teaching strategies (Gay, 2000), aimed at providing equitable educational opportunities to students of all cultural backgrounds.

In the past ten years, education policies in the United States have centered on teacher accountability and standardization; however, the inclusion of popular culture in school curricula and teacher preparation programs may help schools reach students using media content they are familiar with. In 2010, the Kaiser Family Foundation surveyed a national sample of third- through twelfth-graders (ages eight to eighteen) and found that "young people live media-saturated lives, spending an average of nearly eight hours a day (seven hours, thirty-eight minutes) consuming media" (Kaiser Family Foundation, 2010, p. 2). Popular culture is a big part of our children's daily lives, therefore schools should utilize this powerful tool to teach students, using media content they are familiar with. Schools should also find ways to equip students with techniques to decipher images to help them make sense of the world they live in. I strongly believe that schools can and should capitalize on the mass media, I also feel that *Aliens in America* can be a very effective tool in preparing teacher candidates who, in turn will empower younger generations to embrace diversity in our multicultural society.

Notes

1. Available on iTunes, several episodes are also available on Youtube.com.

2. *Skins* aired on MTV from January to June 2011. The series is adapted from the British sitcom *Skins*. The show was very controversial in the United States for its depiction of drug use and teenage casual sex. The show was not renewed beyond its first season in the United States.
3. *Lost* ran on ABC from 2004 to 2010. *Lost* was critically acclaimed for its innovative plots widely popular with television audiences worldwide.
4. *Grey's Anatomy* first aired in March 2005 on ABC; it is currently in its ninth season.
5. *Little Mosque in the Prairie* is now available on Hulu.com.

References

Allen, G. (2005). Intertextuality. *The literary encyclopedia*. Retrieved May 10, 2012, from http://www.litencyc.com/php/stopics.php?rec=true&UID=1229

Apple Inc. (2005, October 12). *Apple announces iTunes 6 with 2,000 music videos, Pixar short films & hit TV shows*. Retrieved February 22, 2010, from http://www.apple.com/pr/library/2005/oct/12itunes.html.

Banks, J.A. (2008). *An introduction to multicultural education*. New York: Pearson.

Barrett, T. (2002). Interpreting art: Building communal and individual understandings. In Y. Gaudelius and P. Speirs, (Eds.), *Contemporary issues in art education*. Upper Saddle River, NJ: Prentice Hall.

Bignell, J. (2004). *An introduction to television studies*. London: Routledge.

Bindig, L. (2008). *Dawson's Creek, a critical understanding*. Lanham, MD: Lexington Books.

Brady, J. (1997). Multiculturalism and the American dream. In S.R. Steinberg and J.L. Kincheloe, (Eds.), *Kinder-culture: The corporate construction of childhood*, (pp. 219-226). Boulder, CO: Westview.

Buckingham, D. (2003). *Media education literacy, learning and contemporary culture*. Cambridge, UK: Polity.

Carpenter, B.S., & Sourdot, L.A. (2011). What are you watching?: Pre-service pedagogy and representations of identity in video and television visual culture. In J, Sandlin, B. Schultz, and J. Burdick (Eds.), *Handbook of public pedagogy*. New York: Routledge.

Cortés, C.E. (2000). *The children are watching: How the media teach about diversity*. New York: Teachers College Press.

Creswell, J.W. (2007). *Qualitative inquiry and research designs: Choosing among five approaches*. Thousand Oaks, CA: Sage Publication.

Denzin, N.K. (1989). *Interpretive biography*. Newbury Park, CA: Sage.

Denzin, N.K., & Lincoln, Y.S. (2005). *The Sage handbook of qualitative research*. Thousand Oaks, CA: Sage.

Duncum, P. (1987). What, even Dallas? Popular culture within the art curriculum. *Studies in Art Education, 29*, 6-16.

Freedman, D. (2000). *(Re)presentations of education: Pre-service teachers' interpretations of Dangerous Minds through the lens of media cultural studies*. Unpublished Doctoral Dissertation, The University of Texas, Austin.

Gay, G. (2000). *Culturally responsive teaching, theory, research and practice*. New York: Teachers College Press.

Giroux, H. (1994). Doing cultural studies: youth and the challenge of pedagogy. *Harvard Educational Review, 64*, 278-308.

Giroux, H. (1997). *Channel surfing: Race talk and the destruction of today's youth.* Toronto: Canadian Scholars' Press.

Giroux, H. (2000). Public pedagogy as cultural politics: Stuart Hall and the 'crisis' of culture. *Cultural Studies, 14*(2), 341-360.

Giroux, H., & McLaren, P. (1989). *Critical pedagogy, the state, and cultural struggle.* Albany: State University of New York Press.

Gross, T., & Miller, D. (Co-Executive Producers). (2007, November, 5). *Fresh air* [Radio Program]. Philadelphia, PA: WFYY.

Guarascio, D., & Port, M. (Executive producers). (2007). *Aliens in America* [Television series]. Burbank, CA: The CW network.

Henry J. Kaiser Foundation (2010, January). *Generation M2: Media in the lives of 8- 18 years olds.* Retrieved March 5, 2012 from http://www.kff.org/entmedia/upload.8010.pdf

Jhally, S., & Lewis, J. (1992). *Enlightened racism: The Cosby Show, audiences, and the myth of the American dream.* Boulder, CO: Westview Press.

Johnson, S. (2005). *Everything bad is good for you: How today's popular culture is actually making us smarter.* New York: Riverhead Books.

Kincheloe, J., & McLaren, P. (2005). Rethinking critical theory and qualitative research. In N. Denzin & Y. Lincoln (Eds.), *The Sage handbook of qualitative research* (3rd ed., pp. 303-342). London: Sage.

Leggo, C. (2008). The ecology of personal and professional experience: A poet's view. In M. Cahnmann-Taylor and R. Siegesmund, *Arts based research in education: foundations for practice* (pp.89-97). New York: Routledge.

Mahiri, J. (2000-2001). Pop culture pedagogy and the end(s) of school. *Journal of Adolescent & Adult Literacy, 44*(4), 382-385.

McKinley, G.E. (1992). *Beverly Hills, 90210.* Philadelphia: University of Pennsylvania Press.

McQueen, D. (1998). *Television a media student's guide.* London: Arnold.

Merriam, S.B. (1988). *Case study research in education: A qualitative approach.* San Francisco: Jossey-Bass Publishers.

Moi, T. (1986). *The Kristeva reader.* New York: Columbia University Press.

National Center for Education Information. *Profile of teachers in the U.S 2011.* Retrieved May 20, 2012, from http://www.ncei.com/Profile_Teachers_US_2011.pdf.

Oceanic Airlines. *Taking you places you've never imagined!* Retrieved February 15, 2009, from http://www.oceanic-air.com/.

The Open Mind (2000). [Television broadcast]. Interview with Carlos E. Cortés, Retrieved May 9, 2012, from http://archive.org/details/openmind_ep275.

Pauly, N. (2006). How might teachers of young children interrogate images as visual culture? In M.N. Bloch., D. Kennedy., T. Lightfoot., & D. Weyenberg, (Eds.), *The child in the world/the world in the child.* New York: Palgrave Macmillan.

Sanderson, J. (2008). The blog is serving its purpose: Self-presentations strategies on 38pitches.com. *Journal of Computer-Mediated Communication, 13,* 912-936.

Sandlin, J., Schultz, B., & Burdick, J. (2011). (Eds.), *Handbook of public pedagogy.* New York: Routledge.

Seid, J. (2006, January 24). *Gilmore Girls meet Smackdown.* Retrieved June 20, 2008, from http://money.cnn.com/2006/01/24/news/companies/cbs_warner/.

Stephan, W. (1999). *Reducing prejudice and stereotyping in schools,* New York: Teachers College Press.

Strauss, A., & Corbin, J. (1998). *Basics of qualitative research: Techniques and procedures for developing grounded theory.* Thousand Oaks, CA: Sage.

Trier, J. (2005). 'Sordid fantasies': Reading popular 'inner-city' school films as racialized texts with pre-service teachers. *Race Ethnicity and Education, 8*(2), 171-189.

United States Census Bureau. (2010). *New Census Bureau Report Analyzes Nation's Linguistic Diversity* Retrieved May 20, 2012, from http://www.census.gov/news room/releases/archives/american_community_survey_acs/cb10-cn58.html.

Watson, E. (Ed.). (2006). *Searching the soul of Ally McBeal.* Jefferson, NC: McFarland.

Wright, R.R., & Sandlin, J.A. (2009). Cult TV, hip hop, shape-shifters, and vampire slayers. *Adult Education Quarterly, 59*(2), 118-141.

Chapter Twelve

"How Does This Sound?" Using Language to Characterize Race in Middle-Earth

Jennifer Culver

My high school celebrates its distinction of being one of the most diverse schools in the area. Our diversity of cultures, incomes, and experiences enriches every classroom and the campus as a whole. Any senior wanting a challenge can choose to take an Advanced Placement (AP) course, and this means for me as a teacher that I need to incorporate a variety of texts and learning experiences to reach a wide range of abilities in my room. Throughout the years my students struggle with syntax and diction, particularly how to understand the ways syntax, the actual structure of the sentence, and diction, the complexities of word choice, create meaning in a text. They also struggle with crafting effective commentary in their writing. In search of an approach that would engage students while helping them learn the importance of syntax and diction in the production of a text, Tolkien emerged as an obvious choice. Movies based on *The Lord of the Rings* remained popular, and more students were reading the books than ever. Accessible and engaging yet also complex and rich in material for discussion and analysis, Tolkien's work provided a vehicle for a project many students felt was their favorite throughout their high school career.

Shippey's (2000) *Author of the Century* provided inspiration for the layout of the project. Shippey wrote that Tolkien's success in individualizing the races of Middle-earth stemmed not only from creating unique languages for each but also from providing each race distinctive speech patterns and diction when speaking in Common Tongue. Shippey attributes this to Tolkien's love of language and Tolkien's insistence that the languages came first and were of utmost importance. This means that students could investigate what made an elf sound like an elf throughout *The Lord of the Rings* without having to learn Elvish. Instead, students would have to learn how syntax and diction help a reader construct ideas about character inside a text.

For help with understanding how language can help construct meaning, the work of Michael Halliday (2004) and the team from *Laying the Foundation* offered ready-made strategies and theory to adapt for the project. Halliday's work focuses on how a text arrives at meaning through language construction. Looking at the function of a word in relation to other words, clauses, and the construction of a sentence does not limit any word to a prescriptive meaning. This means that instead of learning that certain words are nouns or verbs, students can learn the function of nouns and verbs and then identify which words in a sentence perform that function. For example, if I only taught that the word "red" was an adjective, students would not struggle with sentences such as "When she blushed, her cheeks turned as red as a rose." My students might struggle, however, with a more abstract term when reading about finance and encountering the term "in the red." Halliday further examines subjects, themes, and clauses and how a functional grammar can illustrate patterns and insights not easily found elsewhere.

The series of texts from *Laying the Foundation* (2004) seek to prepare students for the rigorous demands of advanced classes, such as Pre-AP and AP level classes, but their work truly includes best practices for all students. In their section centering on syntax, one activity consists of studying the particulars of a passage by gathering data on a chart that looks for information including sentence length, purpose, and imagery. Through the data, the student learns to make observations about connections between sentence length, sentence structure, and meaning. *Laying the Foundation* provides an excerpt from Annie Dillard (p. 228-233) for analysis, and the chapter demonstrates, for example, the emphatic nature of short sentences and the descriptive nature of long, complex sentences. After gathering the data and making observations, the students then begin evaluating the information to find the most significant elements for later commentary. For students who consider themselves more math-science oriented, this approach of gathering data appeals to them because it allows them to employ a more seemingly objective, logical stance to what can be considered an inscrutable task—interpreting literature.

Preparing the Groundwork

Before delving into the project, students learn to work with syntax and diction in a whole-class format with smaller, self-contained texts before working with excerpts from larger passages. By using a short text, usually only a couple of paragraphs, students do not have to worry about whether or not their observations would fit in the larger context of the original work. Any small passage can serve this function, but students generally enjoy working with pieces from *The World's Shortest Stories* series such as the one below:

The Brainiac. The Nerd. Not anymore. A midsemester move to a new school. A
chance for a new identity.
Algebra. First day. First period. Sitting in the back with the cool people, hoping
to clique, I finish my exam long before anyone else.
Doubting my calculations, my teacher grades it aloud: 100. I've failed. (Tray,
in Moss, 1998, p. 199)

With the chart below, adapted from the chart from *Laying the Foundation*, students begin to gather sentence data and look for patterns and significance:

Sen- tence #	Number of words	Part of speech of first word	Subject of the sen- tence	Sen- tence purpose (declar- ative, impera- tive, etc.)	Predi- cate of the sen- tence	Sen- tence struc- ture (simple, com- pound, etc.)	Sen- tence rhetori- cal struc- ture (period- ic, loose, anapho- ra, etc.)

Underneath the chart, students have room to compile words containing imagery
and examples of figurative language. My honor students found this chart challenging, but not daunting, but for non-honor students, columns could be omitted
and then gradually added. Students must then evaluate the data and narrow their
findings down to three significant instances where syntax and/or diction helped
contribute to the meaning of the piece.

In the example above, for example, students first generally notice the rhetorical fragments at the beginning of the piece. By looking for, and not finding a
predicate, students realize the pattern: all the sentences above lack action. They
begin to see the craftsmanship in the mosaic of images that establish the speaker's situation. In addition to this, students then note the short, final sentence following longer ones, noting how the emphatic nature of the short sentence "I've
failed" forces the reader to realize the irony of the situation instead of explaining
it to the reader, letting the impact sink in, allowing for a more dramatic realization. After enough practice with smaller pieces, the students are ready for the
larger project at hand.

Investigating Language and Race in Middle-Earth

Before the project begins, students complete reading *The Lord of the Rings* and participate in various other discussions and assessments. The syntax-diction project is designed to be a group project that can be graded individually. Because students study a race of Middle-earth as a group, the project fosters collaboration. Assigning parts of the project to different individuals allows for differentiation of strengths and weaknesses. Individual grades promote the need for students to own their own learning. This way, students do not suffer if other group members fail to complete their portions of the project, thus relieving some of the angst that accompanies the announcement of group work.

Once groups have been assigned any of the main races of Middle-earth—hobbit, dwarf, elf, human, orc, wizard, or Ent—the students begin to sift through their books for examples of that race's syntax and diction. Each student must find three passages of dialogue to analyze (each for a grade), and to avoid duplication, groups may want to divide the text ahead of time. For each passage, the student must complete the chart and diction analysis, come up with commentary, and discuss those findings with other group members on specifically assigned days. On those discussion days, the group members share their findings and try to look for greater patterns, such as that elves often speak with inverted sentences.

After three sessions of group sharing the group needs to agree on some categories that make up the standardized syntax and diction of their race. Along with inverted speech, to continue the elf example above, students may find that elves use often use nature imagery. Even though students will complete individual pieces of the project, this collaboration serves as a good system of checks and balances to ensure that their findings are on the right track. A student coming to class with the observation that elves prefer choppy language should be challenged by his/her group. This collaboration also helps struggling students reach the depth of commentary they may not otherwise reach alone. Remarking that orcs use exclamatory statements, for example, does not provide much insight. The student needs to understand what it means for orcs to use exclamatory sentences so often.

Producing Drafts

Each group produces a manual detailing the race in Middle-earth that includes several genres of writing, and students are exposed to each genre throughout the process including taking time to assess professional examples. The pieces of writing include: a how-to piece (such as "How to Speak Like an Ent"); an introduction to the race detailing how geographical location, history, and other aspects contribute to language development; a word essay which analyzes a word or phrase that the race repeats throughout the text; and an original piece of fiction written in the syntax and diction of the race. College readiness and state standards encourage students to develop a proficiency in several types of writing, including procedural writing, making students more versatile and less formulaic in their approach to writing in general. With a variety of options, students can explore a new style of writing or rely on an old strength when deciding which piece of the manual to choose from.

Procedural writing can be the most foreign writing for students, yet may also be the one style of writing where most students need proficiency, as there will always be a demand for more technical manuals and the codification of policies and procedures. For the how-to guide, students must start with the data gathered from their passage analysis and decided-on categories. Using those as a guide, the how-to document must conform to the expectations of any procedural text in format and content, which means explicit steps, ample explanations, examples to illustrate difficult points, and some rationale for why a reader would want to undergo this project. An Ent group, for example, recently put together the following step:

> Step Six: Use onomatopoeia
> Ents use onomatopoeia often, particularly terms such as "Hm," and "Hroom."
> This often can add a contemplative aspect to their speech and slows down the
> pacing of the sentence. (Ent Student Group, April 2006)

One way to conduct peer revision for the how-to piece lies in application. Give the procedural text from one race to another group, so the hobbit group may receive the dwarf group, for example. Ask the hobbit group to use the procedural guide to rewrite a fable or nursery rhyme. Because the hobbit group has not been studying the syntax and diction of any race in Middle-earth other than hobbits, the product they create should be a good measure of whether or not the guide works successfully. The hobbit group would then return the exercise to the dwarf group so that the dwarf group members can assess whether or not the guide worked according to plan. To keep with the study of Tolkien, choices from this activity could come from some of the English nursery rhymes Tolkien used in "Songs of the Philologists," a collection of songs included in the Shippey book that Tolkien wrote for fellow lovers of language and they study of language, or songs Tolkien alludes to in the trilogy, such as Frodo's song at the inn before beginning his perilous journey about the man on the moon.

The study of an often-repeated work needs to be included in the manual as well. As the students look at various passages of speech from their respective races, certain words or phrases should appear more often than others. Once the group discusses the options, the student in charge of the word essay needs to go investigate the depths of the word both inside Middle-earth and outside Middle-earth. From this study, the group learns how the meaning of the word takes on the layers of the previous associations with that word inside and outside of the text.

Students also learn about the changing meaning of words over time, and the best example of this lies in the Shire with the hobbits and the use of the word "queer." Students associate the word "queer" now with homosexuality and often add a negative connotation to the word, but Tolkien ascribed none of that to his hobbits, who often spoke as if they lived in an Edwardian shire themselves. While students can hear repeatedly that Tolkien did not use the word "queer" in the same way then as we often hear the word now, investigating the word on their own also provides the students with the chance to own that learning as well.

Using "queer" as an example to help the students see the benefit of investigating a word versus merely understanding that the meaning of a word has changed starts with a trip through the *Oxford English Dictionary (OED)*, and this would be a good time to discuss with students Tolkien's contributions to the *OED* and his love of philology. Showing students that Tolkien loved words and language helps them understand that Tolkien chose his words deliberately, which makes his word choice all the more appropriate for study. The *OED* examines the history of the word, various definitions of the word, and how those definitions change in popularly over time. Students can also explore how famous writers employed various definitions of the word, often in familiar works, to understand the word in a greater context.

The word study allows for an appreciation of the complexity of a repeated word and for how a speaker can employ multiple definitions of the word, sometimes at the same time. The orc group, for example, struggled with the word "kill" when encountering a phrase such as "he's going to kill you." In such a violent culture, the phrase could be literal. In some readings, the line almost always reads as figurative. Which meaning did Tolkien intend? In some cases, the answer is not easy, and this provides for many good discussions about language, meaning, and reader expectations.

Switching drafts with other groups as a means of revision can also work for the word study. In this case, the peer reviewer from another table would not be working on imitation as much as measuring the draft against pre-existing criteria and looking for evidence of depth. As the wizard group reads the orc essay on the word "kill," for example, the wizard group needs to determine if they have gained a new appreciation for that race's use of the word. Did the presentation of the word "kill" only state the obvious—that the word repeats throughout the text and means to extinguish life? If so, the writers need to find more nuances to the word in the text or, even worse, possibly find another word and start again.

Language can be shaped by history and environment as well, and the group member who explores this option spends more time inside the text of *The Lord of the Rings* than the others. This student must understand how setting can affect language and express this in an insightful way. For example, since a dwarf may live underground and/or mine most of his life, his choices of metaphors come from the world he knows. When looking at beauty, the dwarf compares the subject to a gem or to gold, which is what he highly values. Treebeard and other Ents often speak in tree-related metaphors because of their makeup. The metaphors do not only apply to other trees and Ents, however. In fact, Treebeard once said he wanted to curse Saruman "root and branch" after hearing about the cut down forests. Treebeard understands that Saruman does not have branches, but he employs what he knows, tree physiognomy, to Saruman in order to make his point.

History also plays a part in the language development of races of Middle-earth. The hobbit group found, for example, very few references to warfare. This may be because of the Shire's seclusion and roughly 250 years of peace before the Scouring of the Shire in *Return of the King*. This seclusion also offers the hobbits little opportunity for ceremonial language, which appears in their very conversational diction and approach to each other, using more slang than almost every other race. The long lifetimes of the Ents often shapes their language from their contemplative pauses to their flowing, rambling sentences. Because there is no reason for an Ent to be "hasty," he is not going to worry about taking his time with his words, unlike other races who have a briefer lifespan and seemingly constant states of urgency.

Like the word essay, revision for this essay mainly derives from the readers of other tables trying to gain a new appreciation for how the language of one race can be shaped by external factors. Peer reviewers are looking for depth in the understanding of the culture of that race and how that culture brings about nuances of the language. In this case, peer reviewers do not necessarily need to be sure that all aspects of the culture are represented. Instead, they need to be sure that the author chose relevant cultural aspects to include and discuss.

Finally, one student creates a piece of fiction using the syntax and diction of the race at hand. This aspect of the manual intends to take the favorite genre of fan fiction to a more complex level. Jenkins (1992) in his book *Textual Poachers* presented a study of fan fiction, showing the world the fact that fans love to embellish and continue stories of their favorite characters and have loved to do so for some time. While most fan fiction does not have prescriptions in terms of syntax and diction, this piece of fiction needs to mimic that of the assigned race. Hopefully, this student can work with the procedural writer for specific tips when struggling with a concept.

These fictional pieces can stem from a variety of options. Students can continue a character's journey in Middle-earth or beyond, for example. If the students do not want to alter the ending, they may want to add a "missing moment" and cover details of an event only alluded to by Tolkien. Students can also write about events before *Fellowship* begins, or even take characters from the books and imagine them in a different surrounding. Students do not even have to rely on the main characters to write the fiction, they only have to write in the race's syntax and diction. This synthesis-level approach to the data fits the creativity of some students more than others, and letting the group members assign those tasks early on should keep people from working on this piece who do not feel fiction is their strong suit.

Revision for fiction can be undertaken just like any other fictional piece as long as the focus on syntax and diction remains. The peer reviewer needs to come away from the draft feeling as if a hobbit or a wizard wrote the piece. If the believability is not there, then the peer reader needs to determine what aspect of the writing needs to be revised to sound more like that race. Often the syntax can be off quite a bit, as the writer gets carried away with the story and diction and forgets the sentence structure.

Before the drafts are due for any of the pieces, time in the schedule allows for students with similar jobs to meet with each other, share their work, and discuss any difficulties. Since they are the "experts" for that genre of writing, this gives them invaluable time to collaborate with others who are working on the same task. Letting the procedural writers get together allows them to check the conciseness of their steps as well as the overall format, while the word essayists discuss layers of meaning and nuance with each other. Letting these groups collaborate on revision also helps the writers perfect their work, as those who have their particular race in Middle-earth focused on another genre of writing.

Revision activities within the group can also take place. In this case, revision focuses even more on content than it does on format or style. The elf group, for example, will know enough about elves to understand when the procedural text provides a direction towards elf-like speech that does not make sense. Further discussion at the elf table may center around the nuances of the word "light" and whether or not the writer's interpretations of the word throughout the text match their own.

Finishing Touches

Putting the manual together requires the most amount of teamwork. Up until now, the students have worked together but had individual components. Now, the pieces must fit into a larger whole, and decisions must be made. Recently, students started placing their syntax-diction projects together digitally, which allowed for more flexibility, as scheduling time always seemed to be a problem. Even in the digital assembly of the manual, students need to distribute roles that can be assessed individually. Because the bulk of the work and intent lies in the syntax and diction work, some instructors may want to cut down on publication aspects and let students turn in work separately. Others may want the manual to appear like a manual, assigning roles to students such as binding, a title page, a table of contents, and possibly even an afterword that provides a chance for reflection on the process. Some students add a dedication page, with many dedicating their work to the twenty-four-hour copy centers because of their procrastination. Some students divided letters of the alphabet and created a glossary of terms significant to the race in question, offering names, places, items, and expressions that help the reader attain a deeper level of understanding for that race and its complexities.

After the project in their overall course reflections, many students admitted to going through several stages of emotions. They loved Tolkien, feared the work, became frustrated with the complexities, then looked back and felt it was some of the best work they had ever done. In later years, students heard about the project and looked forward to studying their race, digging into the complexities, and producing work like the displays in the classroom. Even better, on essays and timed literary responses to work outside of Tolkien, transfer took effect. Students started to mention diction and syntax and how it contributed to meaning without being prompted to, and they often elaborated in specific and insightful ways. For example, AP exam writing prompts in both prose and poetry sections often require students to discuss a writer's attitude. Implied within the prompt lies the assumption that students will first discern the author's attitude, but students often felt they lacked the tools to discover attitude. Once students realized that evaluating syntax and diction provided them with avenues to determine the attitude of the author with specific evidence and insightful commentary, they became more successful in their analysis. Outside of the AP exam, students began to include elements of syntax and diction in their longer literary analysis pieces. Class discussion over thematic topics and overall texts began to include references to syntax and diction with specific textual references. Students eagerly returned to the text because they realized they possessed the tools to approach complex passages. The goal of the project, to encourage students to see syntax and diction as vital to meaning-making, succeeded, and this was in no small part due to the complexity and richness of Tolkien's work.

References

Hagar, K. (Ed.). (2004). *Laying the Foundation: A Resource and Planning Guide.* Dallas: Advanced Placement Strategies.

Halliday, M. (2004). *An Introduction to Functional Grammar.* New York: Oxford Publishing Company.

Jenkins, H. (1992). *Textual Poachers.* New York: Routledge.

Moss, S. (Ed.). (1998). *The World's Shortest Stories: Murder, Love, Horror, All This and Much More in the Most Amazing Short Stories Ever Written.* Philadelphia: Running Brook Press.

Shippey, T. (2000). *J. R. R. Tolkien: Author of the Century.* New York: Houghton Mifflin.

Tolkien, J. R. R. (1994). *The Lord of the Rings.* New York: Houghton Mifflin.

Chapter Thirteen

"World Goin' One Way, People Another": Using *The Wire* and Other Popular Culture Texts to Teach College Writing

Michelle Parke

When I began teaching College Writing 1 (English 101) at Carroll Community College (Carroll) in 2008, I routinely made references to television and film in an effort, most often, to infuse a bit of humor into class discussions.[1] Sometimes, my *Seinfeld* quotes or gestures to *Buffy the Vampire Slayer* would fall short of my intended impact, but other times, a *Friends* reference or video game analogy would succeed in engaging students with the material. After working with the course textbook and finding it a challenge to sustain students' interest with the readings, I began researching how I could integrate an area of interest to me—popular culture and television and film in particular—into the community college first-year composition course.[2] Through the experiments with different popular culture texts, I discovered that the Carroll population of students whom I encountered in English 101 grappled with the sitcom (*Seinfeld* and *Modern Family*), but the dramatic television programs *The Wire* and *Buffy the Vampire Slayer* proved more effective in addressing the writing and reading objectives, which include "discover topics for academic writing through the critical reading of essays and, perhaps, other forms of non-fiction prose," "engage fully in the writing process," "construct valid arguments based on a variety of evidence," and "engage in academic inquiry and research."

My approach to integrating pop culture texts into the English 101 classroom is informed by my teaching philosophy, pedagogical methods aimed at the community college environment, and television studies. Generally, my teaching philosophy is rooted in creating an active and student-centered learning environment, developing curriculum that supports critical thinking, and integrating the use of instructional technology and multimedia into and out of the classroom. More succinctly, I adhere to poet Mark Van Doren's words: "The art of teaching is the art of assisting discovery" (Famous 2010). Given my background in literary studies, I find upholding these tenets much easier in the literature classroom than I do in the composition classroom. Prior to using popular culture texts, I found that "developing curriculum that supports critical thinking" was the most difficult to implement because students did not engage with the textbook's essays in a critical manner because of, what *seemed* like, a lack of comprehension, lack of interest, and a lack of desire to read the essays at all.

In addition to my general teaching philosophy, my teaching practices are informed by concepts from queer pedagogy. Having worked with queer literature and film, I was drawn to some of the key facets of this method. Queer pedagogy and popular culture can productively collaborate to engage students actively and critically with texts and with the world around them. Queer pedagogy can provide an analytic tool of "interrelated, broad-based pedagogical commitments to free inquiry and expression, social equity, [...] and the broadening of dialogical spheres of public exchange with and beyond the classroom as sites for engaged analyses of social issues" (Spurlin, 2002, p. 10). While broad in scope, this approach informs how I position the study of television programs like *The Wire* and *Buffy the Vampire Slayer* in the English 101 classroom. In this course, I select texts that foreground social issues with the hopes of students engaging in "free inquiry and expression" in their writing and with the goal that students dialogue about the "big" issues during classroom discussion in addition to the elements of narrative.

Further, when considering the course objectives alongside my personal teaching goals, I greatly value William Spurlin's (2002) idea that "students need to be prepared with the necessary tools to question and complicate identity categories and to use these tools *strategically* in those specific *contexts* where they might best work, perhaps by transforming thinking and revising habitual ways of reading texts and reading the world" (p. 12). Though Spurlin speaks of identity categories here, my application of this paradigm extends beyond identity to include the broader social concerns. The study of popular culture texts, such as television, can achieve this revision of "habitual ways of reading texts and reading the world." I mention at the beginning of the semester that students must alter how they watch, setting aside their "fan" hats and donning "scholar" hats. Rather than being passive viewers to which most are accustomed, they must read the episode like they would a work of literature—take notes, make connections among ideas/themes, ask questions, and engage with text.

This queer pedagogical approach aligns with more specific methods of integrating popular culture texts in the community college classroom, particularly those delineated by Lynn Bartholome (2005). The first-year students who enter English 101 vary in age, socioeconomic background, race, and ethnicity (though not much), gender, and sexual orientation. As the instructor, I must account for this range of differences, with age being perhaps the most significant at Carroll. Popular culture extends across these differences, and as Bartholome (2005) notes, studying pop culture is useful because it "teaches us about ourselves" (p.150). At the beginning of the semester, I introduce the course this way, and I see varying looks of skepticism sweep across their faces, but by the end of the term, they comprehend how pop culture can mirror our individual lives and our society.

Another one of Bartholome's observations that speaks deeply to why I believe pop culture can work in the community college writing classroom is that it "provides an opportunity to learn a radically unfamiliar skill (i.e. critical analysis) through deeply familiar material" (p. 151). This is one of the many ideas proffered in her article that drives my desire to teach pop culture in English 101. Many of the students who enter that classroom have a limited ability to think critically. At the beginning of the semester, I mention that analyzing pop culture will be demanding because of our familiarity with it but that by doing so will provide them with skills necessary for the next level of their educational career and for viewing their world with a critical eye.

Finally, Jason Mittell's (2006) approach to teaching television has significantly shaped how I use this medium in English 101. Students can greatly benefit from using his concept of narrative complexity to frame how they write about and discuss television. Mittell's (2006) general ideas center on the narrative structure, production style, and the type of audience of a particular set of contemporary television programs, such as *Buffy the Vampire Slayer*, *X-Files*, and *Arrested Development*. When considering his ideas as pedagogy, I am particularly interested in the role of the audience—the students—and how this perspective can inform how I teach television. Mittell (2006) cites Stephen Johnson's concept of "cognitive workout" when discussing how narratively complex programs encourage "audiences to become more actively engaged" (p. 32). Here, Mittell and Spurlin marry well and, along with Bartholome's perspective, create a practical and robust teaching practice for me.

In addition to offering a "broader range of rewards and pleasures than most conventional programming," complex programs can also contribute to the development of "problem-solving and observational skills" (though Mittell qualifies this latter point by saying that it is unclear whether empirical evidence exists to support these claims) (Mittell, 2006, p. 32). Because this "programming demands an active and attentive process of comprehension to decode both the complex stories and modes of storytelling," I am able to develop writing assignments that will engage the students' critical thinking and analytic skills (Mittell, 2006, p. 32). Moreover, this "active and attentive process" challenges students because they are accustomed to passive viewing, much like they are habituated to reading passively. For my teaching practice, this "decoding" is one of the tools about which Spurlin discusses; it opens the opportunity for students to question and engage with complicated social issues. As I have worked at integrating popular culture texts into this course, I have gradually reassessed my own teaching practices and have constructed an approach that adheres to my personal pedagogical goals while also accounting for the population of students entering the classroom and what texts work in achieving the course objectives.

"Nothing's ever worked out for me with tuna on toast."

One part of the trial-and-error process was using the sitcom *Seinfeld* as a primary text for one semester. I selected several episodes from the acclaimed series, paired them with (mostly academic) readings, and created writing assignments, which emphasized the different forms that were part of the course objectives. Before viewing any episode, we discussed how to read a visual text, how to read the sitcom form, and how to identify the most common types of humor (for example, parody, satire, slapstick, dark, etc.).[3] Overall, I failed to anticipate three major factors: the difficulty that students would have with this form of television, how challenging it would be to analyze—or even discuss—humor in a critical manner, and how much they would grapple with one of the series' central facets—the insignificant. Generally, our discussions about humor were circular ("Why is this moment funny?" and the response was, "Because it is funny."). The exception was slapstick and the character of Kramer; once they had the definition of slapstick and examples from film, such as Jim Carrey in *Liar, Liar*, students were able to clearly articulate, in writing and in discussion, why Kramer's physical mishaps or his signature entry into Jerry's apartment were humorous. A few students even made connections to Charlie Chaplin and classic forms of slapstick comedy. The in-class discussion was one of the most fruitful of the semester.

However, the rest of the "*Seinfeld* experiment" did not proceed as successfully. One episode that I believed would actively engage students, generate productive discussion, and inspire quality written work was "The Opposite." Students were assigned Jason Holt's article, "The Costanza Manuever: Is It Rational for George to 'Do the Opposite'?" prior to viewing the episode. My goals were to encourage students to examine how the narrative is constructed and to consider how a sitcom tackles philosophical, or more abstract, issues about behavior. We spent time working through Holt's article because many students were not accustomed to reading an article of this length or style. The content appeared to challenge them, so we were able to practice active reading and critical thinking skills. Students successfully read the basic structure of the episode, but the impasse occurred when we entered the discussion about how a sitcom (or even comedy in general) could ask its viewers to contemplate philosophical issues.

I asked them to write a brief response addressing whether or not they agreed with Holt's premise: Is it rational for George to do the opposite? The short, two-page essays required them to employ their persuasive writing skills and to actively read both Holt's article and the episode. While students were able to structure their responses in an organized fashion, their thesis statements and evidence from the episode lacked specificity. To answer the prompt, most students spoke generally about the episode rather than honing in on specific scenes, such as the opening scene in Monk's, George and Victoria at the movies, or George's job interview with the Yankees. I asked why there was this lack of specificity, and some students responded that they found it difficult to write with such detail because it was an unfamiliar practice. They also found it challenging to write about humor and how humor allows a viewer to consider abstract questions, like the one posed in "The Opposite." As a result of the discussion and the written responses, I shifted my focus slightly to engage them more closely with specific moments in the episodes, much like they would with a passage or a sentence in a work of prose. In fact, I routinely returned to this analogy when we examined scenes. Yet, the struggle with humor continued. A few students improved and were able to articulate why a moment was funny, but beyond a small group, students could not critically engage with humor in a way that was productive in writing or in discussion.

At the time of the "*Seinfeld* experiment," I had yet to discover Mittell's work, but with this text as a tool, the possibility of returning to the sitcom, from the perspective of narrative complexity, exists. In the fall 2011, I attempted such a revisiting. I began the course with an episode of *Modern Family* ("Fizbo") as a means of introducing television as a text and how we read this medium. I paired the episode with short articles from Popmatters.com to show students how authors write about television beyond reviews and recaps with which students are the more familiar. To prepare students for the short writing assignment, I selected one moment that demonstrates how we could analyze the humor and its contribution to plot and character development: the brief close-up of Fizbo's clown shoe hitting the cement with a thump as Cameron exits the car to defend Mitchell against a bully at a gas station at which they are stopped. I played the entire scene then returned to the close-up of the shoe. We discussed the elements of humor present and how they serve the narrative. I then asked them to consider the remainder of the scene: what is humorous about it, how we understand the characters more definitively, and what larger social issues are at stake. Regarding the latter point, students were able to successfully discuss how the scene works—the non-normative component is Cameron dressed as a clown not the fact that Cameron and Mitchell are a couple. They discussed how the scene subverts the viewer's expectations and how it uses humor to do so. Though, they did clearly struggle with articulating with specificity how humor operates in this scene.

The writing assignment for this episode was brief, and they were asked to draw connections with one of the articles paired with "Fizbo." Overall, the responses were better than I expected, but students still struggled with articulating why a moment is funny, at least one that is not slapstick in nature. They were able to successfully incorporate ideas from the article and could use particular moments from the episode to support their perspective. In the future, I believe a sitcom can work in English 101 when paired with Mittell's (2006) "Narrative Complexity" because I assigned this article for the class following our work with *Modern Family*, and some students seemed to have a greater understanding of the program with Mittell's ideas framing their reading. Because the sitcom has proven challenging, it is perhaps best suited for the end of the semester after students are comfortable working with Mittell's ideas and analyzing more accessible genres of television.

"Got to. This America, man."

Prior to incorporating Mittell's ideas into the English 101 curriculum, I used *The Wire* in a summer course as the primary text, focusing on the acclaimed fourth season. Once again, I view this initially as an experiment but knew that the geographical significance would be at least one appealing factor (Carroll is forty minutes north of Baltimore). I also knew that most students had not seen the series.[4] The fourth season of *The Wire* foregrounds the American education system, and it exposes (my) students to a socioeconomic place that is simultaneously near to and distant from them. Using a one-hour drama for a summer course worked well because attempting to hold the attention of students for four hours is a challenge, and the blending of a visual text with discussion and short writing exercises proved a successful formula.[5] I was able to structure each day around one episode and an article or two that I paired with that episode. The students were asked to not only critically read the articles but also the episodes, which proved challenging for some students because they were shifting the way they thought of "reading." I provided the students with the vocabulary and tools to read a visual text. They were required to write two essays, analytic and persuasive, which reflected the course objectives. Additionally, I assigned daily responses to the episodes that required students to use the discussion forum feature on Blackboard and to write in a concise manner while still providing a critical and well-developed answer to the prompt. The forum posts, I believed, served as a tool of accountability and gave students the ability to practice the different types of writing that we were discussing in class and reading about in their textbook (i.e., *Backpack Writing*).

One of the most productive sets of exercises was centered on the persuasive essay. This research paper is required for the course; I asked students to select a topic inspired by the fourth season of *The Wire*. Additional parameters for the paper included the use of evidence from the show and secondary sources (logos) to support the thesis. Students selected topics such as No Child Left Behind, police corruption, the connection between drug abuse and poverty, and the failure of the American dream. In preparation for writing a persuasive paper, students were assigned two sections from Aristotle's *Rhetoric*,[6] in which ethos, pathos, and logos were delineated. For the discussion forum post about the episode "Know Your Place," I asked students to immediately put their knowledge of the rhetorical triangle to work, and while it was evident that some students were still grappling with some of Aristotle's concepts, many were able to create an argument about the episode using ethos, pathos, and logos.

Following this class, I assigned them three articles from *Dissent Magazine* that focus on the question "Is *The Wire* too cynical?" The articles' authors debate this question from different points of view; John Atlas and Peter Dreier, the authors of the original article, approach the topic from community organizing and poverty advocacy positions while the responders to their article "In Defense of *The Wire*" read Atlas and Dreier's argument and the show itself through an academic sociological lens. In class, students worked in small groups to assess the arguments using Aristotle's rhetorical triangle and definitions of ethos, pathos, and logos. The articles' authors modeled for students how to develop an argument and how a conversation about a complex topic can evolve in writing. They could learn what strategies were effective and what methods of developing argument may fall short in their intent. This exercise prepared students for the writing of their own persuasive essays, which was evidenced in the final product. Generally, students competently connected real-world issues to representations offered on television and did so in well-constructed arguments that demonstrated their knowledge of ethos, pathos, and logos. Not only were students able to achieve the goals set forth for the persuasive essay, they were also able to further understand how television can ask its viewers to consider different perspectives on social and political issues and how, when programs are creative and complex, they provide possibilities rather than concrete solutions to these problems.

Based on the success of using *The Wire* as a text, I have retained its position in the English 101 curriculum, but in the fall 2011, I wanted to shift the focus slightly. I located *The Wire* within our discussion about analytic writing with the goal being that students would analyze an episode using either Mittell's (2006) ideas about narrative complexity or one of the articles about *The Wire* that I paired with the respective episodes. I began with the series premiere, "The Target," and at this point in the semester (week five), I had hoped that students were more comfortable with actively reading a visual text. However, students articulated that watching this particular series was a greater challenge than other shows up to this point, such as *Buffy the Vampire Slayer*. Like Mittell (2006) argues, this show provides a "cognitive workout" for its viewers, and students were unprepared for this level of engagement. As such, I eliminated the other episodes of *The Wire* to focus our work solely on "The Target." We walked through how this complex program demands that we watch actively.

A few students were able to make connections among particular scenes but could not analyze what those scenes were trying to do or say. For example, narcotics officers Kima Greggs, Ellis Carver, and Thomas "Herc" Hauk are writing arrest reports using typewriters, complaining about the lack of computers, and how the failed promise of this technology affects their ability to do their jobs. Later, Detective Jimmy McNulty is visiting an FBI agent at the Baltimore field office to learn about the agency's surveillance of local drug dealers. The offices are well lit and fully equipped with the latest technology; McNulty comments on the quality of the audio and video being received from the bugs placed by the FBI in the dealer's house. We discussed the stark juxtaposition of these two scenes, and while students could see that they were connected, when asked what this connection between these two scenes reveals, they were unable to analyze the larger issues. However, once I walked them through this analysis, they were able to begin to see how an active viewer must engage with this type of visual text.

After we discussed that these two scenes comment on the funding, or lack thereof, at different levels of law enforcement and the effects it has on the officers involved, the proverbial lightbulb went off for many students, and they could return to the episode with more critical eyes. For example, one student examined how he saw the failure of institutions, as discussed by one of the authors whom we read, evidenced in "The Target." He analyzed one scene in which Greggs, Carver, and Herc discuss the war on drugs with Carver mentioning that this is not a war because wars have an end ("The Target"). Based on this scene and his application of the ideas from the article, he concluded that *The Wire* was commenting on the "futility of the war on drugs" (Personal communication, September 30, 2011). Through in-class discussion, modeling analysis, and the use of Mittell's ideas, most students were able to successfully analyze *The Wire* and articulate this analysis in writing. This program is intellectually demanding on students, and it asks that they shift how they "read" television, requires them to employ critical thinking and active reading skills, and demands that they write with specificity and clarity. *The Wire*, in conversation with Mittell's (2006) concepts, can successfully engage students and address many of the English 101 course objectives. With the success in the summer course and more recently, I believe that *The Wire* can best work, at least for this course, in the persuasive writing unit.

"Are you ready to be strong?"

The productivity achieved with using *The Wire* in different incarnations of English 101 inspired me to integrate episodes of *Buffy the Vampire Slayer* into the course. In the fall 2011, I included three episodes of the cult series—"Hush," "The Body," and "Chosen." Of these, "Hush" was the most effective in addressing my personal goals and the course objectives. However, I believe that "The Body" and "Chosen" can also succeed if the focus is altered, specifically moving away from individual articles about the episodes and remaining within the framework of Mittell's (2006) concept of narrative complexity. Students engaged with "Hush" constructively while using Mittell's ideas (2006) and Patrick Shade's (2006) reading of the episode. While some students found the abundant presence of silence in the episode disconcerting, many were able to read the use of silence well and articulate how they viewed its connection to one of the themes of the episode. Additionally, a few students focused on the significance of diegetic sound for the characters' ability to communicate when their voices have been silenced by the villainous Gentlemen.[7] Further, one student approached the episode using Mittell's definition of narrative complexity and examined one scene for how it demonstrated the weaving together of multiple storylines and the effect of coupling humor and drama on the narrative (Personal communication, December 8, 2011). While most students focused on the theme of communication, these other lenses of analysis revealed that students were certainly capable of exploring this particular show productively when given the proper context and guidance.

It was this context and guidance that was needed for "The Body" and "Chosen." For the former, for example, I asked students to read Jesse James Stommel's (2010) article about the performativity of the corpse in this episode. Specifically, the writing prompt focused on Stommel's (2010) idea that Whedon frames death in a particular way in this episode (para. 15). Students struggled with this prompt, and given the difficulty in articulating what they believe Stommel means by "framing death," I believe that situating the episode within Mittell's ideas would be more productive. Students could still focus on a theme, like death, but perhaps discuss the ways in which the audience is being asked to interrogate our culture's practices and rituals surrounding death, using Mittell's (2006) concepts of cognitive workout and "new viewer engagement" (p. 38). Similarly, the series finale "Chosen" could better be understood within Mittell's (2006) broader concepts rather than within a narrower and perhaps more challenging concept of humanism and heroism as discussed in the article that I assigned, written by Candace West. Students found difficulty making connections between the philosophical ideas and the episode. Surprisingly, the readability of the article did not challenge them; rather, it was the content that created difficulty. Again, I believe writing about and discussing "Chosen" within the framework of narrative complexity can be fruitful and provide an opportunity for students to practice a range of writing skills, including analytic and persuasive. Overall, *Buffy the Vampire Slayer* is a valuable text in English 101; in the future, I intend to reframe how we approach this program in order to emphasize Mittell's (2006) concepts and to situate a select number of episodes within the unit on analytic writing.

"This is for the record. History is written by the victor. History is filled with liars."

Finally, I have included video games, though only once, in the English 101 curriculum, so I believe this endeavor is still at the experimental level. However, the small successes in the classroom with video games (and gaming in general) suggest that they could become a fixed feature on my syllabus in the future. I placed the gaming unit at the end of the semester because it was new, and I was uncertain how it would proceed. The short gaming section began around the time that *Call of Duty: Black Ops*, the latest in the *Medal of Honor* series, and the *World of Warcraft* expansion debuted.[8] I assigned Brian Cowlishaw's (2007) article, "Playing War," and we viewed trailers for *Call of Duty: Black Ops* and *Medal of Honor* in class prior to discussion. The article was about the representation of war in video games, and though it was not focused on these particular games, I asked students to consider these new games, their setting (especially *Call of Duty*), and the fact that our country is at war overseas. In a small group setting, I asked students to connect the article and the trailer, and if possible, they could include their own experience with game play. The in-class discussion was lively, engaging, and productive. While many students argued that players could make the distinction between the reality of war and the representation of war in a game, they did concede that the game developers make particular choices when representing war, such as "respawning," the absence of certain depictions of violence (i.e., the player will not see his/her character lose a limb), and the constant engagement in battle, which is certainly not always the case in an actual war setting.[9]

During this particular semester, students had the option to write an analytic paper on one of the popular culture mediums that we discussed, and some students selected video games. Without exception, *World of Warcraft* was the game of choice, and I believe that this MMOPG (massively multiplayer online role-playing game) could be a useful addition to the discussion about the representation of war in video games, given its differences from the standard first person shooters. Based on the class discussion, I believe video games, even simply this small unit on war and gaming, could develop into a productive module. The opportunities to employ different writing skills, including analytic, persuasive, process, or evaluative, are numerous, and combined with another approach to gaming, the gaming unit could be a dynamic one for the English 101 classroom.

One of these other approaches was slated to work alongside the war and gaming class, but we were unable to undertake the material. The third installment of the *Fallout* series, *Fallout 3*, offers the prospect of discussing morality and decision making in video games. Using Marcus Schulzke's (2009) article, "Moral Decision Making in Fallout," I wanted students to reflect on how games can ask us to contemplate how we make decisions, especially those that involve moral or ethical considerations. With samples from game play, students can see how the player must weigh a set of options and decide how to proceed without a clear understanding of the potential consequences of that decision. As a result, the player must "live" with those results and continue playing. For example, one quest, which exemplifies the moral and ethical dilemmas facing the gamer throughout the game, is entitled "Strictly Business." By completing the task set forth by Grouse, the gatekeeper, the player can gain access to the town of Paradise Falls. Grouse asks that the player capture four individuals from his "VIP list" to become slaves. The player must use the slave collar to do so. Slavery and the collar are common in *Fallout 3*, and the gamer must routinely make decisions involving this practice. In this quest, the player does not know the consequences of rejecting the quest or, beyond gaining access to Paradise Falls, the consequences of accepting the task. The decision could affect game achievements, acquisition of equipment or money, and Karma Points (an indicator of the decisions, good or evil, made by the player and how the inhabitants of the Capitol Wasteland perceive them). In addition to the task itself, the gamer can opt to kill Grouse, but once again, the consequences of doing are unknown. Uncertainty in this situation, and throughout the game, puts the player in a familiar situation: weighing potential outcomes in the decision making process.

Working with this game and article can provide an opportunity for students to consider how popular culture texts instruct and ask us to ponder more abstract concepts. I believe that this small module with *Fallout 3* can be more effective in addressing philosophical, moral, or ethical issues than *Seinfeld*. The game play is more structured (the player can only select choices from a few options), which can help students focus their attention on more concrete examples than trying to dissect humor while also attempting to work through the abstract questions posed by *Seinfeld*. As a result, I believe students can write more effectively when much of their intellectual energy is not expended attempting to dissect humor but is instead focused on critically thinking informing the writing skills. In the future, I hope to actually use this in the classroom, and I think expanding the gaming unit to include issues of gender in games, for example, would be productive.

"Yeah, Buffy. What are we doing to do now?"

As an instructor of a first-year composition course at the community college level, I must discover ways to reach a range of students that will actively engage them with the material and will provide them with opportunities to exercise their developing writing skills. Popular culture texts like *The Wire* and *Buffy the Vampire* can accomplish these goals as well as the course objectives with appropriate context and guidance. The familiarity that students have with television is both helpful and initially problematic. While striving to undertake the aims of the course, the active engagement with the prolific medium opens the door for students to take this approach to television outside the walls of the classroom and shift how they watch television in general. On numerous occasions, students have confessed that the course has changed how they watch television, sometimes much to their chagrin. They begin to see how influential popular culture is on their everyday lives and how intimately television and mainstream culture are connected. As a result of the continuing success of using these popular culture texts, I hope to create a professional development session for my colleagues at Carroll to show them how to integrate pop culture into the classroom and to show them how these texts can be useful. I believe the description for such a workshop would draw directly from Bartholome (2005): popular culture allows you to go where your students are (p. 154).

Notes

1. Carroll Community College is located approximately forty minutes north of Baltimore in a primarily rural county and serves nearly three-thousand students. In fall 2009, sixty-one percent of the students were female, and ninety-two percent of the students were white ("Fall Credit," 2011).
2. In the past, I have written about *Xena* fan fiction, the classic rock band Heart, queer issues in *Buffy the Vampire Slayer*, and the influence of Edgar Allan Poe's detective trilogy on *CSI: Las Vegas*.
3. For reading a visual text and doing visual analysis, Jason Mittell's *Television and American Culture* and Laura Gray-Rosendale's *Pop Perspectives* are two useful sources. Also, I routinely give my students the link to the Yale Film Studies Film Analysis Website 2.0: classes.yale.edu/film-analysis. This site includes film terminology along with excellent examples of each element of film technique. Finally, because I could not find an adequate source (a brief and fairly general source) to teach students how to identify the types of humor within a visual text, I created a Prezi presentation in which I define each type of humor and embed YouTube videos that show each type. This was also an excuse to use a clip from *Best in Show* as an example of satire.
4. This fact would later play a role in our discussion in the fall 2011 about Mittell's (2006) idea about the "boutique audience" (p. 31).
5. This combination enabled me to address different learning styles as well, and as more students seem to be visual learners, some form of this combination has almost become an imperative.
6. Rather than asking students to purchase another text for the course, I link them to the two chapters from *Rhetoric* that we read at rhetoric.eserver.org. This source is much more user-friendly and less intimidating than the copy of Aristotle that I use: the 1500+ page *The Basic Works of Aristotle*.
7. Diegetic sound is any sound—voice, music, or effect—that originates within the world of the film or television program.
8. The writing assignment for this unit was broader than video games because of the demographics of the class. I asked students to write about a game that has influenced them or holds a significant place in their lives. The responses varied and included card games, board games, yard games, and video games.
9. Respawning is a gaming term that means to re-create a character or entity after its death/destruction.

References

Atlas, J., & Dreier, P. (2008, March). Is The Wire too cynical? *Dissent*. Retrieved from http://dissentmagazine.org/online.php/.

Atlas, J., & Dreier, P. (2008, March). John Atlas and Peter Dreier respond. *Dissent*. Retrieved from http://dissentmagazine.org/online.php/.

Bartholome, L. (2005). The value of teaching popular culture in the community college: A stew of abstract, concrete, serious, and not-so-serious notions. In Ray B. Browne

(Ed.), *Popular culture studies across the curriculum* (pp. 148-154). Jefferson, NC: McFarland & Company, Inc.

Call of Duty: Modern Warfare 2 [Computer software]. (2009). Encino, CA: Infinity Ward.

Chaddha, A., Wilson, W. J., & Venkatesh, S.A. (2008, March). In defense of *The Wire*. *Dissent*. Retrieved from http://dissentmagazine.org/online.php/.

Corrigan, P., & Walsh, B. (Writers), & Winer, J. (Director). (2009). Fizbo. [Television series episode]. In S. Levitan (Executive producer), *Modern Family*. Los Angeles, CA: Levitan/Lloyd.

Cowan, A., David, L., & Seinfeld, J. (Writers), & Cherones, T. (Director). (1994). The opposite [Television series episode]. In L. David (Executive producer), *Seinfeld*. Los Angeles, CA: Shapiro/West Productions.

Cowlishaw, Brian. Playing war. In Laura Gray-Rosendale (Ed.), *Pop perspectives: Readings to critique contemporary culture* (pp. 630-640). New York: McGraw-Hill.

Fall credit student characteristics: enrollment trends 2007 – 2011. Retrieved from Carroll Community College website: http://www.carrollcc.edu/assets/document/statistics /studentdata/2011%20Fall%20Credit%20Student%20Characteristics%20NEW%20 RaceEthnicity.pdf/.

Fallout 3 [Computer software]. (2008). Bethesda, MD: Bethesda Game Studios.

Holt, J. (2000). The Costanza maneuver: Is it rational for George to do the opposite? In William Irwin (Ed.), *Seinfeld and philosophy: A book about everything and nothing* (pp.121-128). Peru, IL: Open Court Publishing Company.

Mark Van Doren Quotes (2010). Retrieved from http://famouspoetsandpoems com/poets/mark_van_doren/quotes/.

Mittell, J. (2006). Narrative complexity in contemporary American television. *Velvet Light Trap*, 58, 29-40. Retrieved from http://muse.jhu.edu/journals /the_velvet_light_trap/.

Schulzke, Marcus. Moral decision in Fallout. *Game Studies*, 9.2. Retrieved from http:// www.gamestudies.org/.

Shade, P. (2006). Screaming to be heard: Community and communication in Hush. *Slayage*, 6.1. Retrieved from http://www.slayageonline.com/.

Simon, D. (Writer), & Johnson, C. (Director). (2002). "The target." [Television series epi- sode]. In R. Colesberry (Executive producer), *The Wire*. Los Angeles, CA: HBO.

Spurlin, W. J. (2002). Theorizing queer pedagogy in English studies after the 1990s. *College English*, 65, 9-16. Retrieved from http:..www.jstor.org/stable/3250727/.

Stommel, J. J. (2010). I'm not a dead body; I just play one on tv: Buffy the vampire slay er and the performativity of the corpse. *Slayage*, 8.1. Retrieved from http://www.slayageonline.com/.

West, C. E. (2011, March). Heroic humanism and humanistic heroism in shows of Joss Whedon. *PopMatters*. Retrieved from http://www.popmatters.com/.

Whedon, J. (Writer), & Whedon, J. (Director). (1999). "Hush." [Television series epi- sode]. In G. Berman (Executive producer), *Buffy the Vampire Slayer*. Los Angeles, CA: Mutant Enemy.

Whedon, J. (Writer), & Whedon, J. (Director). (2001). "The body." [Television series epi sode]. In G. Berman (Executive producer), *Buffy the Vampire Slayer*. Los Angeles, CA: Mutant Enemy.

Whedon, J. (Writer), & Whedon, J. (Director). (2003). "Chosen." [Television series epi sode]. In G. Berman (Executive producer), *Buffy the Vampire Slayer*. Los Angeles, CA: Mutant Enemy.

Winans, A. E. (2006). Queering pedagogy in the English classroom: Engaging with places where thinking stops. *Pedagogy*, 6, 103-122. Retrieved from http://muse.jhu.edu/journals/pedagogy/.

Conclusion: The Future as Epilogue

Having moved through a variety of chapters meant to be thought provoking and inclusive of practical suggestions, the reader now is about to engage with the final two chapters of the work that were specifically selected to both extend the theme of the work as a whole and serve as a counterpoint to what has come before. It is the hope of the editors that these chapters are read both as extensions of what has been previously outlined, serving to demonstrate what might be when popular culture is infused into a curriculum, and potential backlash to what has been previously outlined, providing an example of what might happen if students are resistant to such infusion.

The first chapter in this section demonstrates one line of potential backlash. When Lynch-Greenberg and garcia argue that one does not need to understand how a cow is butchered to fully enjoy steak, it is difficult to argue against their thinking even after reading previous chapters such as Parke's, which immediately precedes and clearly demonstrates the effectiveness of exactly such an approach. Each reader, and each student, will engage in the pieces on different levels, finding strengths and weaknesses to debate.

Beyond the validity of arguing just how intensive students need to be able to dissect visual media to fully appreciate it, Lynch-Greenberg and garcia's work, used in conjunction with the films cited within, can also be used as an opportunity to open a greater debate on the meaning of art. What is art? What is trash? Why is Kerouac's voice revered as beat poetry and Shakur's voice sidelined as gangsta rap? Should the federal government remain in the business of being the nation's largest patron of the arts? What impact does an artist taking a photo of a crucifix in a jar of urine still have on this debate?

On a completely different note, Benavides' remarkable story rounds out the collection in its own inimitable style. Told from the point of view of a mother who has spent her daughter's lifetime witness to bullying from children and adults alike, her story is a clarion call for all those involved in education that the time to take a stand is now.

Bullying has become an epidemic in the United States (see the trailer for the forthcoming documentary *Bullycide: The Voice of Complicity* on Youtube at http://www.youtube.com/watch?v=dAKMVstGP4c&list=FLGMm4EqQPPl86O 0tZaIC_MA&index=4&feature=plpp_video); indeed, it has even been recognized by the United States Center for Disease Control and Prevention (http://www.cdc.gov/violenceprevention/pub/measuring_bullying.html). Those adults who argue that bullying is just a part of childhood are either ignorant of, or refusing to attend to, all of the new ways children can receive negative attention due to today's hypersaturated mass media market (i.e., Facebook, texting, Twitter, etc.).

Worse, as the case of bus monitor Norma Klein demonstrated, it is not just child-on-child violence that is coming forth. Norma needed her own Ghost Boy Ben that day, and belatedly got him in the form of the thousands of people around the world who supported her emotionally and financially after the incident. Benavides reminds all those in education that everyone is at risk, and everyone must strive to become change agents to stop bullying. Benavides' work provides one opportunity to engage in such a conversation, one launching point from which educators can begin implementing policies that will elicit change.

In the case of both selections, there is no feel-good solution, no happy ending provided. The editors did not select these for the conclusion to provide a set of pithy answers to core questions. They are not clarifying black and white, but increasing the breadth and quantity of shades of gray in the debates, just as popular culture at its best can do. They demand that the reader ask what can be, not what is.

Chapter Fourteen

I Don't Get It and That's Okay: Teaching Experiential Film Interpretation

Jade Lynch-Greenberg and esteban garcia

A journalist in California takes an assignment to cover the Mint 400, which he and his eccentric lawyer declare full of personal danger. Before long, but after a brief delay wherein a stingray kills a pedestrian and Jesus dances in the street, we're off to Vegas in a convertible full of pills, marijuana, cocaine, hallucinogens, alcohol, and even ether. Suddenly, we've entered Bat Country and are forced to contend with human-sized lizards. Later, we take a trip—in multiple uses of the word—to the Circus-Circus, through the eyes of a man in the depths of an ether binge. The film-in-question is Terry Gilliam's 1998 film translation of Hunter S. Thompson's *Fear and Loathing in Las Vegas*; an experience/experiential film thrust upon viewers, sometimes against their will.

In another example of an experiential film, a man with a French accent, lying nude in a bathtub, screws a can of New England clam chowder in and out of a teddy bear's bleeding rectum. A nude, ninety-year-old, alcoholic street person rubs pork rinds over his genitals and smokes a cigarette with a dead pig named "Society," shoots himself, and engages with sex acts with an imaginary woman named "Serenity." In the woods, a down-and-out ex-policeman shares pornography and a diet of raw meat with his son after having his life spared in exchange for his autographed picture of Jesus. And sentient tater tots have unprovoked, stream-of-consciousness conversations wherein every second or third word is either vulgar or obscene. In the end, online reviewer "Mr. Bishop" (2008) says of this particular film, Giuseppe Andrews's 2006 *Period Piece*, "the hard thing to digest is whether or not it is supposed to come off as a comedy, drama, or horror show. Not one scene is ever played out in a way that would indicate how you're supposed to feel about it. [...] The [characters] do and say things that will illicit [sic] some sort of reaction out of you..." (para. 5). With this summary, Mr. Bishop has provided a few key characteristics of film texts exemplified above to which we have given the label "experiential films"; namely, they defy traditional genre labels, do not influence or manipulate viewer responses one way or another, and elicit reactions rooted in each viewer's subjective personal schema.

First, it is important to note that the label "experiential film," and the texts that fall under the label, does not constitute a genre as much as an anti-genre of sorts. For instance, film texts that fall within particular genre labels[1] "follow the same basic pattern and [include] the same basic ingredients" (Petrie & Boggs, 2012, p. 404). Experiential films, by contrast, are all original and different from each other; they avoid preexisting plot lines, generic conventions, and formulaic nature of genre films and, as a result, they share no invariant narrative or iconic attributes. Further, in the case of genre films, the symbolic meanings of characters, settings, and conventions are established through their use across similar texts, and routines are targeted toward anticipated outcomes (Berger, 1978; Grant, 2007). There are no shared characters, settings, or conventions across experiential films; without these points of reference and shared routines, the outcomes of experiential films cannot be anticipated. Overall, they are emotional and spontaneous, not pre-planned and immediately and transparently recognizable in the same manner that traditional genre films are.

That Not-So-Fresh Feeling: Reading an Anti-Genre

Experiential films also tend not to influence their audiences toward a shared response; in so doing, they leave themselves open to any number of possible interpretations; they mean different things to different people and the communication of a neat message is obviously not the filmmakers' intent. Experiential films and their filmmakers achieve this neutrality of sorts in various ways: by not reflecting, representing, or encouraging any singular ideology; by leaving conflicts unresolved and narratives open-ended; by unobtrusively using film techniques (especially in terms of special-effects); by eschewing non-diegetic sound and/or music and voice-over narration. For instance, *Period Piece*, as previously stated, does not contain any scene or repetition of idea that would suggest to the audience how the filmmaker wants it—or, by extension, the viewer—to feel. Additionally, neither Michael Haneke's *Funny Games* (2007) nor *Caché* (2005) contain non-diegetic music, cue reactions from the audience through sound effects or voice-over narration. All are also shot in a non-obtrusive, matter-of-fact, almost documentary, nature. This sort of "slice-of-life" presentation allows experiential films to maintain neutrality, which begs responses that are individual, subjective, and rooted in personal schemata.[2]

But the most important—if not only, definite—characteristic of experiential films is that they elicit responses from their viewers. They do not, however, achieve this in the traditional manner. Traditionally, students respond to textual prompts through objective viewing, but with experiential films, "feelings of personal identification with and pleasure from [films] exist not just because of textual prompts...but also because of the viewer's psychological transaction with these texts" (Fehlman, 1994, p. 39). The psychological transaction occurs when, due to immersion in the film world and the images on screen, viewers experience an emotional, reflexive response (Baird, 1998; Fehlman, 1994; McGinn, 2005). This is easily achieved because experiential film texts are those which truly "communicate on a purely subjective, intuitive, or sensual plane and are meaningful...as experiences"; they bypass the intellect and address themselves directly and substantially to the emotional and visceral through fully engaged, non-distracted by objective and analytical, viewing (Petrie & Boggs, 2012, p. 7). Emotional, non-intellectual viewing allows viewers to more acutely experience the feelings of the characters, to emphasize with them, and respond accordingly.

Unfortunately, students are encouraged to approach film texts with "a high degree of objectivity and critical detachment" (Petrie & Boggs, 2012, p. 5; Buckland, 2003; Corrigan, 2010). Indeed, some film studies texts go so far as to suggest that objective and critical analysis of film texts are necessary for deeper, if not complete appreciation of said texts (Corrigan, 2010; Petrie & Boggs, 2012). Corrigan (2010) stated that "[the] ability to respond with some analytical awareness adds to our enjoyment," and Petrie and Boggs (2012) agreed by stating that our love of movies can be made stronger through analysis.

Even though it is said that critical detachment is intended to deepen, not destroy or replace intuitive and emotional responses, it creates an undeniable gap between viewer and film text that prevents immersion in the film experience through which experiential films elicit responses and communicate their themes (Petrie & Boggs, 2012). Because experiential films do not operate or communicate on an intellectual level, objective analysis strips them of their effectiveness, if not their purpose. This idea is best summed up by noted director David Lynch:

> If you start worrying about the meaning of everything, chances are your poor intellect is only going to glean a little portion of it. If it stays abstract, if it feels truthful, and it hooks you in the right way, and thrills you as it moves to the next idea, and it moves with some intuitive sense, that is a real good guideline. There's a certain logic and truth and right workings that you have to trust. That's all you have to go by. (in Olson, 2008, p.75)

What's more, it is never explained how or why analysis deepens and makes more meaningful the viewing experience, making its necessity seem questionable. If it is not necessary to autopsy a cow in order to fully enjoy and appreciate eating a steak, it should not be necessary to objectively and analytically respond to a film in order to enjoy and appreciate it.

"I Don't Get It": Teaching Our Students with Films, Not Teaching Film Studies

It is certainly no secret that engaging college students in learning—especially in courses that are not part of a students' major, such as the general studies courses—is a hearty challenge for instructors, who are often teaching multiple sections of multiple classes and have little time to cater assignments to students' individual learning styles each semester. One way to appeal to multiple learning styles, as well as capturing (and keeping) students' attention, is through pairing movies with other course material.

Educators who want to connect to students through film in the classroom may realize that many students, especially young (traditional) college students, relate more to visual texts that reflect their own generation and subcultures. These educators should also acknowledge that students can access a broader scope of society's knowledge through material to which they relate, but the inclusion of such material should add on to, rather than replace, the curriculum already present (Duncan-Andrade, 2004). Too often, films shown in the classroom—especially the high school classroom—are treated as a reward for sitting through the books they are based on, rather than being viewed as texts to be studied. Such practices need not be the case, however, as students can analyze films as independent text, compare films to the books they are based on, and/or look for literacy messages present in films (Duncan-Andrade, 2004). Through discussion and utilization of media literacy as part of the overall curriculum, the use of movies in the classroom can help educators connect with students while increasing the acknowledgment of an often-used literacy skill among today's youth.

College students who are unfortunately, all too often, inadequately prepared for higher education, are learning English as a second/other language, or have other academic readiness issues (such as learning disabilities) can especially benefit from writing about and discussing movies, as their knowledge of popular culture is often greater than that of the academic subject matter (Sweeney, 2006). Especially for these less prepared students, visualizing "the rhetorical principles of film composition such as clarity, unity, completeness, continuity, and mechanics—elements in all film types—can be understood more readily by students through watching film than by merely examining model essays" (Sweeney, 2006, p. 29). For example, in Norton-Meier's (2005) article, she discusses the experience of asking students in her literacy methods course to find the literacy messages in scenes from three popular films. She showed a clip and gave students time to write and discuss before moving on to the next clip. After all three movies' clips were complete, the discussion became in-depth and compared the literacy messages in each clip (Norton-Meier, 2005). The students continued to discuss the lesson in the following weeks, relating it to new movies they viewed outside of class and student learning. Norton-Meier (2005) commented, "Media literacy is a powerful tool, and by connecting my students' love of movies to literacy, I helped them learn and extend their understanding. However, they not only learned about content, but they also learned about being media literate" (p. 611). The true lesson, then, is not how to analyze a specific movie, or even a specific genre, but how to think intelligently about a text, regardless of medium.

Making (Sophie's) Choices: Experiencing Film in the Classroom

Rather than prescribing how students should analyze and interpret a particular film, the goal of including movies in the classroom should be to either reinforce understanding the rhetorical situation of any text—and being able to look at a text through both the lens of the original plan for the audience, voice, goal, purpose, genre, or lack thereof, as well as how it is actually received—or to reinforce ideas from a content area. Connecting a film's historical background, original rhetorical situation, and audience reception (both overall, such as may be found by reading reviews or other responses, and by the individual viewers) can help students see similar relationships in other texts. In a non-film course, relating those factors to the content area being discussed—or discrepancies perceived in their comparison(s)—is part of that conversation, which may include many viewpoints. Exploring film in the classroom, therefore, is far less an issue of right versus wrong, and more of a continuum of various, sometimes contrasting, opinions about the same text.

Sophie's Choice (1982), for example, appears formulaic at first. It begins as the story of an idealistic young man, Stingo, portrayed by Peter MacNicol, who moves from a rural area to New York City to write a novel and, upon meeting his neighbors, develops a fast friendship with an eccentric couple: Sophie, a Holocaust survivor played by Meryl Streep, and Nathan, the moody researcher who saved her life years prior, brought to life by Kevin Kline. However, the movie unfolds as Sophie's and Nathan's secrets are unraveled, and the film concludes with a melancholy reminder about the fragile nature of life—which, due to the way it is revealed, after several red herrings, can be confusing to some and vexing to others.

The content of *Sophie's Choice* could be used to enhance a class on history, philosophy, or writing, but has a vastly different impact on audience members based on their own experiences. While students with children of their own, especially older (non-traditional) students may be more affected by the film, its historical content and slow pacing is sometimes lost on younger, less experienced viewers, who may be bored through a large portion of the film but still tend to be shocked at the end. Even groups of students who are shocked, appalled, or saddened by the ending are so for reasons that vary greatly—whether because they sympathize with Sophie, or Nathan, or Stingo, or all three, or because they feel "tricked" by the climax of the film that precedes the final scene.

It is important to note, however, that while teaching experiential film can enhance students' understanding of rhetorical and textual analysis, and can provide students of film—whether in a film class or not—a unique understanding of the subject matter addressed, not all experiential films are appropriate for the classroom. The nature of experiential film leads to many of these movies containing nudity, sexual situations, violence, and coarse language—not because such content is required in an experiential film, but because these qualities often elicit visceral reactions—and may sometimes be, as a result, unusable in the undergraduate classroom. Some, though risqué (or even outright distasteful) in parts, are workable with a mature audience, and sitting through a few awkward moments in the classroom during an on-screen sex act can be well worth it for the overall encounter with the film and resulting discussion.

Drawing Your Own Conclusions (and Asking Students to Do the Same)

Not all grade levels, classes, or institutions of learning are the place to teach experiential film. Of course, this does not mean the only two options are either to teach experiential film as an anti-genre that should not be dissected or to teach more traditional film in a traditional film studies manner. Instead, teaching a more traditional film through the lens of experience—through looking at the film's context (including history, creators, and filming), rhetorical situation, and feelings of the individual audience(s)—provides the opportunity to teach movies (and, by extension, any texts) as experiences.

For example, if one wanted to teach *Sophie's Choice* but found oneself in an educational situation in which the sexual situations and language choices were unacceptable, one might teach *Freedom Writers* (2007) for similar themes of the Holocaust, persecution, unfair imprisonment, and writing as means to social change. While *Freedom Writers* is a traditional, formulaic drama produced for the MTV-generation, it can still be "experienced" rather than "analyzed" (or "dissected") by students who are asked to compare it to other texts or use it as a springboard to a writing assignment intended to provide them an opportunity to change the world (or community, school, or neighborhood, which is a portion of their world, at least).

Using film in the classroom should include a focus on teaching with film instead of just teaching the films themselves. Being able to analyze movies, to dissect them and point to all of their "insides" in an orderly and clearly defined way that features the vernacular of film studies, is not the same as being able to discuss social issues in mixed media. Ultimately, the focus of teaching with film and reinforcing the idea of analyzing the rhetorical situation of a text, rather than the text itself (regardless of medium), is about helping students become media-literate critical thinkers.

Notes

1. For example, mentioning the genre of action films would call to mind certain iconic titles, such as *Robocop* (1987) or *The Expendables* (2010), while most would agree *Frankenstein* (1931) and *The Exorcist* (1973) are staples of the horror genre.
2. Schemata, here, refers to a set of experiences, values, and education (both formal and informal) that comprises one's worldview and understanding of the ideas (and media) one encounters.

References

Andrews, G. (Director). (2006). *Period piece* [DVD]. Available from Troma Entertainment, Inc., 36–40 11th Street, Long Island City, New York, 11106.

Baird, R. (1998). Animalizing *Jurassic Park's* dinosaurs: Blockbuster schemata and the cross-cultural cognition in the threat scene. *Cinema Journal, 37*(4),82–103.

Berger, C. (1978). Viewing as action: Film and reader response criticism. *Literature Film Quarterly, 6*(2), 144–151.

Buckland, W. (2003). *Teach yourself: Film studies*. Chicago: McGraw-Hill.

Corrigan, T. (2010). *A short guide to writing about film*. New York: Longman.

Duncan-Andrade, J. M. R. (2004). Your best friend or your worst enemy: Youth popular culture, pedagogy, and curriculum in urban classrooms. *The Review of Education, Pedagogy, and Cultural Studies 26*(4), 313-337.

Fehlman, R. H. (January 1994). Teaching film in the 1990s. *English Journal*, pp. 39–47.

Gilliam, T. (Director). (1998). *Fear and loathing in Las Vegas* [DVD]. United States: Universal Studios.

Grant, B. K. (2007). Genre. In B. K. Grant (ed.), *Schirmer encyclopedia of film* (pp. 297–308). Detroit: Thomson Gale.

Haneke, M. (Director). (2005). *Caché* [DVD]. United States: Sony Pictures.

———. (Director). (2007). *Funny games* [DVD]. United States: Warner Bros.

LaGravenese, R. (Director). (2007). *Freedom writers* [DVD]. United States: Paramount.

McGinn, C. (2005). *The power of movies: How screen and mind interact*. New York: Pantheon Books.

"Mr. Bishop." (2008). *Period piece*. Retrieved from http://www.infinitropolis.com /reviews/period_piece.html.

Norton-Meier, L. A. (2005). "Trust the fungus": Lessons in media literacy learned from the movies. *Journal of Adolescent & Adult Literacy 48*(7), 608-611.

Olson, G. (2008). *David Lynch: Beautiful dark*. Lanham, MD: Scarecrow Press.

Pakula, A. J. (Director). (1982). *Sophie's choice* [DVD]. United States: Lions Gate.

Petrie, D., and Boggs, J. (2012). *The art of watching films* (8th ed.). New York: McGraw-Hill.

Sweeney, L. (2006). Ideas in practice: Theoretical bases for using movies in developmental coursework. *Journal of Developmental Education 29*(3), 28-36.

Chapter Fifteen

My Conversations with Ben: What This Mother Learned from a Ghost Boy about Bullying

Yvette Benavides

The American Justice Department reports that one in three middle and high school students is abused mentally, verbally, and physically (www.justice.gov). I'm fairly certain that one of those kids is, has been, and will be my own wholly idiosyncratic daughter. Her individual differences run deep. That's true for a lot of children. And she's never going to be what the rest of the world expects. Adolescence is a tough time for everyone. But bullying should not be written off as just an unpleasant rite of passage; it is a public health problem.

This is nonfiction. This story is painfully true. It really happened. I've changed most of the names here—of people and schools—but the story is the same one that teachers and parents and children have heard and uttered over and again. This is the story about the first time I met Ben the Ghost Boy. Some might not agree that a ghost is real, but he is. Ben is real. Ben is a boy. Ben is a girl. Ben is a woman. Ben is a man. Ben is all the children who have ever had the impulse to bully out of the unnamed pain roiling inside them. Ben is the mother and father of the bully and the bullied, the parents who suffer because they can't do enough to help their wounded children. Ben is a pediatrician, a nurse. Ben is a teacher, a principal and school counselor, likewise unable to find any easy answers. Ben is every kid who has been bullied and made sense of it too late. Ben is that kid who scarred over and survived it. Ben is you. Ben is me. This is a true story.

I volunteered to chaperone again, this time at my sixth-grade daughter's first-ever boy-girl dance at St. Mary's School for Girls. The boys from area parochial schools arrived in small groups of four and five. They seemed smaller and younger in their civilian clothes of jeans and T-shirts and out of their white ox-fords and navy blue chinos. They eyed the girls furtively and held their canned goods—the admission to the dance—against their blue-jeaned thighs. Maybe they'd never touched a can of peas or corn before. It occurred to me that there would be many more firsts for these young people in the next few years. The thought hurt something in my chest.

It became increasingly obvious that mothers across the city had cleared their cupboards of the nonperishable rations they'd bought on a whim. The dates on some of the cans revealed that they were likely amassed when these mothers feared that Y2K would bring the world to its knees when these same children were just toddlers. The local food bank would soon house hundreds of dusty cans of unappetizing kippers and unsalted organic kidney beans. One kid with a buzz cut carried a small box of MREs. His friends gathered around him and squeezed the manila brown envelopes of several courses—stew, spaghetti, and apple cobbler.

When Christy and I arrived, night had fallen. I felt invigorated by the cool fall air and even giddy at the heady cloud of baby powder and teen-spirited flowery perfumes that we walked into. But in the lobby, a fog of the usual op-pressive stale school smells engulfed us. There was the same tired plastic Ficus in the corner and the same black and white photo of Sister Catherine—her por-trait as large as the life-sized Bruce Springsteen poster that hung in my room when I was Christy's age. She wasn't just *Sister* Catherine, but *Mother*. She was the boss, the founding Superior General of the Congregation of Divine Interces-sion when the school first opened its doors some six decades ago. And she did look a bit like a man in a habit. I tried to stop the thought from flitting through my mind, but it had taken root there when I first saw the photo months before. Her face and neck were thick and her plain face wide, with not a single hair peeking though the hood. Only her large glasses—unadorned like a pair of boxy Ray-Bans frames—offered the single bit of muted bling to the black and white picture.

I'd long admired her story, although I never really thought about it much. I'd passed the photo dozens of times without a thought to her. Known as a "dreamer" in the long history of the Sisters, she was versed in both English and math. Her name had been Claudia, but she changed it to the more religiously apt and holy "Catherine" during her second novitiate year when she was still in high school. Hers had been an adolescence of challenges. Her family wasn't Catholic, but on her insistence, she was baptized in the Catholic Church in her sophomore year. Her father objected, and she can't have been too popular among her pubes-cent peers for her religious zeal, so incongruous among blossoming teenagers.

Mrs. Sanchez, Alice's mom, welcomed us. Portly and short, she had donned a colorful muumuu and plastic flower lei, though the theme of the dance was "Neon Disco." "Get up and boogie, you all!" she said as she shuffled toward us. With her arms akimbo like a robot, Christy obliged. Alice feigned a look of mock horror, wide-eyed and mouth agape. I could see the purple rubber bands on her braces. She sat on a table, swinging her legs at the same rapid rate that

she chewed gum. The daughter of the PTA president, she carried that Nelly Ol-
sen air of the privileged rich kid of the town on the *Little House on the Prairie*
television show.

"Alice is wearing make-up," Christy stage-whispered in my ear. Alice wore
Candies high heels, a tube top, and short shorts. Unsteady, heavy-handed strokes
of pewter hues shadowed her small eyes. Dark kohl crookedly lining her lids
gave her a look of crazed, sinister innocence. Glittery cherry red lipstick called
attention to her mouth crowded with braces.

The contrast that Christy offered was stark: a long-sleeved teal peasant
blouse over loose-fitting leggings and big chunky low-heel boots. Baby-faced,
but with an understated prettiness that portended a burgeoning classic beauty,
she was tall for her age and usually wore her hair in a pony tail. Tonight it was
loose and long, one strand fastened with a bright green barrette in an effort to
meet the neon theme of the dance.

We checked in. I took my name tag. It read: "Chaperone Mom Candy."

"Um," I objected, waving Alice's mom over and pointing to the sticker
badge. "Is this for someone named Candy?"

Mrs. Sanchez clucked her tongue, waved me off, and sighed. "That's *you*,"
she said impatiently while she tried to make change for a can-less boy.

My duties involved standing behind a table covered from end to end with
candy and rationing out the stuff in fistfuls. One mother estimated the candy had
been in the possession of St. Mary's Preparatory for at least three fall dances. It
was time to move the merchandise—Sour Belts, Starbursts, SweetTarts, and
Twizzlers to awaken the savage beasts in these hormonal teens already hopped
up on too much sugar and other dastardly white foods, energy drinks, and that
strange brand of Disney Channel saccharine cynicism. They mimicked the petu-
lance of the twenty-two-year-old female lead on the show playing a fifteen-year-
old. The teen protagonists rule the households on those shows. Parents are presented as buffoons or not at all.

Their TV watching had led the St. Mary's girls to other more nefarious fare.
One recent October afternoon Christy came home and asked, "Who's Snookie?
All the girls want to be her for Halloween."

Christy wanted to be a butterfly again.

I looked down the long corridor leading to the gymnasium when I heard the
thump, thump, nnnssst, nnnssst, nnnssst, thump, thump of some Rap song I was
certain I'd never hear again after that night.

At Mrs. Sanchez's dramatic "Go!" the gaggle of adolescents filling the foyer moved like a wave and overcame the locker-lined hallway leading to the gym.
It seemed a strange kind of race with no finish line, no goal. Like a herd of os-
triches, the girls ran ahead, all bony limbs and glittered, hair-sprayed curls. Their
strappy sandals slapped across the tile floor as they screamed and giggled. Some
ran arm in arm or holding hands. They pulled up falling spaghetti straps and
held on to their feather-light cross-body purses. I imagined they carried only a
cell phone and lip gloss. The boys followed, not at a run, but a decent unsmiling
and purposeful clip. Something nameless but palpable belied that veneer and

melted their cool. It hurt my heart to see all those young sons trying to be men. Christy trailed behind all of them, trotting now, then stopping, then picking up the speed again. She took a few steps back with every few steps forward to wave me over in her direction.

I shook my head. "Go inside," I said. "Dance with your friends and have a good time." With my arms down at my side, I turned my hands so my palms faced her and waved her in. "Just *go!*" I mouthed. "Have a good time."

I sat at my assigned table where other mothers named Candy joined me. We exchanged that brand of small talk that can be excruciatingly disingenuous. They asked questions like "Which one is yours?" as if claiming a prized calf at the county fair. Most of the moms spent the entire time texting. Some of them flirted with some of the dads who were charged with monitoring the entrances and exits.

I ate a lot of candy and stared at the dark entrance of the gymnasium. I could hear shrieks of laughter piercing Justin Bieber's lyrics. His pleading "Baby, baby, baby" sounded like cruel taunts on a playground. Girls moved in and out of view dancing together. Boys stood around on the sidelines, hands in pockets, their blank expressions penetrating the neon that flashed with the frenetic movements of the dancing children. They seemed much shorter than the girls and much younger, but also much more serious and pensive somehow.

After just a few minutes, Christy came out of the gymnasium. "I'm dancing, Momma!" she said, moving her arms over her head and swaying her hips on the down beat of the Jonas Brothers' "I Wanna Be Like You."

"Great! Go back in there and have fun," I said as I bit into the gum center of my Charms Blo Pop.

Another small herd of boys arrived. The collection of canned sauerkraut, beets, and cream of celery soup had grown to a small pyramid.

Leaning against the doorway of the gym, I turned back toward the hallway to see the other parents munching on popcorn, talking on their cell phones. Through the darkness and apoplectic strobe light flashes in the gym, I saw a couple of the boys spinning around on the floor to the hoots of the other kids. Even a couple of the teachers did their best sprinkler dance and elicited the howls of the vice principal, his large belly quivering. Groups of girls danced together suggestively. They held hands and hugged and giggled loudly. They formed a large circle. Each girl took a turn, jumping in and showing off a signature move. The other girls, bobbing up and down, applauded wildly in approval, eager for their turn.

At last Christy joined in. With her tongue licking her upper lip, she jumped into the middle of the circle of a dozen girls and offered the movements that her body would only begrudgingly allow. Alice laughed, throwing her head back. "Freak!" she shrieked covering her mouth, the unsightly purple rubber bands mingled with red candy, her big painted lips an amorphous blob. "Stupid dork!" another one yelled and mimicked Christy's moves. Everyone laughed. Like a swarm of bees, a giant menacing neon octopus, the girls danced together and floated away from Christy, who sighed deeply and swayed alone into the darkness.

In that moment, I felt paralyzed. Phoebe Prince. Phoebe Prince. Phoebe Prince—that girl from Massachusetts I read about in the paper.[1] Classmates mercilessly verbally abused her. Threats of physical violence created a fear and loathing that strangled the good energy in her soul. Relentless humiliation choked out her will to go on for another day. The photo that accompanied the article showed a girl with long dark hair, a familiar understated prettiness, brown eyes staring straight ahead at the camera, a tender smile that belied that she could ever, ever take her own life. She's a photograph, a memory, a ghost, a whisper I hear now in the locker-lined hallway of St. Mary's Preparatory. *Don't forget about me,* she says. *I was a daughter, too.*

Christy moved to the farthest, darkest corner of the gym rocking slowly to the up-tempo song as if she were hearing some other tune in her head.

For weeks I'd had my own Apache dance with the vice principal of the school. Mr. Hernandez looked like the Santa Claus of my childhood fancies—balding and dark-skinned with a bushy gray beard. I'd reported a number of problems to him regarding the young women at the school. Christy's pencil bag had been stolen from her desk, and seventeen dollars worth of allowance money with it. Her jacket had been buried underneath the fake dirt and moss of the ficus in the lobby. Mr. Hernandez told me that "this kind of behavior" was "normal" in middle school, that I had to keep my distance, "let Christy fight her own battles," and "get a thicker skin."

I didn't agree with him. However, at this moment, I remembered Christy's words to me in the car on the way to the dance: "I'm not going to tell you any more when the girls are mean to me. I'll only tell you when it bothers me."

I returned to my place at the candy table. A moment later, Christy emerged from the darkness holding her green barrette in her hand. "I want to go home right now, Mom."

I said some good-byes, leaving the trove of sweets in the charge of another mother who looked at us askance. "What's wrong?" she asked, peeling apart the red Twizzler plait and sticking a long thread in her drooling mouth. "She sick or something?"

I nodded while Christy bellowed, "No," crossed her arms and looked down at the floor.

"Early day tomorrow," I said.

We rushed down the long, empty hallway toward the foyer. We passed the portrait of the school's founder. A cherry-red moustache and several freckles colorized the gray tones of her portrait. Catherine or Claudia. Our mother, our sister. Phoebe. All the dreamers. We had all been defaced.

In the car on the way home, I told Christy a lie. I'm not sure why I did it. There is nothing to explain it. I was possessed by something, that familiar spirit of good intention that never makes anyone feel better. I told her that one of the boys at the dance had asked me if I knew who the girl in the teal blouse was. "'Know her?' I said! 'She's my daughter!'"

Christy's expression had been hard to interpret until just then—cross, sad, resigned. But now she lit up. "Really?" she said bobbing up and down in her seat.

I lied some more and told her that he wanted to know her name and what grade she was in. "He was really cute," I said. "I mean, cute to me. I don't know if you would think he was cute." But of course I knew.

"What did he look like? Tell me! Tell me!" she screamed, her fists up at her cheeks.

"Oh! You kidding? Like the boy from the *Percy Jackson* movie. Or like a brown-eyed Zac Efron ...but...with curly hair...and...cuter!"

And then the frenetic movement and giggling in the seat next to me stopped. I ran out of ideas. It was a good thing, too, because the needle on my internal self-loathing meter had swung to its limit. I was done. I prayed she wouldn't ask another question about this mystery boy. And she didn't. Not really.

I drove and looked straight ahead, holding my breath to hear her response. But she was quiet for a long time. I drove several blocks. Stopped at two red lights. Neither of us said a word.

"Mom," she said at last, smiling, "I think that boy was a ghost. I think he came here to tell you that everything is going to be okay."

She turned to look at me. I looked away from the road in front of me and looked at her for a second, seeing, not my daughter the twelve-year-old, but my daughter in the future—wise and knowing and healed over. I stared straight ahead and heard her say in a voice deep, certain and assured, "Right, mom?"

The ghost boy was born. I named him Ben.

Teachers were the first offenders to take turns shoving Christy around. I hope she doesn't remember. But she probably does.

What mothers never learn in those birthing classes, in any baby book, baby shower, or hospital is that a child's mind is a singularly complicated puzzle to solve. And we never learn how we should respond when a young woman in her first year of teaching tells you to get ready for a life of special education. She says it about your three-year-old as if she could produce a crystal ball from the ample pockets of her denim skirt and peer right into your future.

At that moment all I want to do is find my daughter, right now sitting in the small cafeteria amid the smells of tuna salad and ripe bananas. She will have trouble opening the Ziploc bag of carrot sticks. The lunchroom teacher's assistants will look knowingly at each other. They both wear sweatshirts, one with a decal of red, white, and blue balloons, one with the words *Happy Haven School for Deaf Children.* Each will recall the short catalogue of students written off over the years—the lost causes of pre-K whose mothers have not yet accepted the realities of the future, swearing their child will develop at her own pace. They will shovel in another fork-full of their micro-waved leftover lasagna and suck on the straw hanging limply from the lip of a Diet Coke can. Christy's small fingers bereft of the fine motor skills required to fasten a button, open the tube of toothpaste, or cut a clean heart shape with scissors, will fail at the latest

test, the Ziploc bag of carrots as impenetrable as a combination lock with no numbers. One assistant will shake her head while she rips open her bag of potato chips with her canine teeth. One will shrug her shoulders and rub at a drop of marinara on her sweatshirt. They will both get on with their lives. No one will eat the carrots.

I don't accept the teacher's recommendation for a speech therapist easily, but in my new role as advocate mom, I'd blindly accepted a number of directives that inured me to any kind of resistance. I did it because it meant I could monitor and mediate the insensitivity, the meanness that seemed to burgeon in every other context outside the classroom. I was the human shield, the bodyguard, the back-up, and the best friend in my many new roles. I was the field trip den mother. I was the Brownie troupe chaperone. I was the catechism teacher. I was the rope-turner in the jump rope camp. I'd speed over from work to the elementary school every Tuesday and Thursday afternoon. In my skirt and heels, with my purse still over my shoulder, I turned the rope with an unusually tall fifth grader, inadvertently slapping every other uncoordinated kid. My daughter tried to balance on a pogo stick. Bending her knees, she sprang up against an unyielding po- with no -go and came crashing down on the floor to the jeers of another gym full of kids.

Ten pounds and almost twenty-two inches at birth, my daughter has always faced the unrealistic expectations of the world. Why the helium voice from this overgrown kid, they wanted to know. Why the cavalcade of imaginary friends? They looked at her sidewise and then at me incredulously: "How old is she again?" At nine months she could recite the alphabet and read small words. But no one, not the teachers or their assistants, seemed too impressed. They expected those benchmarks from such a big kid. But by the age of three, yes, it was true, she would not answer questions. She would not offer information about her time at day-care. She hardly said a word.

I acquiesced and sought the counsel of a series of health professionals. I would come close to depleting my checking account at the end of each month to pay for the out-of-network audiologists and speech pathologists in another part of town I'd never go to otherwise. Designer boutiques and ritzy restaurants with fleets of new-model Jaguars, Hummers, and Land Rovers glinting in the parking lots, guided the way to the speech pathologist's clinic.

Christy played with the Little People farm set. She lined up the animals just beyond the little barn door. She made small pens for the animals out of the chubby board books from a nearby basket.

The therapist, an impossibly tall blond woman in a monochromatic black ensemble and requisite clogs, asked her questions in a lumbering drawl. She wrote down copious notations, but no answers came from Christy.

"What's your favorite animal?" she asked, self-consciously cocking her head to one side for my benefit—an overt show of her interest in the curly-haired subject. She squinted her eyes at Christy's closed mouth.

No answer.

"Christy. Look at me. Look at my mouth. What's your favorite animal?" she asked, cocking her head now to the other side.

"Dog," said Christy without looking at her mouth, without turning from her studious examination of *Good Night, Gorilla.*

"Dog. Gooooood. But, now, listen. Look at my mouth. Look at me. There is no dog on the farm. Which is your favorite *farm* animal?" No answer. The therapist took notes. "What's this?" she asked holding up the horse figure.

No answer. More notes.

I grew to abhor the sight of scrubs with happy, child-themed prints—smiley faces and kittens, Elmos and Doras. They became the incongruous uniform of unmoved, unrepentant drones who casually told me my daughter was overweight and blamed me for having nursed Christy for the first two years of her life, far longer than the recommended six months. "Ooh, she's a fatty," one nurse told me, while I fretted over Christy's ear infection and spiking fever. The nurse looked like she lived a sedentary life, doling out her gloom from a stool in her outsized, formless teddy bear scrubs and blinding white Nikes that looked like casts.

If Ben had been there, hovering over me, floating like a kite in the stagnant air of a doctor's waiting room, or earthbound and sure-footed on the playground or that rare birthday party—vaguely resembling the boy in the *Percy Jackson* movie, or a brown-eyed Zac Efron, but with curly hair—he would have told me to prepare myself to slog through Christy's early years with the unsolicited, unfounded, ineffective recommendations and prescriptions from teachers and doctors and therapists. He would have told me, that with each new condescending pat on the head, Christy would move closer to their "normal" in spite of them. He would have prepared me for the strange brand of unkindness that children can inflict on each other—the name-calling, the preoccupation with weight, the pressure to be pretty, even seductive. He would have reminded me that name-calling comes from dark places of pain and that we must be vigilant and protective of those children, too. He would have taught me that we must protect children—all children—from ever believing the taunts and jeers, from ever succumbing to the humiliation by staying silent, swallowing their words, withdrawing to imaginary, unthreatening worlds in their minds. Yes, he would have told me that children do that sometimes, some terrible times. They close up and close off like a noose around a sweet, tender neck. Gone from here. Like ghosts.

Ben? Are you there? Please come back. I need to talk to you.

Notes

1. The tragic, untimely death of fifteen-year-old Irish immigrant Phoebe Prince occurred in the summer of 2011. One of Prince's last cries for help came by way of a text message where she wrote: "I can't take much more" (Webley, 2011). In a final footnote to Prince's story, the bullies who relentlessly stalked her, tormented her,

and drove her to the desperate measure of suicide over the span of three months were sentenced in Massachusetts Juvenile Court. All five perpetrators made plea deals. The Court agreed to drop the most serious charges: the bullies were charged with criminal harassment, given one year of probation and assigned one-hundred hours of community service. In the courtroom at the sentencing of the bullies, Prince's mother, Anne O'Brien said, "It's is nearly impossible to measure the impact of Phoebe's death upon our lives" (Webley, 2011).

References

West, T. (2012, August 7). Acting Associate Attorney General Tony West speaks at the federal partners in bullying prevention 2012 summit. Retrieved from the United States Department of Justice: http://www.justice.gov/iso/opa/asg/speeches/2012/asg-speech-120807.html.

Webley, K. (2011, May 5). Teens who admitted to bullying Phoebe Prince sentenced. *Time* Newsfeed. Retrieved from: http://newsfeed.time.com/2011/05/05/teens-who-admitted-to-bullying-phoebe-prince-sentenced.

Index

About the Contributors

Editors

Dr. Edward Janak is Associate Professor of Educational Studies at the University of Wyoming. Dr. Janak spent nearly a decade teaching language, literature, and history in the public schools of South Carolina. While teaching, he earned his MEd in secondary education—English and PhD in the social, historical, and philosophical foundations of education from the University of South Carolina. Publishing and presenting in a diverse array of fields related to his work in historical foundations of education and educational biography, he is the "Education, History, and Teaching" area chair for the national Pop Culture/American Culture association.

A former public school teacher, **Dr. Denise F. Blum** is Assistant Professor in Social Foundations at Oklahoma State University and the author of the book, *Cuban Youth and Revolutionary Values: Educating the New Socialist Citizen* (University of Texas Press, 2011) and co-editor of a special issue of *The International Journal of Qualitative Studies in Education* entitled, "Globalization and Education" (May/June, 2012). As an educational anthropologist, her research focuses on how young people negotiate identity and ideology from institutional, media, and informal sources.

Authors

Yvette Benavides' poetry, stories and essays have been published in the *The Red Palm, The America's Review, The Texas Observer, The Austin Chronicle, The Langdon Review of the Arts in Texas,* and *Mothering* and *Latina* magazines.

231

She is a book critic for the San Antonio *Express News*. Her commentaries and reports have aired on National Public Radio's *Latino USA*. She is host of a new Texas Public Radio show, "Fronteras: The Changing America Desk" and co-host and co-producer of "Texas Matters" which has aired for twelve years and is now heard on thirty stations throughout Texas, Kansas, and Oklahoma. In 2008 she received a Lone Star Award from the Houston Press Club for her work on "Texas Matters." Yvette has taught English composition and literature courses since 1990. She is an associate professor of English at Our Lady of the Lake University in San Antonio, Texas.

Jennifer Culver holds an MA in English Literature from the University of North Texas and has over a decade of teaching experience in secondary education. In addition, Jennifer has taught Rhetoric at the University of Texas at Dallas and participated in the first NEH Institute devoted to Tolkien and his works. Currently a doctoral student at UT Dallas, Jennifer continues to teach high school and help write curriculum.

Dr. Joanna Davis-McElligatt is Assistant Professor of Ethnic Studies at the University of Louisiana at Lafayette. Her main research and pedagogical interests include immigrant fiction, literature of the African Diaspora, postcolonial literature and theory, and literature of the American South. She is currently working on a book-length project entitled *Black and Immigrant: African Diasporic Passages in Twentieth-Century American Literature*. In the text, she explores the experiences of immigrants of African descent to the United States, while working to redefine African Americanness in the age of Obama.

Dr. Sheila Delony is an Assistant Professor of education at Abilene Christian University in Abilene, Texas. She teaches literacy education courses, as well as courses in the liberal arts integrated core. Her research interests include teacher professionalism, teacher reflection, and reading assessment. Before joining the university faculty, Dr. Delony was a public school teacher and literacy coach.

Dr. Mikee Delony is Assistant Professor of English at Abilene Christian University. She received her MA and PhD in English Literature from the University of Houston. Her scholarly interests include feminist theory and feminist theology, mythology, Robin Hood and Arthurian studies, medieval literature, especially Chaucer, and contemporary medievalism, particularly adaptations of medieval literary texts. She has published essays on film adaptations of medieval literature in several edited collections and is currently working on a book on the contemporary adaptations of the Wife of Bath.

Brian Duchaney is a graduate of Bridgewater State University where he received a BA and an MA in English. Currently a senior lecturer at Curry College in Milton, Massachusetts, and Bridgewater State University in Bridgewater, Massachusetts, he teaches a variety of writing and literature courses.

Jennifer Edelman is a doctoral student in Mathematics Education at the University of Wyoming. Her research interests include the use of children's literature in the teaching and learning of mathematics, building on her classroom teaching experience as well as her years as an elementary school librarian. She currently works with preservice mathematics teachers at the intermediate and secondary levels.

Richard Ellefritz is entering his last year of Oklahoma State University's PhD program in sociology. In 2008, he moved from Macomb, Illinois, where he earned bachelor and master degrees in sociology, to Stillwater, Oklahoma, to study environmental sociology. Of his many scholarly interests are environmentalism, education, culture, politics, and social structure. He plans on doing research and teaching once he makes his way into the job market.

Jade Lynch-Greenberg is an educator in the Department of English and Philosophy at Purdue University Calumet, where she also volunteers in the Writing Center and advises a student organization. She earned a Master of Arts degree in English with a focus in Popular Culture, and has been a member of the national Popular Culture Association since 2006. Lynch-Greenberg also a member of the National Association of Comics Art Educators and a Teacher/Consultant for the Northwest Indiana Writing Project, a satellite of the highly acclaimed National Writing Project.

esteban garcia is an independent scholar who loves films. He has a Master of Library Science degree from Indiana University and a Bachelor of Arts degree in English: Professional Writing from Purdue University. He has given many presentations regarding the use of comics/graphic novels in the classroom and their promotion in public libraries, and is a strong advocate of non-traditional education methods.

Sylvia Mac is a doctoral student in the Social Foundations of Education program at Oklahoma State University where she teaches a pre-service teacher class focusing on diversity and equity in education. She is also pursuing a CAS in Disability Studies from Syracuse University. Her interests include disability studies, critical pedagogy, and urban education.

Amy Rakowsky Neeman, PhD, is a Professor of English at Johnson & Wales University. She has a doctorate in Linguistics and Cognitive Science from Brown University. In addition to teaching in the English Department, she runs a support program focused on improving the academic language skills of international students.

David D. Newman, MA [Anthropology, Brown University], MA [Social Sciences, University of Chicago], is Associate Professor of Sociology and chair of the Social Sciences Department at Johnson & Wales University. His particular interests are the sociology of food and the portrayal of gender on reality versus fully scripted television shows.

Mwenda Ntarangwi, PhD, is Associate Professor of Anthropology at Calvin College. Ntarangwi's research interests span a wide spectrum including popular cultural expressions, the practice and history of anthropology, inter-cultural engagement, youth and identity, and African Christianity. He is the author of the following books: *Annotated Bibliography on Children and Youth in Africa (2001-2011)* (forthcoming, CODESRIA Books); *Engaging Children and Youth in Africa: Methodological and Phenomenological Issues* (forthcoming, CODESRIA Books); *Reversed Gaze: An African Ethnography of American Anthropology* (Illinois, 2010); *East African Hip Hop: Youth Culture and Globalization* (Illinois, 2009); *Gender Identity and Performance: Understanding Swahili Cultural Realities Through Song* (Africa World Press, 2003); editor of *Jesus and Ubuntu: Exploring the Social Impact of Christianity in Africa* (Africa World Press, 2011), and co-editor of *African Anthropologies: History, Critique and Practice* (Zed, 2006). He is also editor of a special issue of *Africa Development* on "Parent's Involvement in Children's Lives in Africa," (forthcoming, CODESRIA Books).

Michelle Parke is Assistant Professor of English at Carroll Community College in northern Maryland. She is also a doctoral candidate at Michigan State University and is completing her dissertation about post-World War II domesticity and food literature. Her article on *CSI* and the work of Edgar Allan Poe appeared in *Studies in Popular Culture*. As a self-proclaimed television and film geek, Parke regularly incorporates such media as *Buffy the Vampire Slayer*, *The Wire*, *Glee*, *Seinfeld*, and *The Matrix* in the college writing classroom.

Julie Irene Prieto is a PhD candidate in History at Stanford University, currently completing work on a dissertation titled, *Making a Good Neighbor: Public Diplomacy and Development in United States-Mexico Relations, 1926-1945*. *Making a Good Neighbor* argues that the U.S. government began funding cultural exchange, U.S.-style educational programs, and public events in Mexico during the 1920s in response to the perceived radicalism of the Mexican Revolution. Concerned that Mexico would adopt "undemocratic" forms of government or policies, the United States turned to the state control of the dissemination of ideas and of culture as a means of influencing the development of the Mexican state, its national culture, and of guiding Mexico towards a more moderate political expression of the goals of the revolution. This push towards using culture to influence politics was incorporated into the structure of the Good Neighbor

Policy under Franklin D. Roosevelt, ultimately forming the basis of a Pan American system of public diplomacy. Prieto is a two-time winner of the Hoefer Teaching Assistant Partnership Award for her work with Writing in the Major at Stanford University, and has received an Ayacucho Fellowship for Graduate Study and the George Watt Memorial Essay Award, given by the Abraham Lincoln Brigade Archives.

Bob Reese, PhD, is Associate Professor of Psychology and Director of the Health Psychology Program at Jefferson College of Health Sciences in Roanoke, Virginia. His main research focus is on performance and positive psychology and how they may be applied to encourage "Magis Thinking" to thrive and flourish in life. Student performance and teaching excellence fall into this research domain, and, as an educator, Bob is always searching for ways to keep his students engaged to facilitate learning. Bob has been voted "E-Teacher of the Year" twice and thrice nominated for teacher of the year at Jefferson. He is the author of "Develop the Winner's Mentality" (2005).

Forrest Roth is an English PhD candidate in Creative Writing at the University of Louisiana-Lafayette, and the author of a novella, *Line and Pause* (BlazeVOX Books). His creative work in flash fiction and prose poetry has appeared in various print and online journals, including *NOON*, *Denver Quarterly*, *Quick Fiction*, *Caketrain*, and *Sleepingfish*.

Ludovic A. Sourdot, PhD, is Assistant Professor in Curriculum and Instruction in the College of Professional Education at Texas Woman's University where he teaches credential and graduate level courses in education. His research focuses on the pedagogical possibilities popular culture offers for teacher education and visual culture studies. His work recently appeared in the *Handbook of Public Pedagogy*, in the *Journal of Cultural Research in Art Education* and in *Texas Trends*.

Fred Waweru is currently a PhD student in the Social Foundations of Education program at Oklahoma State University. He holds an MA in International Studies from Oklahoma State University and a BS in Social Science from Boise State University. His research interests include examining social factors that inhibit the diffusion of educational technology in Africa. He is also interested in the research of pedagogical approaches that use educational technology as convivial tools in developing countries.